LISTEN TO THE POET

LISTEN TO THE POET

WRITING, PERFORMANCE, AND COMMUNITY IN YOUTH SPOKEN WORD POETRY

WENDY R. WILLIAMS

UNIVERSITY OF MASSACHUSETTS PRESS
Amherst and Boston

Copyright © 2018 by University of Massachusetts Press
All rights reserved
Printed in the United States of America

ISBN 978-1-62534-397-0 (paper); 396-3 (hardcover)

Designed by Sally Nichols
Set in Crimson Text and Avenir
Printed and bound by the Maple Press, Inc.

Cover design by Patricia Duque Campos
Cover photo: *Microphone - Stage Fright - Stock image,* iStock.com/Sean_Warren

Library of Congress Cataloging-in-Publication Data
A catalog record for this book is available from the Library of Congress.

British Library Cataloguing-in-Publication Data
A catalog record for this book is available from the British Library.

Some material in this book was previously published in the following article: Williams, Wendy R. 2015. "Every Voice Matters: Spoken Word Poetry in and outside of School." *English Journal* 104 (4): 77–82. Copyright 2015 by the National Council of Teachers of English. Used with permission.

For Ian

CONTENTS

Acknowledgments   ix

Introduction: Listening to the Poets   1
Chapter 1: Guiding Research and Theory   14
Chapter 2: Studying the Poets   23
Chapter 3: Performing Poetry   33
Chapter 4: Participating in a Community of Practice   49
Chapter 5: Writing and Authorship   79
Chapter 6: Weighing Benefits and Challenges   108
Chapter 7: Exploring a High School Poetry Club   120
Conclusion: Rethinking Writing Instruction   149
Afterword: The Paradox of Emotional Vulnerability   162

Appendix A: Interview Questions   169
Appendix B: Poetry Club Planning   173
Works Cited   175
Notes   187
Index   189

ACKNOWLEDGMENTS

This book would not have been possible without the poets known in these pages as Gabriel, Mark, Brian, Jasmine, Jorge, Nicole, Rafael, Shawna, and Stacey. I thank them for welcoming me into their writing lives. I also thank the two teachers in this book, who are recorded here as Ms. Sanderson and Mr. Casale. They regularly go out of their way to make spoken word poetry available to students at their school.

I appreciate all of the hardworking people at the University of Massachusetts Press for the time and effort they have invested in this project. In particular, I am grateful to my editor, Matt Becker, for his clarity and guidance. I also thank my production editor, Rachael DeShano, and my copyeditor, Jon Berry.

A version of the opening vignette first appeared in the article, "Every Voice Matters: Spoken Word Poetry in and outside of School," published in the March 2015 issue of *English Journal*. I thank the National Council of Teachers of English for permission to use material from that article in this book.

Over the past several years, the Commission on Arts and Literacies (COAL) has provided scholars and teachers with a supportive space at National Council of Teachers of English conferences to discuss arts integration. I thank co-chairs Kathie Macro and Michelle Zoss for including my work on youth spoken word poetry in COAL sessions and in their volume on arts integration.

Long before I started this book, I was lucky enough to study with several people who influenced my work. Dottie Broaddus played a role early on in my college education by encouraging me to go to graduate school. Alleen Nilsen welcomed me into the academy and helped me to think about various aspects of English education; I have always appreciated her keen insights and unfailing humor and support. James Gee taught me to pay attention to the role of identity in learning. Tom Barone introduced me to the world of narrative and arts-based forms of research. Django Paris introduced me to the study of youth literacies and, quite frankly, without him, this project would not exist.

When I was in the early planning stages of this project, Jim Blasingame listened carefully and helped me adjust my path in ways that ended up making all the difference. Josephine Marsh gave me the courage to embrace narrative research, which set me free. Duane Roen has been a helpful guide to me over many years. These days, he is also a supporter of our Sparky Slam at ASU, an event that brings together local poets, high school students, teachers, college students, and professors to celebrate youth voices.

I appreciate that Eric Nystrom provided feedback on an early version of my book proposal. In fact, I am fortunate to have so many fantastic colleagues in the Interdisciplinary Humanities and Communication Department at ASU. In particular, I thank Vanessa Fonseca-Chávez, Manu Avilés-Santiago, Tatiana Batova, Trish Murphy, Lori Eshleman, Leandra Swanner, Claire Lauer, Andy Mara, Eva Brumberger, and Brooks Simpson for their encouragement and support. Furthermore, the College of Integrative Sciences and Arts at ASU provided two summer research grants to help fund the writing of this book.

Jayne Lammers, Tim San Pedro, Meredith DeCosta, Mary Powell, Cynthia Kiefer, Shelly Shaffer, Aron Jones, Melissa Williamson, Alice Hays, Jason Griffith, and Stephanie Reid have been wonderful. I also thank my friends in the Arizona English Teachers Association and the many students I have worked with over the years.

A special thank you goes to Sybil Durand for inviting me to share my work in writing groups she organized in Tempe and Phoenix. She is a thoughtful friend and mentor. I am also lucky to have dear friends like Tracey Flores, April McNary, Kim and Gregory Casale, Cora Fox, Juliann Vitullo, Taylor Corse, Gigi and Bob Bjork, Patty Friedrich, Luiz Mesquita, Nicole and Patrick Bixby, Mary Yu, Lena Hing, and Kristen Dunham. Marcellina and Los Dos checked on me often throughout this project.

Over the years I have received much-needed encouragement from Edward, Alice, and Celia Moulton. Thank you also to Heather Williams-Thoe and Mike, Emily, and Ethan Thoe.

My deepest appreciation goes to my loving parents, Judy and Bruce Williams, who surrounded me with books, music, art, and games. They taught me to value learning and creativity early on.

I am grateful to the talented and clever Sophia Moulton, my daughter who brought laughter and hugs into every day I worked on this project. Finally, I thank my amazing husband, Ian Moulton, for his impressive intelligence, humor, optimism, and thoughtfulness—not to mention, the daily cappuccinos he made for me, which fueled this project.

LISTEN TO THE POET

INTRODUCTION
LISTENING TO THE POETS

We are not approaching young people as if they're lacking.
—Mark

Inside a Poetry Writing Workshop

The poetry workshop begins at noon. As the teenagers enter the space, they greet each other, talking, smiling, and hugging. Several of the adolescents have brought journals, and others turn to a neighbor to ask for a piece of paper or a pen. A few people look at their phones and send a last-minute text. The group is seated in a circular configuration made up of small tables pulled together, and there are additional chairs along the perimeter of the room. Metal scrapes against the floor as latecomers hurry to bring in several more chairs to accommodate the twenty-three teenagers in attendance.

Seated among the group, right at their eye level, is their teacher, Mark.[1] He is dressed casually and has brought his lunch with him. He tucks into his meal despite the fact that food is not allowed here. No one seems to mind. Mark is friendly and jokes with the adolescents, yet he is clearly in charge. Their respect for him is palpable.

He begins the session by asking each teenager to say his or her name and favorite color. Mark takes time with each of them, and sometimes he stops and backs up to previous speakers, reviewing their names and testing himself. He looks into their eyes and listens to their words without writing down anything. This goes on for several minutes, clearly a valued part of the session.

Once Mark is satisfied that he knows their names, he launches into a grammar review.

"Who knows what a noun is?" he asks. "Person, place, or thing, or idea, right?" They review some examples together, and then Mark says, "Write those on the top of your paper, so you know what they are."

"All right, so now I need two verbs. What's a verb? . . . Yes, my friend? . . . Jump. Jump's a verb, right?"

"Adjectives. What are adjectives?" The workshop continues like this.

"So what's going to happen is you're going to take these words, and you're going to put them into a series of sentences. This does not have to make sense, okay? It does not have to change the world. It does not matter really. It's an exercise, okay? So if my words were 'jump,' 'swing,' 'cat,' and 'dog,' and my introductory sentence was, 'Here we go again . . . ,' I'd be like, 'Here we go again. I'm swinging with a bunch of cats, talking to dogs about'—whatever this one was that I forgot, okay? You feel me? It does not have to make sense. In fact, the more out there it is, the more entertaining it's going to be, okay? So don't focus on like 'this sounds *stupid*.'" The group laughs as he says this last part with a high pitch for effect. They seem at ease with Mark. Everyone writes, and after a minute and a half, eight people volunteer to share what they have written.

After this writing exercise, Mark leads the group in a close reading of Julie Sheehan's "Hate Poem." It is a piece in which hatred is expressed to such a degree it is comical, and there are hints that the narrator also feels love for the person described. While they discuss the piece, Mark keeps sending them back to the text, saying things like, "So what part of the poem, if we can look at the text, what part of the poem—or parts of the poem—tell us like, okay, she really doesn't hate this person? What moment? Try to find it right now."

They discuss some of these moments. Then the instructor shares his own feelings about the poem. Mark says, "The beautiful thing about this wonderful woman named Julie Sheehan is that she's bringing you really close to her world. She's saying, 'While you dig through the cashews, I hate you. My breath says I hate you.' What's really beautiful about this poem is when you read through it, it's like, 'Oh, I know more about her. She's like me. We have this human thing.' She does that by adding details: 'The little blue-green speck of sock lint I'm trying to dig from under my third toenail, left toe, hates you.'" The group laughs. "That is detail. That is hilarious. That is what makes it funny."

The writers have half an hour to compose poems of their own, and he encourages them to use sarcasm like the mentor text did. Walking among the writers, Mark occasionally shushes those who are off task or stops to help a writer who is stuck. I hear him reassuring someone, saying, "Just explore it. Have fun."

The thirty minutes go by quickly. Then ten people volunteer to read their work. Mark gives them minimal feedback, sometimes simply saying, "Who's next?" He encourages everyone to read their work but not so he can critique it. Instead, he is trying to get these adolescents to be brave and share something, anything.

As 1:30 p.m. nears, Mark closes with a personal story and some words of advice. He says, "When I was a young person, I had a lot of . . . issues with anger. I think maybe the only thing that really helped me negotiate my world, [because] it was confusing, was writing. There's a lot of things you're not going to have control of. But what's beautiful about writing, and this is what I want you to remember, is that you can control every single element of what you need to say. And that is one of the things that helped me survive. And I'm not saying it's going to help you, but I promise you, the more you write and the more you speak, the easier it's going to be to find who you are and value that thing. Okay? So, again, thank you. Keep writing, and treat each other well."

The session ends without a bell, and the writers disperse until 2:00 p.m., when they will have a chance to perform their poems for a larger audience (observation, October 12, 2013).

The scene described above could have happened in any number of secondary English classrooms in the United States. A teacher guided his students through a poetry workshop, breaking the content down into manageable instructional components and checking for understanding at multiple points along the way. Students reviewed parts of speech, listed examples, wrote, and shared their writing with the class. They read and analyzed a mentor text, and as they discussed that poem, the teacher asked students to return to the text to gather specific evidence in support of their claims. This poem later served as a springboard for a writing activity. Throughout the workshop, writers engaged in close reading, focused writing, careful listening, and frequent sharing. There was a great deal of active participation, and students seemed highly motivated to write.

What is interesting about this scene, however, is that it did not take place in a school; it occurred on a Saturday afternoon in a public library in Arizona. The adolescents attended voluntarily, and Mark was not paid. Mark is the founder of Metropoets, a youth spoken word poetry network[2] that offers free monthly events like the one described above. Adolescents write and perform poetry in this group. In addition, Metropoets sends teaching artists into about ten schools to assist with after-school poetry clubs, and they conduct summer writing camps in partnership with a charity for youth who have faced economic hardships and abuse.

The Metropoets network helps young people gain confidence, and it provides spaces for poets to challenge injustices. The group is inclusive, welcoming poets of all races, ethnicities, languages, socioeconomic classes, religions, genders, sexualities, and levels of education. Latina/o, white, African American, and Indigenous (Native American) writers are present in proportions that roughly reflect the populations of the urban areas where Metropoets operates. Typically more girls than boys attend.

Some of the poets who shine on the Metropoets stage previously failed a high school English class or even dropped out of high school altogether. In fact, Gabriel, who runs the group with Mark, dropped out of high school when he was a teenager. Today he has a GED and is working toward a college degree while helping to expand this literacy organization for adolescents.

What is Spoken Word Poetry?

Spoken word is poetry that is performed. As such, it "tends to forefront rhythm, improvisation, free association, rhymes, and the use of hybrid language, from rich poetic phrasing to the gritty imagery of the vernacular" (Weiss and Herndon 2001, 118). Often spoken word poems are political and comment on current issues. This form also has musical aspects (Fisher 2007b). It has been influenced by hip-hop culture and rap music, not to mention blues and jazz traditions (Beach et al. 2016; Chang 2005; Weiss and Herndon 2001).

Oral poetry has a long history and can be found in many cultures. We may read poems like *The Odyssey* and *Beowulf* on the page today, but these poems circulated orally first. Richard Prince (2003) situates today's spoken word poets within a tradition of oral storytelling, arguing that spoken word poets "are part of the old bardic or folk tradition of people gathering to sing, tell stories, and share with words what they think and feel. This tradition encompasses the Homeric epic, medieval ballads, the English broadside, and any culture's folk songs and folktales" (141). Texts shared orally also allow for some degree of improvisation. For example, while *The Odyssey* follows a structured meter throughout (i.e., dactylic hexameter), poets likely improvised lines and phrases within this structure and delivered performances with some variation (Knox 1996). Recitation can involve sophisticated processes, and even metered lines allow for flexibility and improvisation.

Many movements, individuals, and spaces have shaped the spoken word we hear and see today. In particular, the Harlem Renaissance, the Black Arts

Movement, the Beat Poets, the Last Poets, and the Watts Prophets have been influential (Jocson 2008; Lee 2008; Rivera 2013; Weinstein 2009; Weiss and Herndon 2001). Also, the creation of the poetry slam as a contest profoundly changed this art form. Marc Smith is credited with coming up with the first poetry slam in Chicago during the eighties (Eleveld 2003). The Nuyorican Poets Café in New York has been an important space for spoken word over several decades, and television shows like *Def Poetry Jam* brought spoken word to a larger audience (Jocson 2008).

Drawing on several African American traditions, spoken word employs practices such as call-and-response, as well as testifying and witnessing, "narrative practices [that] can be located within the homiletical tradition of the Black church" (Hill 2009, 71). Soraya Sablo Sutton (2008) suggests that such practices have helped "African Americans learn to value the creative use of oral language for the purpose of socialization and cultural survival" (215). The practice of call-and-response involves interaction between the speaker and the audience. Geneva Smitherman (1977) describes this practice as "the congregation's way of 'talking back' to the preacher, the most well-known example of which is 'A-men'" (104). Geneva Smitherman (1977) describes this practice as "the congregation's way of 'talking back' to the preacher, the most well-known example of which is 'A-men'" (104). Smitherman explains that this practice can be traced back to slavery and "this singing pattern [can be found] in old plantation work-song styles" (112). In the context of the current studies, at a Metropoets slam, a host might say, "Can I get a yeah, yeah?" and the audience would know to reply, "Yeah, yeah." These events are interactive. In the context of the current studies, at a Metropoets slam, a host might say, "Can I get a yeah, yeah?" and the audience would know to reply, "Yeah, yeah." These events are interactive.

Poetry slams draw on witnessing and testifying traditions. That is, poets go up to the mic to testify, sharing their personal stories, while audience members listen (Fisher 2003; Weinstein 2009). Smitherman (1977) defines "testifyin" as a "concept referring to a ritualized form of black communication in which the speaker gives verbal witness to the efficacy, truth, and power of some experience in which all blacks have shared" (58). In short, "To testify is to tell the truth through 'story'" (150).

Although spoken word has been shaped by African American traditions and history, young people from many different cultural and ethnic backgrounds use this medium today. The two youth poetry groups discussed in this book are majority Latina/o, but poets from many other backgrounds participate as well. Django Paris and H. Samy Alim (2014) suggest that adolescents' cultural identities are fluid, and it is not enough "to sustain African American, Latina/o, Asian American, Pacific Islander American, and Indigenous American languages and cultures in our pedagogies[;] we must be open to sustaining them in both the traditional *and* evolving ways they are lived and used by young people" (91, emphasis in original). In other words, young people's ideas about what it means to be Latina or African American or Navajo are not static. Adolescents are "forging dexterous linguistic identities that belie easy categorizations of what it means to be Black or Brown" (Paris and Alim 2014, 91). This perspective on youth culture matters for the current research. Poets from a variety of backgrounds are embracing spoken word poetry, using it to examine who they are, where they come from, and how the world should be. In Arizona's Sonoran Desert, writers who are Latina/o are using spoken word to comment on the challenges they face in this setting, including racial profiling, English-only mandates in schools, and a border wall that already cuts many families into two. They are testifying about injustices that are specific to their lived experiences.

In fact, spoken word poetry has much in common with the Latin American *testimonio*, or life story genre (Gutierrez 2008; The Latina Feminist Group 2001). A testimonio can be shared orally, in writing, or online, and this form "incorporates political, social, historical, and cultural histories that accompany one's life experiences as a means to bring about change through consciousness-raising" (Delgado Bernal, Burciaga, and Flores Carmona 2012, 364). As with spoken word poetry, "When people share intimate or vulnerable parts of themselves, testimonio pedagogy asks the listeners for openness, respect, and self-reflexivity to forge connections between people who otherwise might never coalesce or build solidarity" (369). Kathryn Blackmer Reyes and Julia Curry Rodriguez (2012) insist that the testimonio is written to be shared. Testimonios and spoken word poetry are resistance literacies with much in common.

Young people are learning to resist and to speak out through the medium of spoken word poetry, thanks to organizations like Youth Speaks and Young Chicago Authors, as well as many other youth poetry groups. Adolescents from around the world, including those in the current study, aspire to compete in the Youth Speaks international poetry competition known as Brave New Voices (Eleveld 2003 and 2007; Jocson 2011; Youth Speaks 2014). To get a sense of what is involved in preparing for major competitions, videos on the Brave New Voices website (Youth Speaks 2014) and the movie *Louder*

Than a Bomb (Jacobs and Siskel 2010) are both enlightening. As poems in these contests show, spoken word can be used to address any topic: gender, race, sexuality, class, family, education, beauty, love, loss, religion, discrimination, abuse, etc. In addition, poems can be delivered individually or with a group. With such versatility, spoken word is a form that many adolescents appreciate. Through it, they are able to examine personal challenges and social issues and even envision new possibilities. Many young people also appreciate the immediate feedback they receive from the audience.

James Kass, founder of Youth Speaks, has compared spoken word to the poetry he experienced as a younger person. Kass (2003) reflects, "I learned . . . that poetry wasn't necessary . . . [and] was tucked away high up on the dusty shelves. Today's generation of poets and poetry organizations is working to change that" (223). In fact, Kass has helped make poetry accessible to a phenomenal number of adolescents through the Brave New Voices (BNV) contest. Jill Tucker (2014) reported that "a quarter-million kids from around the world participate each year" in Youth Speaks programs, and the organization "has raised more than $20 million dollars" since Kass founded it in 1996. Organizations like Youth Speaks have tapped into the excitement and opportunity that spoken word has to offer.

Korina Jocson (2011) has speculated on some of the reasons for spoken word's growing popularity among young people. She points out that this form "exposes social realities that are often steeped in the margins," "is accessible to experimentation in a way that prose is not," and "blends elements of literary precision and performance with . . . hip hop music, language, and style" (156). She adds that thanks to advances in technology poets can now take a poem "from the page to the stage and onto the screen" (158).

Increasingly, spoken word videos are going viral online. For example, the YouTube video "Can We Auto-Correct Humanity?" received more than seventeen million hits within two years (Prince Ea 2014). This poem critiques the social media age and longs for people to make deeper connections face to face. The work includes not just the performance of a spoken word poem, but also music that changes with the mood, cut-away scenes to illustrate points, and animated text for emphasis. Videos like this one demonstrate how spoken word can tap into a range of literacies at once.

While some in literary circles still see spoken word as a lesser art form (Frost 2014), others have argued that spoken word and formal poetry are not so different (Weiss and Herndon 2001). Former U.S. poet laureate Ted Kooser (2007) has praised the "energy overflowing from performance poetry" (xix), and former U.S. poet laureate Billy Collins (2003) has celebrated the oral aspects of spoken word, writing, "To hear a poem is to experience its momentary escape from the prison cell of the page, where silence is enforced" (3).

Unlike formal poetry, spoken word is an accessible and inclusive medium. Young people from all backgrounds are sharing stories, celebrating language, and examining social issues through spoken word. They are learning to be expressive, rhythmic, physical, interactive, political, critical, profound, and entertaining with their words. To imagine poetry as inaccessible except to the educated few is to close one's eyes to the magnitude of the current youth poetry movement.

Scope of Listen to the Poet

This book discusses writing, performance, community, and authorship in two youth spoken word poetry groups in the Metropoets network. I first spent one year (September 2013–September 2014) examining the Metropoets group, an out-of-school group that met monthly on Saturdays at a public library. In this qualitative case study (Hancock and Algozzine 2011; Yin 2006), I looked at the group's practices and adolescent poets' attitudes toward their writing. I found that Metropoets writers composed meaningful texts and shared them with others in a supportive "community of practice" (Wenger 1998). The poets credited several benefits to their participation in this group, including becoming more confident, developing leadership skills, experiencing healing, and learning empathy. They also talked about improving their writing skills and feeling more comfortable at school. This study found that these youth poets have distinct writing practices and attitudes, and they see themselves as writers.

During that yearlong study, the youth poets praised their high school poetry clubs. School poetry clubs are smaller, weekly writing groups where writers do more focused work on their poems. Metropoets teaching artists would visit these clubs to teach lessons and coach students. In response to participants' comments about the value of these clubs, I decided to design a semester-long (January–May 2015) follow-up study of one of these school clubs, Palo Brea Poets Club. In this second qualitative study, I was primarily concerned with learning about how the club operated in comparison to the Metropoets group that met at the public library. Together, these two studies allowed me to consider the possibilities and limitations of literacy learning in two types of contexts (after-school versus out-of-school). I found that Palo Brea Poets Club faced different challenges than the Metropoets group, including issues with censorship, bureaucracy, and attendance. Comparing spoken word in these two settings also revealed the importance of access to mentors who are writers themselves.

One purpose of this book is to show how urban youth who are ethnically and linguistically diverse enact literacy in their lives. I seek to draw attention to adolescents' extracurricular and out-of-school success with writing (Hull and Schultz 2001), as many of these poets craft sophisticated pieces on their own time and perform them for large crowds. Although some of these poets have had negative experiences with school, within this poetry network, they write voluntarily and make valuable contributions to the group.

This book also examines voluntary writing to better understand how schools can make writing instruction more meaningful for secondary students. As it turns out, the sense of community in Metropoets and the sense of authorship poets develop are unlike anything I have seen in schools. When writing is taught in schools, typically the emphasis is placed on the writing process or on the final written product, rather than on the community within which a person writes or how a person feels about him/herself as a writer. The Metropoets network fosters safe spaces for writing, inspiring teenagers to tell their stories. Participating in these spoken word communities seems to transform how adolescents feel about writing and about themselves as writers.

Contributions to the Youth Poetry Conversation

Previous books on youth poets have examined different configurations, settings, and populations of poets. For example, in *Youth Poets: Empowering Literacies in and out of Schools,* Korina Jocson (2008) discusses the implementation of a Poetry for the People program, which involved a partnership between a university and local schools in the San Francisco Bay Area. The majority of poets in Jocson's study identified as black or African American. In *Writing in Rhythm: Spoken Word Poetry in Urban Classrooms,* Maisha Fisher (2007b) explores a school-based spoken word club in the Bronx led by a dedicated teacher-poet. Most poets in Fisher's study identified as Dominican, Puerto Rican, or African American. Finally, in *Feel These Words: Writing in the Lives of Urban Youth,* Susan Weinstein (2009) investigates individual youth songwriters and poets in Chicago. These poets identified as African American or Latino. These three valuable books examine the importance of poetry and literacy in the lives of diverse youth.

Listen to the Poet adds to previous scholarship by examining a network of poets with a unique configuration, setting, and population. Regarding configuration, this book looks at two groups in the same poetry network: an out-of-school group at a public library and an after-school club at a high school.

In addition, the setting for this research is unlike the settings of the three studies mentioned above. Metropoets and Palo Brea Poets Club operate in Arizona, a traditionally conservative-leaning state with a poor record of treatment of historically marginalized groups, including those who have emigrated from Mexico. Readers may have heard of Maricopa County's former sheriff, Joe Arpaio, who served from 1993 through 2016 and made national news for immigration sweeps, racial profiling, and poor treatment of prison inmates (Hagan 2012). It is worth pointing out the vastness of the county he oversaw. Maricopa County has approximately four million people and spans nine thousand square miles consisting of multiple cities (e.g., Phoenix, Mesa, Tempe, Scottsdale, etc.), not to mention several rural areas, the Salt River Pima Maricopa Indian Community, and the Gila River Indian Community (U.S. Census Bureau 2014).

Arizona is an interesting place to conduct youth literacies research. The area was part of Mexico until the mid-nineteenth century, and it only became a state in 1912. The population of the state is nearly one-third Hispanic or Latino. According to U.S. Census Bureau (2014) figures, the state population is 56.2 percent white, 30.5 percent Hispanic or Latino, 5.3 percent American Indian and Alaska Native, 4.7 percent black or African American, and 3.3 percent Asian. The urban areas in which these studies took place have proportionally greater ethnic and linguistic diversity.

Many members in the Metropoets group and Palo Brea Poets Club are part of families with roots in Mexico, and they identify as Hispanic, Latina/o, Mexican American, Chicana/o, or Mestiza/o. Situated within a border state, Metropoets members engage in several practices rooted in Southwestern and Mexican traditions. For example, poets make references to coming-of-age events like *quinceañeras,* and the group's call-and-response practice to warm up the crowd includes a *grito,* a cry often used in *mariachi* music. Poets use this space to address injustices to the Mexican American community in Arizona, including bills that have limited people's rights, language use in school, and access to curriculum.

The Political Aspects of Literacy in Metropoets

The political aspects of literacy are at work in Metropoets. In this group, freedom of speech is encouraged, and poets regularly share poems that argue for justice and equality for all. Women, people of color, LGBTQ members, and members practicing different religions are valued. Furthermore, all members have access to literacy, and they are expected to cultivate reading, writing, listening, and speaking skills as they develop the agency and voice to stand up for what is right. In Metropoets, diverse youth are empowered through literacy. This is especially important given the political context in which Metropoets operates.

Arizona has had an English only mandate for schools since 2000, which means that English must be the language of instruction. In addition, three years before my first study of spoken word poets, two controversial bills went through the state legislature. In 2010, Arizona lawmakers passed SB1070, a bill allowing racial profiling, and HB2281, which banned the teaching of ethnic studies in schools. When SB1070 passed, I was a high school teacher in Phoenix, and many of our students participated in a walk out, leaving campus to join other activists from around the state at a protest. (For a description of that protest, see Django Paris's 2012 article.) During my study of Metropoets, the Arizona legislature also passed SB1062, a bill that would have permitted discrimination against gay and lesbian customers; however, Governor Brewer ultimately vetoed this 2014 bill. These controversial laws, even when overturned in whole or in part, have rattled many members of Metropoets. The themes of equality, sexual orientation, and ethnic pride in their poems need to be understood as occurring in conversation with the unique political context in which these writers live.

Unfortunately, this legislation has reified the racism and tension present in this border state. Writing about life along the U.S. and Mexico border, Gloria Anzaldua (2012) describes what it is like to be a person of color living in the borderlands: "Gringos in the U.S. Southwest consider the inhabitants of the borderlands transgressors, aliens—whether they possess documents or not . . . The only 'legitimate' inhabitants are those in power, the whites and those who align themselves with whites. Tension grips the inhabitants of the borderlands like a virus. Ambivalence and unrest reside there and death is no stranger" (25–26). Anzaldua suggests that life can be uncertain and scary in the borderlands for people of color.

Operating in the U.S.-Mexico borderland that is Arizona, the Metropoets network provides safe spaces for young people to speak out, and some of its members believe that spoken word is even changing the culture of the state. It is vital to research youth literacies in the borderlands to bring resistance literacies and counter-narratives to light. In fact, several recent studies of youth literacies in Arizona have examined the safe spaces that have formed in response to structural injustices here (Durand, Flores, and Williams 2015; Nicholson 2011; San Pedro 2013).

Listening to the Poets

Like others before me (Intrator and Kunzman 2009), I believe it is essential to bring students' points-of-view into education research and to re-envision new possibilities for English education with young people themselves. For this reason, I incorporate the voices of the poets often in the chapters that follow.

Metropoets members sometimes use the expression, "Listen to the poet!" At poetry slams, judges who do not know the performers and who are sometimes unfamiliar with spoken word poetry altogether are called in to assign scores to each poem. It is the audience's job to try to let the judges know when they have made a bad call. They can do this by booing or yelling out complaints. One phrase the audience might use is, "Listen to the poet," which means that the scores indicate the judges did a poor job of hearing the poet's message. They undervalued the poem and therefore disrespected the poet.

"Listen to the poet" is used as this book's title to honor the young people who are out there "spitting" their poems and sharing their stories. Diverse youth are engaging in literacy practices on their own time and creating powerful writing on their own terms. Working from an asset-focused (rather than a deficit-focused) approach, I suggest that schools and policymakers are failing to acknowledge and value the rich and varied literacy practices that young people participate in with great dedication. Each week brave poets are speaking out at writing workshops and slams all over the United States. This book is an invitation to listen to the poets.

Outline of the Book

Chapters 1 and 2 provide background for the yearlong study of Metropoets. Specifically, chapter 1 shares influential research and theory, and chapter 2 explains the study's design.

Chapter 3 takes readers inside a Metropoets poetry slam and introduces study participants as they enter the scene. This chapter closes with a discussion of poetry slams, performance, and authentic writing.

Chapter 4 looks at the group through Etienne Wenger's (1998) "community of practice" lens, discussing the group's purposes, practices, and tools. The chapter also examines Metropoets in terms of forms of participation, trajectories, global connections, and boundaries and brokering (Wenger 1998). The second part of the chapter focuses on how Metropoets builds a safe space for adolescents to engage in literacy learning. Language use, ground rules, and supportive practices are explored. Examining the structure of Metropoets to this extent can be useful for those who teach writing or work with young people.

Chapter 5 turns to the youth poets' poems, writing practices, and attitudes toward writing. This chapter explores their prewriting, topics, tools, schedules and locations for writing, and whether poets write alone or with others. Also, the poets discuss their writing histories, most powerful writing experiences, motivation to write, sponsors and role models, experiences of flow (Csikszentmihalyi 1990 and 1996), writing challenges and pet peeves, and predictions about future writing. This study found that the adolescent poets have distinct writing practices and preferences, as well as a strong sense of authorship. This work suggests that schools could draw on students' writing practices and preferences in formal instruction to create opportunities for students to identify with their writing and to see themselves as writers.

Chapter 6 takes a look at some of the personal, academic, and writing-related benefits participants have experienced in the Metropoets group. It also looks at challenges the group has faced (i.e., dealing with growth, space issues, and lack of funding). This chapter calls for greater support of literacy groups that empower diverse youth.

Chapter 7 takes readers inside Palo Brea Poets Club, a high school poetry club in the Metropoets network. The chapter explains the design of this semester-long follow-up study and shares key findings about the club's practices, benefits, challenges, and changes over time. The chapter closes by comparing the Metropoets group to Palo Brea Poets Club to explore the limitations and possibilities of literacy learning in out-of-school versus after-school spaces.

The conclusion takes both studies into account and shares some implications for education. In particular, the chapter considers what schools can do to support writing, performance, community, and authorship. In line with the book's theme of listening to the poets, this chapter closes with advice from the young poets themselves about how to improve education.

Finally, the afterword looks back on the poetic journey I took during the year I studied the Metropoets group. I situate my own experiences writing and performing a poem for this group with findings from my research. As it turns out, sharing my wounds within a supportive community was a powerful experience for me. I can understand why so many young people are drawn to spoken word poetry.

CHAPTER 1

GUIDING RESEARCH AND THEORY

I write basically every day.
           —*Stacey*

Various studies and theoretical perspectives have shaped the research presented in *Listen to the Poet*. In the sections below, I highlight influential research in the areas of literacy in communities, extracurricular writing, youth literacies, and spoken word groups. I also address sociocultural theory and the concept of "communities of practice," which are useful for shedding light on literacy learning in these two diverse youth poetry groups in Arizona.

Guiding Research
Literacy in Communities

Literacy research experienced an important shift when Shirley Brice Heath (1983) turned to communities to study literacy learning. Her ethnography, conducted from 1969 to 1978, examined three groups of families living in the Piedmont Carolinas: those from Trackton, an African American working-class community; Roadville, a white working-class community; and townspeople, African American and white professionals. Heath discovered that all three groups had different ways with words, resulting in varying levels of academic preparedness and advantage as their children entered school. She argues that if schools do not adapt to students' cultures and ways with words, they will "continue to legitimate and reproduce communities of townspeople who control and limit the potential progress of other communities and who themselves remain untouched by other values and ways of life" (369). Heath's ethnography continues to be relevant in literacy studies to this day, as additional research on class, race, family, and community emerges (Delpit, 2006; Lareau 2011; Yosso 2005).

Brian Street's (1984) research in Iran in the 1970s also looked at literacy in communities. His work highlights the social dimension of literacy practices. In later research, Street (1995) looks at how unofficial literacies are "marginalized against the standard of schooled literacy" (128), and he calls for future research that locates "forms of resistance and alternative literacies alongside 'schooled literacy'" (124). Resistance literacies are certainly at work within the Metropoets network.

Heath, Street, and others helped to usher in the "New Literacy Studies" movement of the 1980s. This movement brought with it the understanding that there are multiple ways to be literate, in some ways challenging the oral-versus-written debate (Collins and Blot 2003; Gee 2012). This work paved the way for later studies of literacy in homes and communities.

Extracurricular Writing

The writing that young people engage in outside of the formal curriculum goes by many names such as extracurricular writing, out-of-school writing, unsanctioned writing, voluntary writing, and self-sponsored writing (Abbott 2000; Hudson 1986 and 1988). On their own time, writers choose their topics, practices, and communities rather than have teachers decide these things for them. Judy Abbott (2000) found that "self-sponsored writing at home featured a wider range of audience, purpose, and genre than both assigned and self-sponsored writing at school" (56). She also discovered that some of the work described as self-sponsored actually originated in school as work assigned by teachers, something I found as well with a young rapper who wrote a song about the Holocaust after reading the book *Night* in his high school English class. His school experience influenced his voluntary writing (Williams 2013). In other words, dividing writing into "school" or "out-of-school" is not as clear-cut as it may appear because writers move across different spaces and take ideas and techniques with them (Gutierrez 2008).

In her discussion of extracurricular writing, Anne Ruggles Gere (1994) explains that people have gathered "in living rooms, nursing homes, community centers, churches, shelters for the homeless, around kitchen tables, and in rented rooms to write down their worlds. These writers bear testimony to the fact that writing development occurs outside formal education" (76). People write and learn in a variety of contexts besides schools. Conducting research in these nonschool spaces can yield important findings about learning, literacy, and community that may also have relevance for schools.

There seem to be some key differences between school-sponsored and self-sponsored writing. Janet Emig (1971) found that her participants' out-of-school writing focused on the writer or on society. It tended to involve more prewriting, was usually shared with peers, and typically involved a strong moment of completion, pauses and reflections, and revisions. This stands in stark contrast to the writing participants composed for school, which typically accompanied literary study or responded to issues selected by the teacher, who was also the primary audience for the work (91–93).

Many scholars have commented on the gap between students' interest in their voluntary writing and their lack of interest in writing for school (Mahiri and Sablo 1996; Weinstein 2009). Perhaps students view school assignments as mere exercises, favoring voluntary writing instead, which may be based on their lives or offer "a partial refuge from the harsh realities of their everyday experiences" (Mahiri and Sablo 1996, 174). Voluntary writing often explores topics that schools will not go near (e.g., violence, drugs), and it appears to offer benefits regarding "identity construction," "personal status," and "personal satisfaction" (174).

Studying voluntary literacies can uncover stories of success from a broader range of students and in a broader range of settings. In their review of out-of-school literacies research of the 1980s and 1990s, Glynda Hull and Katherine Schultz (2001) noted that researchers have investigated voluntary writing for multiple purposes, including to "decouple the effects of literacy from the effects of schooling," "account for school failure and out-of-school success," and "push our notions of learning and development" (602–3). Going outside of school to study adolescent writing removes a complex array of factors associated with the classroom context (e.g., school rules, a fixed schedule, mandated attendance, homework, classwork, tests, standardized curriculum, etc.).

When out-of-school youth literacies combine with academic learning, a "third space" can result (Bhabha 1994; Gutierrez 2008; Moje et al. 2004; Soja 1996). That is, unofficial (home/community) and official (school) spheres overlap in a hybrid space, creating new opportunities for participation and learning. Palo Brea Poets Club and the Metropoets group both operate in third spaces in which teaching artists make poetry accessible to adolescents. Many studies have examined this type of bridging between school and out-of-school literacies (Alvermann and Hinchman 2011; Gutierrez 2008; Hull and Schultz 2001 and 2002; Sweeny 2010). It is worth mentioning that such bridging does not mean teachers should lead kids into academic learning with their out-of-school interests only to discard that piece once the academic material is introduced. Rather, students' out-of-school literacies themselves are worthy of exploration—and therefore, critique—in the classroom (Kirkland 2008).

Glynda Hull and Katherine Schultz (2002) have called for research that explores partnerships between schools and communities, and they have pointed out that if divisions must exist between schools and communities, more work is needed to understand how these divisions should work. The studies in this book, which examine both an out-of-school group and an after-school club, demonstrate useful points of convergence and divergence between schools and communities (see chapter 7).

When young people engage in unsanctioned writing, they do so by choice, rather than for an academic reward or out of fear of punishment for noncompliance. A student may struggle to produce a paragraph on a set topic in school only to stay up late that evening, captivated by the art of writing fan fiction, a rap, or a blog. The more teachers know about the writing young people are drawn to during their free time, the better they can shape curriculum to engage all writers in the classroom.

Youth Literacies

In their lives outside of school, adolescents are engaging in a wide range of writing practices for multiple purposes and audiences. Some of these forms of writing include drama (Winn 2011), autobiography (Wissman and Vasudevan 2012), graffiti (Chang 2005; Cintron 1997), texting (Paris 2010), fan fiction (Trainor 2008), blogs (Blinka and Smahel 2009), and new technologies (Kafai and Peppler 2011; Knobel and Lankshear 2007; Lankshear and Knobel 2011). Some adolescents write a great deal in their lives outside of school, yet adults do not always recognize the forms of writing as legitimate (e.g., texting, social media).

Young people are writing about topics that are important to them in their own words, sometimes even moving between different languages. Many scholars (Alim 2007; Harris 2006; Kinloch 2005a; Morrell 2005; Paris 2009) have stressed the importance of honoring and cultivating linguistic diversity in student writing. In one study, Korina Jocson (2006b) found that a poet sometimes used African American Vernacular English and "incorporate[d] a Chilean way of talking in his poems" (142). Unfortunately, students may feel that they are not free to express themselves or to play with language in school settings. Valerie Kinloch (2005b) recalls students' shock at her "invitation to expressive freedom—freedom to manipulate the 'standard' or 'proper' or 'linear' way to write by playing with style, arrangement, and language forms, particularly home languages, or the 'Mother Tongue'" (102). Furthermore, Marcelle Haddix and Yolanda Sealey-Ruiz (2012) have called for more student freedom and teacher imagination in classrooms, and Haddix recommends that teachers allow students to select "the topics, the genres, and the mediums and tools they use when composing in school" (190). These viewpoints honor students' perspectives, experiences, and words.

When Jabari Mahiri (2008) examined video essays, raps, screenplays, and poems in which youth writers described their experiences, he found that these "street scripts" enabled adolescents to think about their experiences and engage in social critique. His participants attempted to gain greater control of their lives by "actively conceiving and critiquing the nature of their experiences by naming and explicating the paradoxes that clouded their lives" (38). Writing street scripts can be transformative. Pedro Noguera (2008) adds, "these scripts reveal how young people attempt to challenge the larger societal script which positions them as 'at-risk,' troubled and dangerous" (43). Noguera explains that street scripts can be critical, reflective, and hopeful.

Similar to street scripts are "youth space identity texts," which Django Paris (2012) defines as "texts inscribing ethnic, linguistic, local, transnational, and political affiliations on clothing, binders, backpacks, signs, public spaces (e.g., walls and benches), youth authored rap lyrics, and electronic media (e.g., cell phones, Facebook)" (1). Paris suggests that literacy instruction should include the reading and writing of such texts.

When studying youth literacies it is worth acknowledging the importance hip-hop culture has for many adolescents. Adam Bradley (2009) writes, "Hip hop emerged out of urban poverty to become one of the most vital cultural forces of the past century" (xiii). It grew out of the South Bronx "in defiance of inferior educational opportunities and poor housing standards" (xiv). Hip-hop includes elements like dance, graffiti, rap, beat making, freestyle, and rhyme. For some Metropoets members, the poetry slam is a natural extension of the hip-hop culture they are already part of. For example, Metropoets teaching artists use mentor texts by rappers, play familiar songs at poetry slams, and encourage dancing.

Teachers and researchers have begun to explore possible connections between hip-hop and literacy education (Alim 2007; Beach et al. 2016; Morrell and Duncan-Andrade 2002; Sitomer and Cirelli 2004). However, Jung Kim (2011) cautions against "programs [that] package hip-hop in overly simplified ways" and instead recommends using hip-hop to explore "a culture or movement" and to restructure approaches to teaching (173).

Ernest Morrell and Jeffrey Duncan-Andrade (2002) have designed a hip-hop unit for adolescent students that involves poetry study, side-by-side analysis of hip-hop and canonical texts, and the critical reading of a song. David Kirkland (2008) asks, "Why aren't we using hip-hop anyway to help students make sense of the world and make meaning of their lived situations?" (74). He recommends that teachers "incorporate the artifacts of student life (e.g., rap, body art, graffiti, and so on) into classrooms to not only help advance students' academic literacy development but to ultimately adjust how literacy is conceived of, practiced, and assessed" (73). Kirkland makes a strong case for attending to youth literacies in the classroom.

Spoken Word Groups

Spoken word research has found that this medium can offer poets an array of benefits. For example, young writers may come to identify more with writing and literacy as they share their spoken word poetry (Fisher 2007b; Jocson 2008; Weinstein 2010). Some poets conduct research for their pieces, and their commitment to writing may transfer into other settings as poets reach for a thesaurus or carefully revise work for their classes (Jocson 2006a and 2008). As one youth poet attested, "The opportunity of performing was a great help in strengthening my writing" (Weiss and Herndon 2001, 23). Youth spoken word groups can even motivate students to stay in high school and encourage them to move into higher education (Fisher 2007b). These are exciting findings.

In addition, poets may experience a range of personal benefits through spoken word, such as overcoming shyness and gaining self-confidence, and many youth find that spoken word can be therapeutic as well (Weinstein 2010). These works tend to be hopeful even as they address bleak situations (Sutton 2008), and poets seem to develop empathy as they share their stories with each other. James Kass (2007) writes, "I never imagined a girl would read a poem in class about how painful it was for her to choose to have an abortion and that, the next day, when she showed up for class she'd find a bouquet of flowers on her desk paid for by her classmates" (Eleveld 2007, 198). Sharing stories can strengthen community in a group.

Spoken word groups typically bring people of different ages together. Group leaders might be classroom teachers, college interns, or professional poets (Fisher 2007b; Jocson 2008). Open mics and poetry slams can also attract audience members with different backgrounds and experiences. Maisha Fisher (2005) writes that spoken word groups allow for "the inclusion of intergenerational perspectives" (128) and may connect younger members to history, culture, and music (Fisher 2003). Older poets may serve as "literacy activists and advocates," "practitioners of the craft," and "historians of the word" (Fisher 2007a, 157–58). In these spaces, people of different ages are seen as having much to offer each other.

Spoken word has been found to appeal to many young people who did not enjoy writing in school. Soraya Sablo Sutton's (2008) participants expressed that poetry in school was "alienating and uninspiring because it had little to do with their daily lives" (223). In contrast, spoken word gave them a chance to perform poetry about real issues in front of a real audience. A participant in Maisha Fisher's (2007b) study expressed, "Poetry is about us. In English class the reading and curriculum is about them. The school's work. I don't like that at all" (93). Many young people identify with spoken word at a time when high-stakes test preparation is draining and uninspiring.

Despite these benefits, Javon Johnson (2010) argues that scholars need to notice the problems in these poetry groups as well. For example, more work is needed to uncover the homophobia and sexism in slam communities. He reminds scholars to attend to the "racial, gender, class, and sexual dynamics between and among various performers, whereby the notion of community is always a contested concept" (397). Members of a group may very well experience the same community differently, and not everyone will feel welcome. Johnson (2010) adds, "With all the progressive politics many slam and spoken word poets live by, it is somewhat astonishing how frequently queer folks are pushed to the margins" (415). While the issues he brings up may be more prevalent among adult communities of poets, Johnson nonetheless offers a caution that researchers should take seriously as they study young people as well.

Youth poetry groups are certainly not without their challenges. Susan Weinstein and Anna West (2012) have pointed to some of the difficulties adolescent spoken word poets may face in these groups. In particular, poets may be unfairly associated with the poems they write, some poets in a group may be given a higher status, and even the popularity of spoken word poetry in the media can be a negative force. It is necessary to see both the benefits and challenges of these groups for a more complete picture.

Guiding Theory
Sociocultural Theory

Sociocultural theory, which can be used to highlight the social nature of literacy learning (Goncu and Gauvain 2012; Prior 2006), has influenced both of my studies of youth spoken word poetry groups. Applying this lens to studies of youth poets can illuminate the ways that writing happens with others. Specifically, young writers may teach each other techniques, share tools, write works together, adjust their writing based on audience feedback, and write in response to others. Even an author working independently uses preexisting building blocks, including a socially constructed language (Bakhtin 1986; Volosinov 1973), to create something "new." A sociocultural perspective can reveal how socially mediated tools and processes support writers.

A sociocultural perspective can also highlight the communication at work in spoken word spaces. Multiple conversations are in play as poets and poems respond to each other, popular culture, and the social conditions in which poets live. After all, "language is a continuous generative process implemented in the social-verbal interaction of speakers" (Volosinov 1973, 98). M. M. Bakhtin (1986) used the metaphor of communication as links in a chain and argued that utterances occur within larger conversations: "Utterances are not indifferent to one another, and are not self-sufficient; they are aware of and mutually reflect one another . . . , [and] each utterance is filled with echoes and reverberations of other utterances to which it is related by the communality of the sphere of speech communication" (91). These echoes can occur across time and space, with creative people looking to the past for mentors, as Barbara Rogoff (1990) and Vera John-Steiner (1997) have argued. "Exceptionally creative writers, painters, and physicists discover their own teachers from the past" (Rogoff 1990, 198). Moreover, even printed text is situated within a conversation. It is a "verbal performance in print" (Bakhtin 1986, 95).

Young writers learn from more advanced poets in these spoken word poetry groups. A "zone of proximal development" may be at work, which Lev Vygotsky (1978 and 1986) describes as "the distance between the actual developmental level... and the level of potential" (Vygotsky 1978, 86). Often teaching artists are important literacy sponsors (Brandt 2001) for young poets, offering support and resources to mentees.

Paul Prior (2006) has summarized some of the contributions sociocultural theory has made to writing research, and they are of particular use to these studies of the Metropoets network: (1) writing is never a solitary act, even if it appears so; (2) writing results in artifacts that encapsulate culture; (3) resources for writing derive from multiple literacies and ways of knowing; and, (4) although the act of writing happens in measurable units of time, the influences and experiences that culminate in that writing stretch back into the writer's past—even into the history of his or her culture. Amy Burgess and Roz Ivanic (2010) add that notions of the future also affect how writers write. In other words, writers imagine future contexts in which their work will be read or heard.

Communities of Practice

The two youth spoken word groups examined in this book are both examples of communities of practice. A "community of practice" (Lave and Wenger 1991; Wenger 1998 and 2000; Wenger, McDermott, and Snyder 2002) is a group in which members gather around a common endeavor—in this case, writing and performing spoken word poetry. Communities of practice are similar to "affinity groups" (Gee 2004). Members learn from each other and through participation in the practice. "Legitimate peripheral participation" (Lave and Wenger 1991) is often at work in a community of practice, meaning that even novices can participate in the practice in valued ways. In fact, all members can participate in different ways and to different extents. In a spoken word group, this means that novices may choose not to perform. On the other hand, more advanced poets may perform every time, take on leadership roles, mentor younger poets, and eventually become teaching artists themselves. Some of Etienne Wenger's (1998) ideas about communities of practice are applied to the Metropoets group in chapter 4.

CHAPTER 2

STUDYING THE POETS

Energy. Love. We are celebrating young people's voices.
—Gabriel

I pull off the freeway and make my way toward the library, eager to meet the poets. The road alternates between five and six lanes across. This is an urban area with a hospital, medical offices, fast food restaurants, a large grocery store, smaller ethnic grocery stores and restaurants, a beauty college, a uniform supply store, strip clubs, and loan stores. Some of the buildings I pass house organizations that offer resources to women, children, and families in need.

Large, colorful murals are painted on some buildings. As I get closer to the library, I near museums, theaters, and arts organizations of various kinds. Some downtown skyscrapers are visible. People are out walking, waiting along bus routes and rail lines, and getting around on their bikes. At a bus stop, two police officers are talking to a man with a shopping cart.

This library is near a light rail stop, yet the parking lot is relatively full of cars. I find a spot and make my way toward the entrance. There are several people sitting outside. Someone asks for change. Other people are visible in a nearby park, sitting with their belongings. Near the library entrance, a man with a clipboard is calling out for people to come over and sign a petition.

The doors to the library slide open, and I go in search of the poets.

Metropoets

The Metropoets network, a spoken word poetry organization run by poets Mark and Gabriel, began in 2009 when a teacher asked Mark for help coaching students for the Brave New Voices poetry competition. Mark worked with a group of ten to fifteen kids, but after a while, the teacher who invited him left the school. Mark continued volunteering with the school club, but he grew tired of the other teachers' lack of support, not to mention the district bureaucracy involved with taking a group of kids out of state to compete. He decided to move the group outside of the school setting, and they started meeting in a room at an art museum. At that time, there were five to seven members, and Mark prepared them for competitions and helped them raise money to travel to events.

Gabriel came on board in 2011. The two men had attended some of the same adult open mic events around town. They got to know each other when Gabriel invited Mark to participate in a play that he was organizing for youth. Their friendship grew out of that collaboration, and Gabriel is now the executive director of Metropoets, which means that he runs the day-to-day operations and is in charge of marketing. Mark's growing popularity as a rapper and poet has meant that Gabriel has had to take over the running of the Saturday workshops and slams. Mark still maintains the role of visionary for the group, designing curriculum, training teaching artists, and refining their philosophy for the work they are doing with kids. When my study began in fall 2013, Mark and Gabriel said the group was beginning its second season in its current iteration, which they defined as a school year that included a Town Slam event (i.e., an annual two-day workshop and competition that Mark and Gabriel host to bring together poets from the school clubs).

During the 2013–2014 season, they typically held one Saturday event per month, consisting of a 12:00–1:30 p.m. writing workshop and a 2:00–4:00 p.m. slam. While a workshop might attract twenty-five young writers, slams typically attracted at least fifty audience members (sometimes as many as eighty). Between ten and twenty poets would perform. These Saturday events were free and open to the public. Most adolescents learned about them through their school poetry clubs. Others would attend because they did not have clubs at their schools, and this was their only opportunity to perform spoken word. Sometimes people who happened to be in the library at the time would drop by. Hearing the music and energy of the slam, they headed upstairs to see what was happening.

Gaining Access

I first became acquainted with Metropoets when Mark, Gabriel, and Jorge (a youth poet in this study) performed at an English teachers' convention I attended in 2012. Their poems were emotional and powerful. As I was later planning a yearlong study of youth literacies, Metropoets seemed an obvious choice because of the group's reputation for making a difference in the lives of teenagers. When I visited Metropoets at the library in the beginning of the 2013–2014 season, Gabriel met me at the door. Rather than questioning who I was and what I was doing there, he immediately welcomed me, expressing appreciation that I was interested in studying them. He said he saw my presence as a benefit to the group.

The adolescent participants I recruited were equally friendly and eager to talk to me about their writing. The fact that Gabriel and Mark were on board with the study seemed enough for them to trust me, and they said as much. Part of this is likely due to the community norms already established within Metropoets. The group encourages poets to get up and meet new people, including adults, after every slam.

The first few times I attended Metropoets events, the group leaders allowed me to blend into the background. Eventually Gabriel asked me to introduce myself at a writing workshop, and I said I was a doctoral student and a former high school English teacher. I told them I was visiting Metropoets to learn about their spoken word poetry group and to try to discover ways to make high school English classes more relevant for students.

As an adult who was not a teaching artist in the space, I was automatically positioned as an outsider. This position can sometimes offer the researcher "the advantage of noticing what insiders do not notice" (Anderson-Levitt 2006, 286). To be fair, few adults attended these workshops for adolescents, and when adult guests did visit, they were not expected to write and perform unless they were teaching artists from school clubs. Visiting teachers, professors, parents, and other adult guests were welcome, but their age marked them as distinctly outside the scope of this youth spoken word poetry group.

At Metropoets workshops and slams throughout the year, I typically sat at the back of the room with my research equipment. When I noticed some members were arriving without paper and pens, I started bringing extra supplies to workshops. I also chatted with participants at breaks, commiserating with them when they drew a poor slot (e.g., going first in a slam usually guarantees low scores), offering words of encouragement or praise for a great performance, or asking them how things were going. When I first attended slams, I was slow to participate as the audience members around me did. Snapping and shouting out encouragement during a poem are common practices at slams. However, my own cultural experiences had conditioned me to be a silent audience member. Even though I knew the audience was expected to respond, I was afraid that I might distract the poet and make him or her forget lines. It took me several months to get over this fear and feel comfortable with slam norms. Now I snap and make utterances in response to poems without worry and long for these practices in other situations, such as academic conferences.

During the yearlong study, I wanted to give the poets a poem in return for the stories they had shared with me. It seemed only fair that I would share something meaningful and real with them. This development was not a part of my original study design, but it emerged from spending time with the group. I recalled Marc Lamont Hill's (2009) description of Mr. Colombo, a teacher who listened to students' stories without contributing any himself. He "was often positioned within the class as a voyeur who engaged in one-sided storytelling for the purpose of what Foucault (1990) calls 'the pleasure of analysis,' or a self-centered obsession with the sources of pleasure (or in this case pain) of another person. It was this type of surveillance, or at least its perception, that further marginalized Mr. Colombo within the class" (89). I did not want to be a Mr. Colombo in this study. At the same time, everyone knew I was no spoken word poet. Eventually, with repeated exposure to spoken word and hearing from Gabriel that my presence mattered to the group, my poetic confidence grew. I ultimately did write and perform a poem for the poets, a journey I reflect on in the afterword of this book.

Researcher's Stance

I am a white middle-class female who was born in Arizona. My path to studying youth literacies can be traced to my own adolescence, when I performed in my high school's talent show. Jamming out on my electric guitar and singing a song I wrote to an auditorium full of people in 1994 was the highlight of my high school years. When I later taught high school, I organized a school talent show to make this opportunity available to students at our school. Two rappers in that show impressed the audience with their intriguing lyrics and fascinating beats, and they left me wanting to find out more about them and their writing. The following year, when I took a doctoral seminar on youth literacies with Django Paris, I realized I needed to track them down and learn more about their literacy practices through a formal study (Williams 2013). Investigating youth songwriting showed me how complex and sophisticated extracurricular writing could be. My study found value in venturing outside of school to understand the literacies that young people practice and identify with.

The move to studying spoken word seemed like a logical progression from studying youth songwriting, as both forms involve performance, poetic phrasing, and artistic use of voice. In addition, they both demand creativity, something I am willing to fight for, for both students and teachers, in this era of standardization in education. For several years, I have been a member of the Commission on Arts and Literacies, a group of teachers, teacher educators, and researchers within the Conference on English Education and the National Council of Teachers of English. Arts-based pedagogies (Emert, Macro, and Schmidt 2016) that encourage creative, multimodal expression are central to my teaching and research. The arts have been important to me personally, and hobbies like writing, photography, and the culinary arts have deepened my appreciation for creative expression. Rather than buying into the idea that the arts are only for certain people born with natural talent, I believe that everyone can benefit from creative expression and encounters with the arts. Spoken word is an incredible art form.

I am not a spoken word poet myself, but I believe we must meet kids where they are. If adolescents are interested in spoken word poetry, researchers should study this writing phenomenon because it matters to young people. While it can be humbling to venture into the unfamiliar, it is exciting also as we trust young people to teach us about literacy. Jen Weiss and Scott Herndon (2001) write, "When you encounter unfamiliar terrain, you must listen instead of seeking refuge in what you already know" (60). This theme echoes throughout this book as I turn to the poets for answers.

Research Design

My yearlong study of the Metropoets group employed qualitative case study methodology (Hancock and Algozzine 2011; Yin 2006). Sharan Merriam (2009) describes case study as "an in-depth description and analysis of a bounded system" (40), and Robert Yin (2006) argues that case studies are appropriate when a researcher needs "to illuminate a particular situation, to get a close (i.e., in-depth and firsthand) understanding of it" (112). Case study methodology allowed me to study the entire group as a case and to examine individual cases within the group as well.

Three research questions guided the yearlong study: What are the characteristics and practices of the Metropoets group?; How do adolescent members of this group view their writing and themselves as writers?; and What changes, personal or writing-related, do adolescent writers attribute to their experiences in Metropoets? As these questions demonstrate, the study was concerned with understanding both the structure of the group and the experiences of individual members.

Site

The study took place in an urban area of Arizona. The workshops and slams that ran from September 2013 to September 2014 were almost always held in the same public library. The library is made up of several floors, and Metropoets workshops took place in one of two rooms. Usually they were in the teen wing, a space that also houses young adult literature, computers, study group tables, and televisions. At the back of this wing is an area with many small café rounds and chairs. Metropoets usually met back in this semi-private space. To accommodate up to thirty attendees, the group would pull the café rounds together into a big circle. A few times, a large room was available on the same floor, so workshops and slams were held there.

Slams usually took place in a lecture room on the same level. This wood-paneled room seats about eighty people. Gabriel and friends carried in their equipment from the parking lot. At minimum they needed a microphone, a stand, and a speaker for the slams. The microphone and stand were set up in the front of the room right in the center. A table at stage right was set up with a speaker, and the deejay would operate from there. Deejays brought their own music on their phones, tablets, or laptops. Usually the group displayed a professional-looking Metropoets banner with the group's logo at stage left. Judges for the poetry slam would sit in the front row, facing the deejay table. Hosts would go back and forth between the microphone and a seat in the audience, often sitting in the very back of the room and blending in with other audience members during poems. On those occasions when shirts, sweatshirts, or Mark's album were for sale, they would be sold from a table in the back. Gabriel's mother or one of the teaching artists would handle the money and merchandise.

I conducted most of the interviews in study rooms in this library. These rooms have glass walls, a table, and four chairs each. The rooms could be reserved in blocks of two hours per day, and four people were allowed in them at a time, which worked well for the small focus group interview that I conducted with three of the participants. While most of the adolescent interviews took place in these study rooms, there were some exceptions. I interviewed Shawna at the charity where she works because transportation was an issue for her. In fact, her mentor waited for her in an adjoining office, ready to drive her home when our interview concluded. I once met Jorge in a mall food court close to his house because he was having a hard time getting transportation to the library that day. I interviewed Gabriel in an office at the university where he works and goes to school because that was most convenient for him, and I interviewed Mark at a coffee shop within biking distance of his home.

Participants

After my university's institutional review board (IRB) approved the study, I began recruiting participants. Two adult leaders of Metropoets (Mark and Gabriel) and six of the adolescent members (Shawna, Jorge, Rafael, Jasmine, Nicole, and Stacey) participated in the yearlong study. All participants signed consent forms—and in the case of minors, their parents signed forms as well—before they were able to participate in the study. Group leaders assisted me in identifying adolescent participants according to the following criteria: (1) ages thirteen to nineteen, (2) a cross-section of the group, representing the range of races, ethnicities, genders, and ages present, and (3) diversity in experience: at least one beginning, one intermediate, and one advanced poet (see table below). Each participant is described in more detail in the poetry slam narrative in the next chapter.

Adolescent Participants in the Yearlong Metropoets Study

Name*	Level**	Experience	Age	Grade	Gender	Race/ Ethnicity
Shawna	Beginner	3 months	19	GED in progress	Female	Black
Jorge	Advanced	2 years, 1 month	18	1st year college	Male	Hispanic
Rafael	Beginner	1 year	18	12	Male	Latino
Jasmine	Intermediate	1 year, 1 month	16	11	Female	Hispanic
Nicole	Intermediate	1 year, 8 months	16	11	Female	White
Stacey	Beginner	2 years	15	9	Female	Hispanic

* Participants had the opportunity to select their own pseudonyms.
** Information was reported by participants at the beginning of the study, with the exception of "level," which was determined by the teaching artists.

Data Collection

The yearlong study drew on multiple forms of data, including observations, interviews, and artifacts.[1] These different sources allowed for triangulation of data (Calfee and Sperling 2010; Denzin and Lincoln 2008), which Robert Stake (2008) describes as "a process of using multiple perceptions to clarify meaning, verifying the repeatability of an observation or interpretation" (133). Seeking out multiple perspectives can make case study findings more robust (Yin 2006) by providing both confirming and disconfirming evidence.

Between September 2013 and September 2014, I attended thirteen Metropoets events. Most of these events consisted of a ninety-minute writing workshop, a thirty-minute break, and a two-hour poetry slam. Occasionally I photographed participants while they were writing, discussing poems, preparing to present, or "spitting" their poems at the microphone. I also wrote ethnographic field notes (Emerson, Fretz, and Shaw 1995) at these events to capture my impressions of what was going on in the space and to record observations that my videocamera and audiorecorder would not record (e.g., the number of attendees, conversations with participants at breaks). I transferred audio files to Express Scribe and used a foot pedal to do my own transcription, omitting nonparticipants at the point of transcription. In July 2014, after I had collected most of the data for the study, I went back and viewed all of the videos and wrote additional notes.

Interviews were an important data source for this study. The interviews were semistructured (Merriam 2009), which "has the advantage of asking all informants the same core questions with the freedom to ask follow-up questions that build on the responses received" (Brenner 2006, 362). I audiorecorded the sixteen interviews and transcribed them in full. Occasionally my questions prompted participants to tell a story. Irving Seidman (2006) recommends this technique because stories can reveal details about plot and character and may "lead to treasured moments in interviewing" (88).

I interviewed Gabriel and Mark separately in June 2014, and these interviews were approximately ninety minutes each. For the adolescent interviews, I invited the youth to take part in a series of three interviews, consisting of two individual interviews each and one focus group interview. The three adolescent interviews explored the following topics: (1) their writing lives (average length: fifty minutes), (2) their participation in Metropoets (average length: ninety minutes), and (3) performance and discussion of two of their poems (average length: sixty minutes). All six adolescent poets participated in the three interviews except for

Shawna, who only participated in the first interview. The second interview was meant to be a focus group interview with all of the youth poets, but I ended up interviewing Jorge and Stacey individually, as they preferred, and I conducted one focus group interview with Jasmine, Nicole, and Rafael together. This arrangement worked nicely because the focus group participants were from the same high school poetry club and knew each other well. Because of their prior familiarity, they had much to say about each other's development. At the third interview, I asked participants to perform two of their poems, and I recorded these performances using iMovie on my laptop. Then, each participant played back his or her recordings, stopping the videos periodically to comment on them. (See appendix A for interview questions used.)

I collected several artifacts as well. At the beginning of the study, each adolescent completed a participant information form.[2] At two different points, I collected social media posts from the Metropoets page. These posts often served to communicate information about upcoming events. In fact, social media correspondence was a valuable data source because it represented official communication from Gabriel to the group, a space where the group's goals, values, and attitudes were reified (Wenger 1998). I also collected handouts that were distributed at workshops and slams. These tended to be notices of upcoming events, such as adult poetry slams happening around town, and occasionally Mark distributed a poem at a writing workshop.

Data Analysis

I used grounded theory (Charmaz 1983; Corbin and Strauss 2007; Glaser and Strauss 1967) to make sense of data collected in this study. A grounded theory approach enables the researcher to build theory out of the data. The process is inductive and recursive (Dyson and Genishi 2005). Furthermore, a constant comparative method allowed me to "[employ] cycles of data collection, analysis, and interpretation . . . to compare data more or less continuously" (Sowell 2001, 147).

During open coding (Corbin and Strauss 2007), I read through materials several times and wrote descriptive tags in the margins next to the text.[3] Throughout this process, I reduced chunks of content to the fewest words possible. For example, the recommendation "read ten poems for every one you write" was labeled "advice." Whenever possible, I used an in vivo code (Saldana 2009), which is "taken directly from what the participant says" (3). "Safe space," a term participants used frequently, became an in vivo code, for example.

I combined and collapsed the codes and organized them into categories. Then I looked for relationships between categories. This process resulted in categories such as context, goals, tools, and practices. Peter Smagorinsky (2008) reminds researchers to apply their selected theoretical framework throughout all stages of the study. The categories that resulted from my data analysis were congruent with the sociocultural lens I was using.

At various points in this study, I conducted member checks (Merriam 2009). For example, I shared participants' interview transcripts with them and asked for their feedback. This process encourages participants to make "corrections to the transcript or even further elaborations as an informant reflects on what was said during the interview" (Brenner 2006, 368). Also, in the second interview, I asked youth participants to comment on preliminary findings. At the last workshop of the study, I shared a sampling of findings with participants and asked for their feedback.

Constructing Narratives from the Data

I have employed narrative tools (Barone 2000; Clandinin and Connelly 2000) to make data more accessible to readers and to attempt to capture the complexities and multiple truths that arose during these investigations. Cathy Coulter and Mary Lee Smith (2009) write, "The dominant stream of narrative research theory in education denies the existence of a single, external reality and declares that the pursuit of objective methods and single, definitive knowledge claims is therefore impossible" (40). By presenting the stories of multiple people in the Metropoets space—group leaders, adolescent participants, and me—I attempt to employ polyphony, or many voices (Bakhtin 1986). Ideally, "no voice, including the author's, is privileged over others" (Barone 2001, 157).

Narrative tools can be useful in spoken word poetry research. Polkinghorne (1995) argues that in a narrative "a new level of relational significance appears" (7). Narrative research certainly has the potential to invite the reader into a larger conversation, as works by Tom Barone (2000) and Denise Clark Pope (2001) have shown. *Listen to the Poet* includes narratives of a writing workshop (introduction), a poetry slam (chapter 3), a school poetry club (chapter 7), and my own poetic journey (afterword). I present this material in narrative form in an attempt to take readers into these moments with me, as the next chapter will show.

CHAPTER 3

PERFORMING POETRY

Streetlight's on, poet.
 —*Nicole*

Inside a Poetry Slam
Gabriel, Executive Director of Metropoets

Gabriel stands at the front of the room, ready to start the Metropoets poetry slam.[1] As he counts down from ten, the audience goes quiet. The man takes a deep breath and launches into a poem about his last visit with his now-deceased grandfather. It is an emotional piece. Gabriel's hand is in his pocket as he starts reading, and eventually he takes it out to gesture for emphasis. With the other hand, he holds up his phone, reading from the device. This poet wears a t-shirt, sweatpants, a backwards baseball cap, and glasses. He sports a short hipster beard, and some of the tattoos on his arms are visible.

Audience members snap in response to Gabriel's words, and then the poet finishes to applause. Mark, who is serving as the deejay of this slam, plays a song. Gabriel is hosting today's poetry slam. A host's responsibilities include explaining slam norms to the audience, welcoming poets to the microphone, reading out the scores for poems, making announcements, and maintaining the atmosphere of the slam.

Before directing Metropoets, Gabriel worked at a Boys and Girls Club, which gave him valuable experience interacting with kids. He also trained as a motivational speaker and worked as a realtor during the housing boom. Gabriel is a thirty-four-year-old male who identifies as white. He was raised in a single parent home with his mother, who is white. His father is Puerto Rican.

Gabriel grew up in an urban area of Arizona in the nineties, and he did not feel safe going to high school because of the racial tension. Eventually, he dropped out of school. In an interview, he explained,

> I figured out that the high school didn't really give a crap whether I was there or not. I stopped going, and I learned how not to get caught because it was that serious for me.... The neighborhood I grew up in was predominately African American, and so there was this riot between the black gangs and the Mexican gangs, and I remember just being terrified.... It was just easier to take the risk of dropping out of school, and that's exactly what I did.... It was really easy for me to just fall between the cracks.... I went my entire four years of never really going to school, having major conflict with my mom, keeping a lot of emotional stuff in, a lot of fear, a lot of confusion, you know. I essentially just kept it all bottled up. (Gabriel, interview, June 5, 2014)

Since dropping out of high school, Gabriel earned his GED and is now close to completing a bachelor's degree in the arts. These days, he is a role model who encourages teenagers to continue on to college.

"Thank you," Gabriel says in response to the crowd's applause. "That's a poem I wrote for my poetry class, so I'm glad I got to share it. They don't really like spoken word poetry in my poetry class. 'Stop reading it so loud. Stop doing such a good job reading it,'" he imitates. People laugh. "I'm just kidding. My poetry class is amazing."

"Um, how is everyone doing? Can I get a 'yeah, yeah'?" Gabriel asks.

"Yeah, yeah," the audience repeats.

"Can I get a 'yeah, yeah, yeah'?" he asks.

"Yeah, yeah, yeah," says the audience.

"Can I get an 'aaaaaaaaaaaaaaaaaaaaaaaaaaaaaaaah ha ha ha hiiiiii'?" He does the *grito*.

"No," the audience says. They are shaking their heads and laughing.

"No? That was a good one. That was a good one, yo? I'm practicing for tonight. I'm going to a *quinceañera*. I'm just kidding." The audience laughs because it is funny to imagine him at a party for a fifteen-year-old girl.

"All right, so welcome to the first [Metropoets] slam of the 2013–2014 season. We are super excited for this season, mostly because this year's Brave New Voices festival is in Philadelphia.... I see a lot of new faces in the crowd, and that means there's potential for new people to be going on the trip."

Gabriel asks which audience members have never been to a poetry slam before. Many young people sitting in front of me raise their hands. He says, "Excellent. Welcome. Okay, your life will forever be changed, and nothing will ever be as cool." Gabriel explains that poetry slams are contests. Poets read their poems, and judges score them. A couple of audience members behind me boo in response to the idea that their art will be reduced to a score.

He emphasizes the importance of responding to judges' scores: "Your job as an audience member is to let these judges know how you feel about what they just did. For instance, if they score a poem extraordinarily low, let's give an example, okay? Uh, for instance, I come up here and I do a poem about how dolphins shouldn't be extinct in North Korea." People laugh at this. "You're like, 'Damn, dolphins shouldn't be extinct, and I can't believe they're killing dolphins over there in North Korea. . . . And then [Jorge] over here, who's one of our judges, is like, 'I don't care about dolphins.' So he's like, 'That's a horrible poem,' and he gives me a 7.5, right? Now, what you are supposed to do is to let [Jorge] know how you feel by doing a couple of different things. The funnest thing to do is to boo him. So everybody try that." The crowd boos.

Gabriel says, "How you boo is up to you. You can add your flavor to it. Mark says he likes to boo like he's falling down stairs." Gabriel imitates this sound, and they laugh. "Another thing. If you were raised properly—like um, my mother would be very disappointed if I was booing people in public—you can say something like, 'Listen to the poet.' So you can be like, 'Listen to the poet, man. Come on!' . . . Your job is to persuade them to score these poems higher, all right, so do not miss out on your opportunity to do your job."

Now Gabriel looks at the row of judges. "Judges, you're the only people brave enough to do what you're doing, okay?" He whispers and motions to the rest of the crowd, "They don't know anything." People laugh. "They're just here. You are the only people who count, so do not be persuaded by the audience, cool?"

Then he looks at the rest of the crowd and whispers, "Audience, they really don't know how to count, so make sure you let them know. All right?" The crowd laughs.

Gabriel explains that poets will come up to the microphone to perform. He acknowledges that this is terrifying for a lot of people. Some people are afraid of public speaking, but it is also hard to stand before an audience and read something emotional and something that required a lot of time and effort to create. He says, "So your other job, other than to boo the judges, is to give some mad energy to the poets. . . . We're in a library. Just for the sake of yelling in a library, you should do that, okay? So when the poets come up, you're going to be like, 'Yeah, yeah, yeah, let's go.' You can say things like, 'Spit that.' You can say, 'Put the bun in the oven and turn it up.' You can say, 'Mother's sick.' Like 'Listen to the poet,' you can say, 'Peanut butter and jelly sandwiches.'" They laugh at this. "Whatever. It's all right. If that gets you hyped, it might get the other person hyped."

Then Gabriel says that all of their poetry slams for the year lead up to a slam-off to select their team of four poets for Brave New Voices. Even people who are new to Metropoets can make the team if they work hard. He points to Nicole and Jasmine (poets in this study), who earned spots on the team as new poets. He explains, "The reason why it's important to [slam here] is practice, but also every time you [slam], you get a point. . . . Then you get three points if you win, two points if you get second, one point if you get third. So if you win, you get a total of four points. During the slam-off, the person who has the most points [for the season] gets to go last. Everybody knows the person who goes last is in the best position because the judges do what's called a 'score creep.' So, the more you participate, the better the chances you have."

"So, now . . . we're going to have a couple of performances to warm you guys up. Uh, then we're going to have a sacrificial poet who's going to warm the judges up. All right. So are you guys ready to get this poetry slam started? Can I get a 'yeah, yeah'?" The group repeats this.

"Can I get a 'yeah, yeah, yeah'?"

"Yeah, yeah, yeah," the crowd says.

"Can I get a 'put the bun in the oven and turn it up'?" They repeat this.

Gabriel says, "Can I get an 'aaaaaaaaaaaaaaaaaaaaaaaaaaaaaaah ha ha ha hiiiiii'?" Many audience members do the *grito*.

"That's what I'm talking about," Gabriel responds.

Jorge

Gabriel calls Jorge to the microphone. Jorge has been a member of Metropoets for approximately two years. At eighteen, he is the second oldest of the six adolescent participants in the yearlong study and the most advanced. He has competed in Brave New Voices twice. A college freshman who reported earning an A in his first-year composition class, Jorge was majoring in business when this study began. As the year went on, he switched to studying immigration, economics, and Spanish (simultaneously). Jorge identifies as Hispanic, and both English and Spanish are spoken at home. His stepdad is a teacher, and his mother is a certified nursing assistant. He loves art, basketball, comedies, and cooking, and he says that diversity is important to him. In an interview, Jorge explained to me that he has a multicultural family that is made up of Navajo, African American, Hispanic, and Caucasian members.

When Jorge was a baby, his biological father was murdered. His mother later remarried. Jorge has used poetry to work through the loss of his father and the acceptance of his African American stepdad. He believes poetry has helped him mature and become a man.

In high school, Jorge was in AVID, and he now works as a mentor in that program. By the end of this study, Jorge was also working in a warehouse. During the 2013–2014 season, time and transportation limited Jorge's involvement in Metropoets. I saw him at only a couple of events and at our interviews.

As Jorge walks up to the microphone, the crowd cheers and Gabriel gives him a fist bump. Before he begins the poem, Jorge says to the crowd, "What's up, everybody? How y'all doing?" He seems at ease and flashes a warm smile. He reads a bilingual poem (i.e., English-Spanish) by another author. It is about racism and what it means to be a black Puerto Rican.

Jorge's experience shows when he performs. Typically this poet recites his original pieces from memory and includes carefully considered arm gestures. Today, Jorge holds up a book to read from, but he still looks out at the audience. His voice is strong and clear and full of emotion. He looks professional, wearing a white button-down shirt and black pants.

The crowd snaps at various places in the poem and then gives him a round of applause at the end. As Jorge goes to sit back down, Mark plays the song "Black or White."

Gabriel says, "Give it up for my deejay one time, [Mark]. Give it up for [Jorge] one more time." The crowd is cheering. Gabriel continues, "One thing I love about poetry . . . is that it tells stories that aren't often told and that are sometimes uncomfortable to hear, right? But the one thing that is beautiful about this community is that it is a safe space, right? We're coming here to share our stories and . . . if [a poem] makes you a little uncomfortable, good. . . . Think about why it makes you uncomfortable, right? Examine that."

Gabriel gestures to the back of the room and welcomes the large group of teenagers that has just entered. He says, "Right now I think we have ninety percent young people in this room, and that's crazy because most of the time it's either fifty-fifty or sometimes it's, we don't do math that well, but give it up for math club in the building back there." He motions toward the table where the math club is sitting, ready to tutor people, and says, "We should have had you guys as the score keepers." Today's slam is being held in the large room of the library. The math club is positioned in the center of the room at a u-shape formation of tables. We are in a far corner that has rows of chairs set up for the slam. In other corners, there is a computer lab, a conference table, and offices. Along a back wall is a storage area. There are at least fifty audience members present and ten poets performing today.

"What is really beautiful is that this event is for the community . . . of young people," Gabriel says. He tells them to clap for themselves, and Mark plays "What's Love Got to Do with It." At this point, Gabriel introduces Mark, who is sitting at the deejay table.

"What's really important about the deejay is this person extends the conversation of the poet, right? The poet did this really interesting poem about race and color . . . and what did the deejay play?" Gabriel imitates the singer, "It's black, it's white." He continues, "You won't even know that it hit you upside the head, but you're like, 'Dang, I feel like that poem went on longer.' And that's when you have a good deejay."

It is now time for the sacrificial poet. Gabriel explains, "The sacrificial poet gets up here and sheds blood and doesn't get anything in return for it." This is practice for the judges. The sacrificial poet is not actually competing in the slam.

Mark, Founder and Visionary of Metropoets

As Mark, the sacrificial poet for this slam, walks up to the microphone, he is playing one of his own songs from his recent album. He wears a black button-down shirt and gray jeans. Like Gabriel, he sports a short hipster beard. The crowd cheers. Nicole, a poet in the audience, shouts out, "Let's go, poet. Streetlight's on, poet. Turn it up."

It goes quiet while Mark adjusts the microphone stand. He rubs his hands together and takes a pencil out from behind his ear and places it on the deejay table. He rolls up his sleeves and then launches into his poem, a piece about how there is no light rail in the poorest areas of town. Mark has the piece memorized, and he delivers it with gestures for train tracks and prison bars. He varies the volume of his voice to emphasize his points, and at times he is quite loud. This is a powerful political piece about poverty, slavery, immigration, and equal rights. There is a strong rhythm, like a song, and people are nodding and clapping. All of a sudden, Mark stops. "Uh, I messed up."

"Keep going," the crowd says. Mark jumps back into his poem.

A little later, he stops again. Mark hesitates and says, "Oh, man. Dang. I haven't done this one for so long."

Gabriel, who is sitting at the deejay table with Mark's computer, tries to help Mark find his place in the poem. Meanwhile, Mark scans the room, looking past us as if searching for the part of the poem he has forgotten. "I feel bad," he says. Mark is laughing, though, so the group laughs along with him. After a few seconds, he remembers the lines and continues with the poem.

After a few moments, he stops again. Now he asks outright, "How does it go, [Gabriel]?" He laughs with the audience.

Gabriel says, "You think you can." (This poem alludes to the children's book, *The Little Engine That Could*.) Mark gets back into the poem, chugging on toward the end, and when he finishes, the group claps and cheers. Gabriel gives Mark a handshake and hug, and they exchange places.

"Give it up for [Mark]," Gabriel says. He recalls that this was the first poem he ever heard Mark perform, and it had impressed him.

Although Mark stumbled during his performance today, this is unusual for him. His poems are typically not only eloquently written but also meticulously performed. He travels all over the country performing and teaching, an up-and-coming talent on the spoken word scene who competes in national and international slams. At twenty-seven years old, this founder and visionary of Metropoets has a bachelor's degree in creative writing, an album, several music videos, and a published book of poems. Mark is brave as well, confronting Arizona politics head-on in his poems, sometimes calling out elected officials by name. A strong voice in his community, Mark inspires young people to educate themselves and speak out against injustices. Some of his poems deal with racism, sexism, corruption, incarceration, and immigration.

Mark identifies as Chicano. His mother is Chicana and his father is white, and both of his parents have doctoral degrees. In an interview, Mark talked about growing up and coming to accept his identity as a person of color:

> I was fortunate because my parents taught me to be proud of . . . all the things that feed into who I am. My mom . . . would put her forearm to mine and we'd look at our forearms together, and she'd go, '*Mira*, look, you're brown. You're lucky. Brown is beautiful.' So I grew up believing that. . . . I think I was incredibly fortunate, but that also made high school crazy. It made me more of a target because the other kids of color in my school would stick to the wall and be silent, whereas I was instructed not to be that way. In high school I ended up defending every single ethnic group in the world. . . . My

senior year of high school I almost didn't graduate because I had like twenty-two absences in my first hour class. . . . I was super disconnected from my teachers the last semester. I had all kinds of issues. I didn't even take my SATs or ACTs. I didn't know where I was going to go to school. And I know they were super worried about me because I was going through this identity thing about the politics of race because in Idaho often I was way too brown, but in New Mexico and in other scenarios, you know, I was plenty white. So too-much-and-not-enough-and-in-between-and-no-place was sort of overwhelming. (Mark, interview, June 24, 2014)

Similar to Gabriel, Mark found that school was not a safe space. Mark struggled with his identity regardless of where he was and felt like an outsider. The empathy he developed as a young person is still evident today as he connects with diverse youth in Metropoets.

Back at his deejay station, Mark plays a song from his own album. In it, there is a part in which he says his name over and over. It is funny to hear his recorded voice singing his name, so the audience laughs. Gabriel announces the scores (9.5, 9.5, 9.6) and then calls the first official poet of the slam to the microphone.

Stacey

"Give as much energy and love as you can. It is hard to be the shotgun poet. Please give it up for [Stacey]. Yeah, let's go." The crowd is cheering, and music plays as Stacey walks up to the front of the room. Gabriel lowers the microphone to Stacey's height and pats her on the shoulder.

At fifteen, Stacey is the youngest of the six poets enrolled in this study. However, she is by no means new to the group. She started going to Metropoets functions two years prior when she was attending junior high school. Stacey is a freshman at a Catholic high school, and she reportedly earned an A in English. She enjoys writing, cooking, and volunteering. Stacey identifies as Hispanic, and Spanish is her home language. Her father is a piano mover and her mother stays home to care for Stacey's sister, who is autistic.

Stacey is the only poet in this study who resisted attending the poetry writing workshops that precede slams. She would perform at slams, but the idea of attending a writing workshop with a lot of other people terrified her. During the 2013–2014 school year, she attended only one writing workshop, the first she had ever been to; however, I noticed Stacey did show up to the first workshop of the following season, which may foreshadow more serious participation to come.

Nicole, shouts out, "Let's go, [Stacey]. The streetlight's on."

Gabriel chimes in, "Come on. Don't be nice."

Stacey pushes her glasses up on her nose, brushes her bangs to the side, and holds her hand up to her mouth, hiding part of her hands inside the sleeves of her Metropoets sweatshirt. Mostly looking down at her black journal, she appears nervous. In fact, Stacey often looks scared when she performs her poetry. Her voice goes very quiet, and her hands visibly shake. Still, she gets up there and pushes through, which is brave in a room packed with so many audience members.

Her poem begins with the line, "You are known to be scary and fierce." The poem mentions a man with no name. At one point, she turns the journal ninety degrees so she can read something she has written in the margins.

Afterwards, the group claps and music plays. Gabriel is back at the microphone, saying, "Yes, yes. Give it up for [Stacey] one time. Beautiful. You're growing. That's good. She's always so scared. You look like you're going to pass out."

The group says, "Oh."

Gabriel continues, "That's good. You capture that. Don't ever lose that feeling," Gabriel makes a circle on his stomach, "that burning sensation when you get up. It's a sad thing when you're not afraid to do this. It's not really fear. It's just energy, and you put it out. And that was a beautiful poem. Thank you. That's the other side of what we do, public speaking, but also emotional literacy, talking about things that are important."

Mark plays the song, "I Will Survive." The group laughs, and Gabriel says, "Nice!" He starts dancing to the song.

Stacey's scores are 7.6, 8.3, and 9.0. Gabriel calls up the next poet.

Shawna

As Shawna approaches the front of the room, she is smiling and appears remarkably confident, considering this is her first time on the Metropoets microphone. At nineteen, Shawna is the oldest of the six adolescent poets in the study. She has only been in Metropoets for three months, which makes her one of the newest members of the group—at least of those enrolled in the study. (New members seem to walk into every workshop and slam.) Shawna identifies as black. Her home language is English, and she does not live with either parent. On her information form, she wrote that her father is "disabled/unemployed," and her mother works in a bank. This poet reported earning a B in her senior English class. She did not finish high school.

Her shirt advertises a soft drink, and she wears a pink baseball hat backwards.

She has a dog tag necklace and glasses. As Shawna reads her poem from a journal, people snap in response. The poem is about how someone responds to a friend's suicide. At one point in her poem, she says, "I never thought it would be your feet that would walk all over me." Later in the poem, she says, "Letters are sorry ass goodbyes," and the crowd responds with an, "Oh!" She steps away from the mic, and the group cheers.

In addition to writing and reading, Shawna likes to cook, create art, and help others. On her information form she wrote, "I like learning new things and meeting new people. I don't like sitting around, so I try to get out of the house every chance I get. I'm funny, can ease tension, . . . [and I am] really peaceful [and] serious when I need to be. And I'm very responsible. People call on me for [a lot] of things. And I'm well liked." Shawna participated in only the first of the three interviews for this study, not responding to invitations for later interviews. She seemed preoccupied and busy with the responsibilities of her adult life. Shawna works for a charity for children who have been abused or have faced other challenges, and she seems to enjoy being a mentor there. She also has a supportive network of her own. I noticed several women from her work attending Metropoets events to cheer her on.

Shawna's poems tend to deal with serious issues like abuse. She talked to me about a difficult childhood, being placed in foster care, and dropping out of high school. During her adolescence, she moved a lot and changed schools. In her senior year, she was finally starting to feel comfortable and settled into her new school when an administrator from that school visited her home and told her she would have to switch to a charter school. Apparently Shawna did not have enough credits to graduate that year. Of course, Shawna was behind on credits from all of her moving around. That administrator's action, reportedly to boost the school's graduation rates, was as good as throwing Shawna out completely. Displeased with the charter school where she was placed and missing the stability she had finally found in her previous school, Shawna eventually dropped out of high school altogether.

Shawna's relationship with her mother is not a happy one, and this theme appears in her poetry. Despite the challenges she has faced, Shawna comes to Metropoets events with a positive attitude and a warm spirit. During the yearlong study, she was enthusiastically working on her GED.

Gabriel says, "Give it up for [Shawna] one more time." The group cheers. "I've been telling her to come, and now she's here. She's showing up. Excellent. Part of a community. All right." Shawna's scores are 8.7, 9.0, and 9.6.

Gabriel makes an announcement about the upcoming Town Slam, a citywide competition that Metropoets sponsors as part of its residency program. Metropoets is active in approximately ten school poetry clubs, and at the Town Slam these school teams compete against each other. During the school year, Metropoets assigns a teaching artist (e.g., Gabriel, Mark, and other adult poets they have trained for this role) to each club, and clubs hold writing workshops, slams, and other events on their campuses. Some youth poets from these school clubs attend the Saturday workshops and slams at the library, but others never make it to Metropoets events, perhaps because transportation poses too much of a challenge.

Nicole

The next poet to the microphone is Nicole. Nicole has been in Metropoets for close to two years and has competed at Brave New Voices once. She identifies as white, is sixteen years old, and is a junior in high school. Her home language is English. On her information form, for parents' professions, she wrote "unemployed/[delivery] driver." Nicole reported earning an A in her last English class, a dual enrollment honors class. She described herself as someone who likes to play basketball and volleyball, read to her younger cousins, and play the piano and flute.

This poet has a Brave New Voices shirt. She wears glasses and has added blue streaks to her hair. As she holds up her blue phone to read from it, her hand shakes even though the poem sounds polished. Nicole has control over her timing, volume, and emphasis.

At Metropoets events, Nicole goes out of her way to support fellow poets. She is often heard encouraging performers with a "Streetlight's on, poet." This lets the poet know the audience is ready to hear that person's story. With her snaps and eagerness to reach out to newcomers, Nicole is a leader in the group who strives to make others feel welcome. Her leadership and empathy are traits she has cultivated at least partly through her high school. Nicole talked about a special school camp she participated in that helps adolescents explore diversity and leadership. The poem she shared at the camp talent show is the same one she is sharing today. The piece has the refrain, "Swim the hallways." It is about high school cliques and the various challenges teenagers face.

Nicole's scores are 9.2, 9.4, and 9.8. Gabriel says, "I forget where I heard it, but when you come up here on the mic, it's often like, 'What am I going to give you?' You know what I'm saying? This is an altar where you're leaving something here for us. Do you know what I mean? So thank you. Thank you for coming up here and baring your soul."

Jasmine

The next poet to the microphone is Jasmine. Nicole shouts, "Come on, [Jasmine]. Toast that bread."

Jasmine, who identifies as Hispanic, is sixteen years old and a junior in high school. She reported earning a B in her previous English class, AP Composition. Her home language is Spanish. Her father is a chef, and her mother is a stay-at-home mom. On her information form, Jasmine mentioned being interested in guitar, theatre, tennis, ceramics, and psychology.

Although Jasmine has only been in Metropoets for one year, she has already competed at Brave New Voices. Her poems are incredibly thoughtful, and she delivers them with careful attention to timing, pacing, and emotion. Jasmine said it was practically unheard of for the group to select someone so new to be on the Brave New Voices team. She attends the same high school as Nicole and Rafael (other poets in this study). In fact, they are good friends, and Jasmine and Nicole co-run the spoken word poetry club at their school.

Although Jasmine reads from her phone, she looks up from it often, making eye contact with people in the audience. She has wavy hair and wears large glasses. The rhythm of her poem is almost musical. Later in the season, she will start to sing some of the stanzas of her poems. Today's piece is an advice poem for someone with depression. She smiles and seems at ease throughout the performance. Jasmine's scores are 9.5, 9.6, and 9.8.

One last adolescent poet performs in the poetry slam after Jasmine. Then, Mark shares some beats he made, and a friend of Gabriel's from college gets on the microphone to share a poem, which gives the judges time to calculate final scores and determine the winner.

Gabriel thanks people for coming out and reminds them, "Find [us on social media]. Let people know about what's going on. Invite a friend. . . . The more people here, the livelier it gets, right? The more attention that we bring to this, to your guys' voices, the more opportunities that come available, right? This is for you. I can't stress that enough. So take ownership of your community and let's continue to build this and to grow this. We got some amazing things happening this year."

Before he announces the winners of the slam, Gabriel says, "It's always super, super close. Remember, being the winner doesn't make you any better than anyone else; it just means that this particular day, you were on. And if you didn't win, just remember, it's all good. Keep writing. Keep coming here. The point is the poetry and not the score. Can we all say that together?" The group repeats it. He asks the crowd to clap for the judges, and then he announces the results. Shawna is in fourth place, Nicole is in third, Jasmine is in second, and the poet who read last is the winner. There does seem to be some truth to "score creep," or a tendency for scores to rise throughout the slam.

Gabriel reminds people that the library gives them the space for free, so they need to take care of it. "Let's make sure that we clean it up and respect the space," he says, asking them to stack chairs in the closet. He adds, "Meet someone that you don't know. Say hello. High five. It's cold and flu season, so you can give the knuckles. All right? And you can hang out for a little bit. Have a beautiful weekend. Stay safe. Peace." The poets and audience members mill around the room, chatting with each other and stacking chairs.

Rafael

Of the six adolescent poets in this study, Rafael was the only one who did not compete in this poetry slam. However, he did compete at the next slam on October 26, and he placed third in that event. Rafael is eighteen years old and a senior in high school. He has attended Metropoets events for one year.

During his freshman year of high school, he failed his English class and had to take summer school. That was a turning point for him because his summer school teacher was also the school's poetry club sponsor. She helped bring him into the school club, and he eventually started to participate in Metropoets events at the public library as well.

On his information form, Rafael reported earning a C in his most recent English class, a dual enrollment honors English course. Also on that form, Rafael identified as Latino and wrote that his home language is Spanish. For parent profession, he wrote "janitory." In his free time, Rafael likes to spray paint, skate, and play videogames. He also takes care of his younger siblings on weekdays. By the end of this yearlong study, Rafael had graduated from high school and was working as a carpenter. He talked about how exhausting the job was, and he looked worn at our last interview. In earlier interviews, Rafael had talked enthusiastically about his plans to go to a community college and then transfer to a university. He hoped to become a teacher of English or history.

Rafael reported that he began reading at an early age, and he credits this to his older siblings. Rafael also said that his older brother is an activist who used to take him along to rallies and protests. A strong political awareness certainly comes through in Rafael's poems. For example, in his *Mestizo* piece, he writes, "I am the product of *los conquistadores* stepping foot on new ground. I am the product of pillaged villages, raped women, and lost culture. Spanish blood flows through these veins and Aztec skin keeps it all in. *Yo soy Mestizo.* I am the product of two worlds colliding. I am the product of years of oppression, colonization, and revolution" (observation, January 18, 2014).

Putting the Event into Context
The Poetry Slam

When poet and construction worker, Marc Smith, invented the poetry slam in the eighties, he transformed dull, endless poetry readings into a competition and a show (Gonzalez 2007; Smith 2003). Guy Le Charles Gonzalez (2007) speculates that Smith had "grown tired of the stale politeness of the academic poetry reading, where the poet was placed on a pedestal and had no obligations to [the] audience" (24). The three-minute time limit helps audience members stay focused, even if the poem is less interesting or less developed. Daniel Ferri (2007) attests, "as long [as] you keep it short we will listen because you might have something to say" (84). Poetry slams can be exciting and fun (Smith 2003; Weiss and Herndon 2001). They may even veer toward the "carnivalesque" as audience members animatedly respond to judges' scores (Rivera 2013, 116), scores that do not necessarily reward the best poems (Taylor 2007).

Marc Smith (2003) writes, "Slam has moved everyday people to be passionately involved with art and performance, with words and ideas, with the people who speak the words and the people who come to listen" (120). Furthermore, Luis Rodriguez (2003) has argued that spoken word can benefit all people, including "populations normally not considered poetic, such as the homeless, gang members, midwives, prisoners, carpenters, etc." (210). Through spoken word, people from all backgrounds can share their experiences, grapple with complex issues, and argue for a more just world.

Performance

When spoken word poets perform, they communicate messages through their voices and bodies. Words are brought to life, enacted. While writing requires decisions about topic, message, form, devices, and word choice, performing a piece also involves determining rhythm, speed, volume, emphasis, facial expressions, and gestures. In a study of spoken word poets, Soraya Sablo Sutton (2008) found that participants memorized their works so they would have "the freedom to experiment with ... linguistic variation, ... eye contact, body gestures, and facial expressions to draw the audience into the experience" (228). It is true that a memorized piece frees the poet's hands and can inspire a more physical performance.

The audience plays an important role at a poetry slam. After all, poets speak to real people sitting in front of them who respond to their words (Prince 2003). Many writers feel energized and validated through this sharing because they can hear audience members snap, clap, cheer, gasp, and comment. Performance "turns the idea of audience into something concrete and participatory" (Fishman et al. 2005, 228). When poets perform, they can actually see the audience for their writing. Jenn Fishman and colleagues add, "To the performer, the difference in performing for a dynamic audience as opposed to performing for a lifeless piece of paper or computer monitor is immense" (238). Performing can be powerful.

There may well be a relationship between performance and identity. Glynda Hull and Mira-Lisa Katz (2006) point to "the power of public performance in generating especially intense moments of self-enactment" (47). As writers go public with their works, they may reveal who they are and who they hope to be. Over time, they may even come to identify as certain kinds of people (e.g., writer, spoken word poet, rapper, activist, etc.). Ann Marie Smith (2010) found that using poetry slams in school encouraged "students to perform identities and create authorial voices" (207).

Authentic Writing

Spoken word poets write for authentic purposes and audiences. In fact, this is a key difference between writing in Metropoets and a lot of writing in school. Janet Emig (1971) argues that with school-based writing, "Too often the [audience] is a teacher interested chiefly in a product he can criticize rather than in a process he can help initiate through imagination and sustain through empathy and support" (97). In contrast, Metropoets writers perform in supportive spaces, and they are highly motivated to write for these poetry slam audiences.

Youth poets write in order to share messages that matter to them. Their words may reach dozens or hundreds of people at a slam, and videos of their poems may reach many more than that. This writing can even personally impact members of the audience, as Jorge reveals in chapter 5. In these youth poetry spaces, writing is so much more than an exercise. Lev Vygotsky (1986) has criticized learning exercises that are disconnected from authentic situations: "Instead of being founded on the needs of children as they naturally develop and on their own activity, writing is given to them from without, from the teacher's hands. This situation recalls the development of a technical skill such as piano-playing: the pupil develops finger dexterity and learns to strike the keys while reading music, but he is in no way involved in the essence of the music itself" (105–6). Students need opportunities to make decisions about their writing.

James Britton and colleagues (1979) argue, "Work in school ought to equip a writer . . . to write as someone with something to say to the world in general" (192). When teachers dictate topics and enforce formulaic structures, they limit students' creativity and shut down opportunities for meaningful experiences with multiple literacies. In contrast, youth poets in groups like Metropoets explore who they are and what they care about as they write and perform. Educational theorists (Dewey 1938 and 2009; Tyler 1969) have long stressed the need to connect curriculum to students' lives. Writing needs to matter to the person crafting the piece.

Conclusion

While youth poetry slams across the country may share similarities, each event is situated within a specific sociocultural, historical, and geographic space. The local context, group customs, and even the individuals who are present that day shape the slam. Also, the poems that are shared and the audience's responses make each slam unique, a special experience that can never be replicated exactly.

In Metropoets, young people are not forced to write on a set topic. In addition, they do not have to fear correction by a teacher. These poets are driven to write about subjects they select, and they look forward to participating in slams to share their stories with larger audiences. Writing is both personal and social in this group. If we really listen to the voices of youth writers, we can begin to think about new directions in writing instruction that would better support today's secondary students. As we have seen, authentic writing and sharing can be powerful for young writers.

CHAPTER 4

PARTICIPATING IN A COMMUNITY OF PRACTICE

If you don't have the community, maybe you wouldn't really have a reason to write. If you don't have a sense that other people are listening, you wouldn't be motivated to keep writing.
—Jasmine

As the poetry slam in the previous chapter demonstrates, members of Metropoets perform poetry in a supportive community. The youth poets said that in this space they could express themselves without worrying about being judged by others. They also said the Metropoets group is like a family. This is not an accident or a coincidence. Gabriel and Mark actively work to nurture this group of writers, and the language, goals, practices, and tools they employ shape the community in specific ways. This group is an example of a "community of practice" (Wenger 1998) or what Maisha Fisher (2007a) terms a "participatory learning community." Members gather around the practice of writing and performing spoken word.

The first part of this chapter investigates the structure of this community of practice to understand how writing and learning work in this group. The second part of this chapter identifies some of the features that contribute to a safe space for storytelling, features that could be employed in other settings to foster positive, welcoming, and supportive spaces for young people to share their stories.

A Community of Practice for Poets

In Metropoets, young people become poets as they participate in a community of practice, writing, performing, and listening. As Etienne Wenger

(1998) has pointed out, "Learning [occurs through] social participation" (4). Like other communities of practice, the Metropoets group has "routines, words, tools, ways of doing things, stories, gestures, symbols, genres, actions, [and] concepts that [it] has produced or adopted in the course of its existence" (Wenger 1998, 83). Below, I examine the purposes, practices, and tools that define the Metropoets group. In addition, I look at possibilities for participation in this group, common trajectories, local-global connections, and boundaries and brokering.

Purposes

According to its mission statement, Metropoets seeks "to create a safe space for young people to find their voice through spoken word poetry in an effort to combat illiteracy and silence but also to help empower these young people to be productive and caring citizens of the world" (Gabriel, interview, June 5, 2014). In fact, this community of practice has multiple purposes, including improving writing, celebrating marginalized voices, developing emotional literacy, encouraging active citizenship, creating bridges to higher education, and providing a space for competition.

Improving Writing

One of the main purposes of Metropoets is to teach adolescents to write spoken word poetry. Teaching artists do not expect writers to enter as accomplished poets, but they believe young people can improve with guidance and practice. As Gabriel explained in a writing workshop, "The workshop is designed for you to become more comfortable with writing and expressing yourself through the written language, which eventually then will turn into the oral language, if you so choose to spit your poetry. But it's really designed for you to grow as a writer.... All great writers will tell you the same thing: 'Nothing happens overnight. It's a process of writing, revision, working at it over and over and over again'" (observation, February 15, 2014).

Saturday writing workshops provide opportunities for focused practice. Poets come into contact with more experienced mentors and mentor texts, which offer young writers glimpses into possible future selves. Teaching artists create "zones of proximal development" (Vygotsky 1978) for learners as they meet writers where they are and guide them toward new understandings, understandings that the adolescents may not have even realized were within reach.

Celebrating Marginalized Voices

Another purpose of Metropoets is to celebrate the voices of diverse youth. According to study data, teaching artists talked about "sharing voices" about four times as often as "improving writing." Gabriel believes that encouraging young people to tell their stories can improve their public speaking and lead to social change. He said, "Energy. Love. We are celebrating young people's voices. And public speaking is the number one fear in the world, but we really believe that if we can teach these young people and empower them to exercise their right to speak, . . . we believe we can create a change in the world that we live in" (observation, October 26, 2013). Celebrating youth voices empowers these adolescents. At the same time, their messages enter the community and are absorbed into it, potentially effecting change. It seems that the poems shared in this space are utterances that are part of a larger conversation, evoking M. M. Bakhtin's (1986) metaphor of communication as links in a chain.

Mark discussed the importance of celebrating adolescents' voices. In an interview, he said:

> The reason why I wanted to start [Metropoets] is I knew what it was like as a young person to feel isolated and have no real outlet to speak about my own pain, my own issues. [Performing for] an audience . . . changed me. And it made me heal to a degree because I was like up, facing it. I'm visible, you know? This idea of invisibility dictates so much of how young people live their lives. Teen suicide. Car wrecks. Teens are the most at-risk population. And a lot of it is because young people feel so often that they're isolated. And these kids go, "No one will understand this about me, but this is just how I am, and my pain is so unique or so different, or can't be understood. . . . When you take this poetry culture and you put it in a room and you develop a safe space for young people to speak to each other, then you see some kid read a poem about abuse or whatever and you see the minds of their peers open up. And they go, "Oh shit. Your parents got a divorce too? Wow. Except for my mom is actually more like your dad in my situation." But then they go, "We're not alone. We're not alone. And our stories run together and they're similar." You know? And then you have this incredible . . . sense of community and appreciation for everyone's story. (Mark, interview, June 24, 2014)

Mark believes that sharing a poem can be therapeutic for the poet. In addition, it can provide relief to a listener, who may realize he or she is not alone.

Gabriel agrees that the voices of young people are routinely silenced in our culture. He said that Metropoets works to remedy that:

We're not looking for one specific kind of youth, one demographic. It's open to anybody. But what you find . . . is the young people . . . who come to these spaces are ones whose voices are marginalized. Their stories aren't being told . . . , or they're being told through one particular lens, a stereotypical lens. So it really is about de-marginalizing these voices and these young people. I think it doesn't matter what your gender or ethnicity or race is. I think, as young people, you are automatically marginalized because you're a young person. What you have to say isn't important. How could you possibly have anything important to say? You're a young person. You know nothing yet. And I wholeheartedly disagree with that. I think to have a healthy world, you have to be able to listen to everybody's story. (Gabriel, interview, June 5, 2014)

Gabriel hopes to empower adolescents by teaching them that their voices matter.

In this poetry group, adolescents "construct their own voiced response[s]" (Dyson 2005, 155) to issues and events that are larger than any one person. At the same time, their poems reflect their cultures, languages, and experiences. Metropoets has much to teach schools about the power of celebrating young people's voices.

Developing Emotional Literacy

Metropoets strives to help adolescents develop emotional literacy. They try to get kids in touch with their feelings, help them reflect on personal experiences, and develop empathy for others. When I asked Mark if Metropoets helps members with anything other than writing, he replied, "Yeah. Life. Addiction. Abuse. Trauma. Reflection. Making decisions. Navigating the future. Expressing themselves. Navigating fear. Embracing their own unique output of thoughts and energy and all that" (Mark, interview, June 24, 2014). Presumably, if these writers are emotionally in touch with themselves and others, they can overcome any obstacle life throws at them. Ernest Morrell (2008) has similarly suggested that writing can be used to help people think through issues, "relieve pain," "deal with stress, loss, anger, etc.," and "cope with otherwise overwhelming emotion" (169). Writing to understand ourselves and others can be incredibly powerful and useful. Unfortunately, this type of writing is often neglected in schools.

Encouraging Active Citizenship

This group seeks to create "caring citizens of the world" (Gabriel, interview, June 5, 2014). Mark said they aim to not only "cultivate the minds of new, emerging artists" but also to encourage adolescents to contribute something to the world (Mark, interview, June 24, 2014). For example, at the final slam-off of the season, Gabriel told the audience that it is not enough to talk about injustice. Adolescents also need to get involved: "If all you're doing is talking, then don't expect to see too many changes. . . . Be an active citizen in the world. Go out there. Do your community service. Be a part of something" (observation, May 10, 2014). Words should not be a substitute for action.

Creating Bridges to Higher Education

Metropoets aims to create bridges to higher education. During this study, Gabriel invited a professor to lead a workshop on applying to college, and then poets toured a college application center. A social media announcement prior to this event emphasized the workshop's importance: "Education is very important to us, so this Saturday we are dedicating our workshop time to a college readiness presentation! Please come out and/or let any student (no matter what grade level) [know] about this opportunity" (online post, accessed October 24, 2013). In the workshop, Gabriel warned the youth poets that applying to college could seem overwhelming. He told me he was giving the poets this opportunity because he hoped to be the person in their lives whom he never had growing up. As other research has shown (Fisher 2005), spoken word poetry groups can play a powerful role in motivating adolescents to go to school and to pursue higher education.

Providing a Space for Competition

Finally, this group facilitates competition through monthly poetry slams. The teaching artists played up competition in the group several times, especially at the beginning and end of the 2013–2014 season. Gabriel was upfront about what was at stake: a key purpose of the slams is to select the team that will represent Metropoets at Brave New Voices. During the preliminary slam in April and the final slam-off in May, twenty poets would compete for just four places on the team.

Gabriel believes the competitive aspect of the slam motivates young people, creating energy and excitement around writing. (The youth poets I spoke to agreed.) While competition defines the arc of any Metropoets season, teaching artists would emphasize that competition was not the end goal. Even while announcing winners, the host would deemphasize the importance of placing, simultaneously humbling those who won and lifting up those who lost. For example, Mark announced:

> Just remember this about the poetry slam: It doesn't matter. Seriously. I've seen all kinds of slam greats do nothing with their careers because they

think they're hot on the mic, and all of a sudden, they can't go anywhere. This is a nice crowd. They're here to support you, right? This is where you want to get nurturing. . . . It takes work and work and work and work. You need to bring your poetry everywhere, [to] all kinds of rooms. So it's good to feel proud, but ultimately, separating first, second, and third place is literally a tenth of a point: 29.1, 29.2, 29.3. . . . It doesn't mean anything. . . . Victory is like that . . . . The order you go in determines a lot, so don't put too much value into this whole game. It's a fun game, a cool game, but it's a game. It's a gimmick. That being said, if you don't win, that's all right. You won because you got up here . . . on the mic. That's what it's about. (observation, November 23, 2013)

Paradoxically, teaching artists caution participants to see beyond the game at the same time everyone is wrapped up in playing it.

Practices

As I attended multiple writing workshops and slams during the yearlong study, I found that Metropoets events typically followed a predictable pattern. Readers have already seen a Metropoets writing workshop (introduction) and a poetry slam (chapter 3) in action. This section looks across multiple workshops and slams to identify patterns and variations.

Writing Workshops

Writing workshops tended to begin with introductions. A poet would share his or her name and grade or favorite color, something low-risk enough that everyone would be willing to do it. Teaching artists invested time in learning names, even though a writer might never return.

Several writing workshops involved language review of some kind. In the workshop described in the introduction, participants reviewed parts of speech, synonyms, and antonyms. Sometimes poets considered the value of different parts of speech. For example, during a workshop in March, Gabriel asked poets if adjectives or verbs were more important, and he suggested that using "strong verbs" in their poems can "keep it moving" and strengthen the "dramatic arc" (observation, March 15, 2014).

Teaching artists consistently set aside time in these workshops for participants to work with mentor texts. In the writing workshop described in the introduction, Julie Sheehan's "Hate Poem" was used as a springboard for writing. In November, Mark read Ted Kooser's "The Abandoned Farmhouse," and then writers brainstormed abandoned places they could feature in their poems. Mark, who has a degree in creative writing, would spend a lot of time immersing students into the language of these poems. With Kooser's poem, Mark said, "Okay, so something bad happened. Do we know what happened? . . . Why? How is this being communicated to us?" (observation, November 23, 2013). Mark constantly had students going back to the text—or when he did not bring enough copies for everyone who showed up, he would ask them to think back to a place in the text—to collect evidence. Mark demanded careful reading and listening.

The identification of poetic devices was never approached in a tedious way. For example, when teaching "The Abandoned Farmhouse," Mark asked, "What's 'like branches after a storm'? What kind of poetic device is that? Simile. A comparison" (observation, November 23, 2013). When he introduced the writing activity for this poem, he said, "Point of view. This is an exercise in point of view. You're using the viewpoint of the space to tell the story" (observation, November 23, 2013). Literary terms were introduced into discussions as needed.

Teaching artists did not only select published poems to serve as mentor texts. Once Gabriel showed a video of a group poem from a Brave New Voices competition. Then he led a discussion about the techniques the poets used, such as repetition, humor, and timing. He also used this piece to talk about the differences between narrative and lyrical poems.

Teaching artists' own poems sometimes served as mentor texts for students. In July, Gabriel performed a poem about his grandfather and then asked the audience to recall crucial details: "Where was love? . . . Yeah, when I was holding his hand, right? Was there sadness in that story? . . . What were some of the sounds that you heard? . . . The oxygen machine, right? What did you see? . . . A cigarette butt, right? I took these five senses, and I grounded this story in very concrete details. So I want you to show me where the story *is*" (observation, July 19, 2014). Poets then crafted their own works about how home smells, looks, sounds, tastes, and feels.

Guest instructors occasionally led the writing workshops, as in the case of the college workshop. In addition, a well-known poet from California led a writing workshop and had students do tongue twister warm-ups and writing exercises based on key words. In February, a Metropoets teaching artist and her former professor led a workshop that explored the humanities. In March, students brought their poems to the workshop and revised them in pairs. Finally, at the July workshop, participants had the chance to tour an art gallery, hear poems about the artwork by Metropoets "ambassador" poets, and write poems of their own based on a collection of photographs in the museum. As these variations suggest, Metropoets members had access to a range of people, resources, and writing experiences throughout the year.

Many of these activities—including language review, mentor text work, revision workshops, college application preparation, and writing in response to art—look similar to activities used in schools. Metropoets teaching artists bridge the worlds of school and out-of-school, fostering a "third space" (Bhabha 1994; Gutierrez 2008; Moje et al. 2004; Soja 1996) where literacy learning is engaging and relevant. In this space, adolescents are excited to write—and on their Saturdays, no less.

Slams

Slams varied less than workshops did. As readers saw in chapter 3, the host would begin a slam by counting down and then performing a poem. Starting a slam this way would quickly grab the audience's attention. After the poem, the host would greet the audience and explain how slams work (e.g., scoring, reacting to scores). Judges were typically gathered at random from the library during the break and would have no knowledge of the group or the poets, a selection method that is supposed to have the effect of valuing the most powerful poems in any slam. However, "score creep" is a very real phenomenon, and the poets who went later in a slam would usually end up with higher scores than those before them. Scores tended to range from 7.5 to 10.

As scoring practice for the judges and reaction practice for the audience, the host would bring up a "sacrificial poet." As Gabriel said, "We have to warm the judges up . . . so we have a sacrificial poet who is not a part of the slam, who doesn't win anything. . . . They shed blood for the sake of the poetry slam" (observation, January 18, 2014). In practice, the sacrificial poet tended to be an adult teaching artist from Metropoets or a former member now in college.

The host would devote some time to warming up the crowd, perhaps asking for a "Yeah, yeah." Group traditions like using the phrase, "Put the bun in the oven and turn it up" would be introduced, and audience members would be encouraged to do the *grito*. These call-and-response practices would get the audience enthused and reinforce the idea that their participation mattered. Audience members were reminded to snap, clap, cheer, and comment in response to poems. As Gabriel said, "If . . . you enjoy what they say, please do not wait until the poet is done to share the love. We're at a poetry slam, and part of the culture is you let the poet know right there in the moment that they are doing a great job, that you appreciate what they say" (observation, January 18, 2014). Gabriel compared this to the call-and-response practices used by some congregations: "When you go to church, ... you don't wait for the pastor to be done before you let the pastor know that you are appreciating what is being said. If you like what the pastor's saying, and you like what the poet is saying, you can give them that energy, right? You just snap your fingers. You're like, 'Yeah, say that. Spit that. Uh. Yeah.' You know what I'm saying?" (observation, May 10, 2014). When a crowd needed some help getting reenergized in the middle of a slam, the host would encourage people to stand up and dance or stretch, do a "soul clap," or shout back a "Yeah, yeah." These breaks occurred more frequently as the season progressed, more poets were scheduled to read, and the length of the slams increased.

Poets were called to the microphone one at a time. The host would announce who was "on deck" (next) and who was up, the deejay would play music, and the audience would clap and cheer as the poet made his or her way to the microphone. The audience would react audibly to poems, and music would play as poets finished and returned to their seats. Back at the microphone, the host might thank the poet, say a few words about the poem or the poet, tell a funny story, or make an announcement to fill time if judges were still scoring. Then the host would read the scores from low to high, and the audience would react accordingly. As the final scores for the slam were tabulated, a visiting poet or teaching artist would perform a piece. Before announcing the winners, the host would remind everyone that winning did not matter. Finally, audience members would be asked to clean up the space and meet someone new, and music would play as everyone mingled.

Tools

In this community of practice, technology and music are important tools. Jen Scott Curwood, Alecia Marie Magnifico, and Jayne Lammers (2013) write, "Today's technologies have forged new ways that young people can engage with words and ideas" (677). As an example of this, many poets use their phones throughout the writing process, from brainstorming to drafting to researching to revising to performing to posting.

Technology is seen as a useful tool in the Metropoets group. Gabriel would ask the audience to pull out their phones, take pictures, and post them online to help spread the word about Metropoets. In the weeks between functions, Gabriel would use social media to communicate with members. Announcements celebrated the success of a past event or reminded members to come to the next function. Sometimes announcements recognized sponsoring organizations or promoted poetry or hip-hop events going on around town. Etienne Wenger (1998) writes, "Any community of practice produces abstractions, tools, symbols, stories, terms, and concepts that reify something of that practice in a congealed form" (59). The group's online presence served to reify the values and expectations of the group in a written form.

Although the group seemed to appreciate technology, sometimes there were issues with it, as when Gabriel showed a video of a group poem. It was difficult for everyone in the room to see the poets on his laptop screen. Because he did not bring external speakers, it was also difficult to hear the poets. At the May event, Mark forgot the charger for his laptop and had to ask the audience if he could borrow one.

Music was another important tool in the Metropoets group. Deejays brought their music libraries with them on their phones, tablets, or laptops. Rafael explained that deejays need to choose the "right song," and Jasmine added that the music "keeps the vibe going" at the slam. Furthermore, Nicole pointed out that there is an "awkward silence" when the music does not start soon enough after a poem (interview, focus group, March 22, 2014). Music also breaks up the slam and energizes the audience. At one slam, Gabriel said, "I encourage you to just get up. Stand. Don't go nowhere. Stay in your zone, okay? Shake it off. Just close your eyes. Dance like no one's watching" (observation, January 18, 2014). People did get up and dance. At the Town Slam, I noticed that music contributed to the festive atmosphere. At this event, songs were played longer between the poems, and people jumped up and started dancing when the deejay played a song from Mark's album.

Music seemed to really matter to Metropoets members. Five of the six adolescent participants in this study mentioned an interest in music or songwriting. Jasmine sings and plays guitar and keyboard, and she started singing some lines of her poems by the end of the season. Nicole and Shawna also play guitar, and Jorge, Nicole, and Rafael write raps. Despite their interest in music, the adolescent poets in this study did not perform raps or other songs in place of poems at slams. When outsiders would come in and perform a song instead of a poem, the performance always seemed out of place. For example, three visitors once shared a song they had heard on the radio. Gabriel was kind in his response, but he encouraged them to do more next time:

> Um, so this is beautiful, and I love singing other people's stuff. I listen to it. I want you to examine that song and why you connected to it and just understand that you can write a song just as important as that one in your own language. A lot of times we feel like we can't do it because we hear it on the radio, but that's not true. You can write your own language. You can

write your own story. That was a story with a message. But you write your story. You got stories. I know the three of you got stories, so I want you to see why you connected to that song—what was the emotional connection—and then find your own story, and then I want you to bust a move the next time with your own personal stories. (observation, October 26, 2013)

Gabriel tried to use this moment as an opportunity to get them to reflect on why they liked that song. He never criticized them for singing it, but he did encourage them to write their own pieces the next time around: "You got stories." His response demonstrates his confidence in them as writers.

Forms of Participation

In a community of practice, members may participate to different degrees. On their website, Etienne Wenger-Trayner and Beverly Wenger-Trayner (2011) have illustrated several levels of participation that are possible within a community of practice. In the center, they show a core group. Moving outward are decreasing levels of participation: active participants, occasional participants, peripheral participants, and transactional participants. They point out that the ability to support all types of members is crucial to making a community of practice work. In addition, all members, not just those at the heart of the organization, will need to get something out of their participation. Even first-time attendees and those who attend sporadically can participate in the practice in valid ways.

It is common for a community of practice to have a "core group" made up of "people whose passion and engagement energize and nurture the community" (Wenger-Trayner and Wenger-Trayner 2011). In Metropoets, Mark and Gabriel are the core.

In the next level, "active participants" are "members who are recognized as practitioners and define the community (though they may not be of one mind as to what the community is about)" (Wenger-Trayner and Wenger-Trayner 2011). Many of the adolescents enrolled in this study were active participants who reliably showed up to workshops and slams. However, within this category, I did observe some variation in participation. For example, Jasmine and Nicole seemed closer to the group's center. Gabriel called them the group's "go-to poets" (Gabriel, interview, June 5, 2014). They represented Metropoets at a gala and were leaders in the group, cheering and snapping for other poets and mentoring them. Gabriel and Mark were grooming them to be teaching artists. Jasmine said, "We're teaching, like we're actually going to be teaching in [Metropoets] soon, and we're doing events outside of it, just really getting the community into spoken word poetry since it's starting to expand" (Jasmine, interview, March 22, 2014). Nicole and Jasmine were even looking into opportunities to lead a spoken word class for teenagers at a local arts center.

Jasmine and Nicole seemed to have a special status because they had represented Metropoets at a Brave New Voices (BNV) competition. Mark believes the BNV experience changes poets. Part of this is likely due to the intense practice sessions Metropoets holds, which can last four hours each. "The BNV kids, because they go through that training, are on a certain level," Mark said (Mark, interview, June 24, 2014). Jorge, the most experienced adolescent poet in this study, went to two Brave New Voices competitions. Once an active member, he started to cycle out during the 2013–2014 season as he became busy with the demands of college and other adult responsibilities.

Rafael and Shawna were more typical of active members. While they participated in most workshops and slams, they were not asked to represent Metropoets, nor did they compete in BNV. Both of them became active members in Metropoets only during the year of this study. Mark said of Rafael, "He's just behind [Nicole and Jasmine] as a writer. He has had far less practice" (Mark, interview, June 24, 2014). At the beginning of the 2013–2014 season, Shawna was nineteen, and Rafael was eighteen. Because of their ages, it seemed unlikely they would become "BNV kids" and move into the types of participation Jasmine and Nicole were experiencing. Rafael was clear-sighted about this reality: "I see that if I was dedicated earlier on, I would be at a whole new level than I am right now, which I kind of regret, but at the same time, everything happens for a reason. I guess I wasn't mature enough to do this [before], and I feel like I am now" (Rafael, interview, March 19, 2014).

The next type of member is the "occasional participant," or those who "participate when the topic is of special interest [or] they have [something] specific to contribute" (Wenger-Trayner and Wenger-Trayner 2011). Jorge took on this role, attending few Metropoets events. Stacey, the youngest poet enrolled in this study, was another occasional participant. She attended just one writing workshop during the 2013–2014 season, but she did regularly perform at slams. Teaching artists from the school clubs were another kind of occasional participant. While they were core members of their school clubs, at Saturday functions, their presence was less consistent. When they did show up, they would participate in writing workshops alongside adolescent poets. At slams, they performed as sacrificial poets or served as deejays.

The next category of membership is the "peripheral participant." This level includes those "with less engagement and authority, either because they are still newcomers or because they do not have as much personal commitment to the practice" (Wenger-Trayner and Wenger-Trayner 2011). Every time Metropoets gathered, new members participated, including people who happened to be in the library that day, friends of members, and other youth groups. Newcomers would begin on the periphery. They could participate in workshops and slams to whatever degree they chose. Some returned; others did not. Over time, they could move into more central forms of participation in Metropoets, attending occasionally or actively. What is interesting is that newcomers could enter the space and immediately participate in the group in legitimate ways, what Jean Lave and Etienne Wenger (1991) term "legitimate peripheral participation." During the study, I noticed that when there were many peripheral participants present, it would change the atmosphere of events. For example, the audience at an event at an art museum across town used less snapping, probably because the peripheral participants, who were definitely in the majority that day, had not yet learned the norms of the group.

Finally, "transactional participants" are farthest out from the core; they are "outsiders who interact with the community occasionally without being members themselves, to receive or provide a service" (Wenger-Trayner and Wenger-Trayner 2011). Transactional participants tended to fall into one of three groups: (1) one-time guest poets visiting the space to perform or teach, (2) university partners coming to offer advice or other support, or (3) family members, teachers, or community members who attended to show their support. As a researcher, I saw myself as a transactional participant. Although transactional participants are farthest from the group's center, this does not mean their participation is irrelevant. After all, the group's connections to a university put adolescents in touch with higher education and financed some of the group's travel to BNV.

At events, all of these different kinds of participation were valued, from Gabriel running the day-to-day operations to the casual passerby who dropped in to sit in the back and listen. A "red flag is when there is no movement across levels, no one from the periphery moving in, the same old core group, or no new blood among active members" (Wenger-Trayner and Wenger-Trayner 2011). In Metropoets, members could move across these different levels of participation. In fact, this is one of the advantages to communities of practice: members can participate a little or a lot and still get something meaningful from the experience. Also, someone may participate on the periphery for a while until ready to commit more fully to the practice.

It is fascinating to compare this model of participation to classrooms, where fewer types of participation are available and participating less may result in some form of punishment. If a student in a classroom is perpetually disengaged, it seems worth exploring what would motivate that person to move into more central forms of participation. In Metropoets, a genuine interest in the practice seems to propel youth toward deeper participation and increased learning.

Trajectories

In a community of practice, members travel on different types of trajectories. Etienne Wenger (1998) uses the term "trajectory" to mean "a continuous motion—one that has a momentum of its own in addition to a field of influences," but he emphasizes that a trajectory does not "imply a fixed course or a fixed destination" (154). In Metropoets, adolescent participants tended to travel on three distinct types of trajectories: inbound, insider, and outbound. Examining these movements can shed light on how learners enter a group, participate as insiders, and exit a group.

Inbound Trajectories

An inbound trajectory is a path a member takes into a group. Wenger (1998) explains, "Newcomers are joining the community with the prospect of becoming full participants in its practice. Their identities are invested in their future participation, even though their present participation may be peripheral" (154). I asked the six adolescent poets how they came to participate in the Metropoets group to get a sense of their inbound trajectories.

Jasmine and Jorge described their inbound trajectories in ways that were strikingly similar. They both began their stories by stating that a friend encouraged them to go to their school poetry club. This supports other research indicating that students' social lives can influence their literate lives (Smith and Wilhelm 2006). Along with extending these invitations, these friends praised their writing. Jasmine recalled, "She was like, 'I think you should share your poem. It's really good.'" Jorge remembered, "He was like, 'Hey, dude. You're actually kind of good.'" Once at the school poetry club, they were challenged by a mentor. For Jasmine, teaching artists encouraged her to share her poem at the Town Slam, and her initial reaction was, "Oh, I don't do poetry. I'm not used to this." For Jorge, it was coming into contact with a more experienced poet (via a video of B. Yung) and not understanding what the poet was saying (i.e., Jorge recalled, "I really started to question myself."). Finally, they both described experiencing a transformation. Jasmine said, "As I kept progressing, I was like, 'Oh, I can write poems now out of anywhere.'" Similarly, Jorge remarked, "And that's when . . . a fire struck inside of me, and it was like, '. . . I have to be able to learn to write that way because I want to be that smart.'"[1]

In these clubs, a more experienced poet confronted them with a challenge that took them out of their comfort zones, but they were ultimately motivated by this opportunity, and it propelled them toward deeper participation. It seems that Jorge and Jasmine are describing "zones of proximal development" (Vygotsky 1978). It is worth noting that in both cases, these zones involved challenge and discomfort for the adolescents. Another poet also described being confronted with a challenge. Stacey said, "I was expecting like two people, and I see this whole crowd. I was going to die. And then I went up there. My hands were shaking. My voice was cracking. But then I started reading out my poem" (Stacey, interview, January 18, 2014). This unease did not scare them away from spoken word. It motivated them. Performance played an important role in their inbound trajectories.

Their early encounters with spoken word involved "just in time" instruction (Gee 2004). Jasmine and Jorge could see that learning spoken word had practical value in the present as well as in the near future. They did not have to invest in learning "just in case" they might need it several years down the road in college or in a career, as is often the case in schools. Michael Smith and Jeffrey Wilhelm (2006) write, "Effective learning situations must approximate as closely as possible what real practitioners know and do in the world. This requires a culture of immediate use" (156). Even writers who were new to the group encountered literacy learning that was timely, practical, and useful.

Other stories of poets' inbound trajectories show the expanse of the Metropoets network. For example, Mark led a poetry workshop at Stacey's middle school, a school that does not have a poetry club. Afterwards, the school librarian took a group of students to a Metropoets event. For Nicole and Rafael, their English teacher encouraged them to attend a school poetry club meeting, and that was how they found out about Saturday Metropoets events. Shawna heard about Metropoets events when Mark and Gabriel held camps at a charity for children who had suffered abuse and other hardships.

When discussing their inbound trajectories, the poets identified literacy sponsors (Brandt 2001). These sponsors included school clubs, the teachers overseeing these clubs, friends, a school librarian, an arts charity, and, of course, Mark and Gabriel. People and institutions in these adolescents' lives created opportunities for them to pursue this literacy learning. Teaching artists, especially, encouraged them. Susan Weinstein (2009) suggests, "This direct correlation between having someone young writers care about value and encourage their writing and coming to value their writing themselves seems hugely important . . . as an indicator of what makes young people believe in their own talent and potential" (145). Their writing trajectories depended, to some extent, on others.

These stories also demonstrate the importance of intergenerational interactions (Fisher 2007a) and access to experts. Teaching artists, in particular, provided writing guidance and emotional support. Having access to such people at schools created opportunities for students. Even videos of poets were influential. When Jorge heard a poem by someone he related to, as opposed to the white canonical poets he had previously encountered in his English classes, he realized he could be a poet too.

Some poets were initially so intimidated by their peers' skills that they did not stick around. For example, Rafael said, "I [thought], 'This really isn't for me' because I would write stuff and then I would hear other people like [Jasmine] and [Nicole] and I would just be like, 'No, I can't do that. That's way out of my league.' And junior year, I reconnected with [Nicole] and she invited me back" (Rafael, interview, March 19, 2014). While Rafael was intimidated by the group at first, his attitude changed over time. Similarly, Shawna said, "I convinced my house a couple times to go down [to the library] and . . . watch. Sometimes I read. Sometimes I didn't. . . . I felt very anti-care because a lot of the kids that I see now were reading back then, and they were still like really good at what they do. I stopped going for a while" (Shawna, interview, December 27, 2013). However, at a later point, Shawna saw these same kids and was inspired by them:

> I met [Jasmine] and [Nicole]. . . . I was like, "Whoa. I want to do this so bad." And I [thought], "They are so good at it. I want to do it." . . . When I finally moved out this way, I was like, "The library's right there! I can go whenever I want," so I went [to the poetry slam] and it was cool. I slammed, I placed fourth, and I was like, "That's awesome." I walked in, and [Gabriel] was like, "I am really happy to see you here." And I was like, "I'm really happy to be here." (Shawna, interview, December 27, 2013)

For Rafael and Shawna, their inbound trajectories were not as smooth, quick, and direct as some of the other poets' trajectories. An inbound trajectory might zigzag into and out of the group over the course of several years. These stories are important because they reveal that even if a community is welcoming, a poet may feel out of place. And of course, this study only examined poets who persevered and stayed, not those who attended once and never returned.

An inbound trajectory to the Metropoets group does not require previous success with writing or school. Recall that Shawna dropped out of high school. In addition, Rafael failed English, and it was his summer school teacher who encouraged him to check out the club. Rafael said, "I failed out of mainstream English my freshman year, so I had to take summer school.... We went over a poetry unit. [The teacher] read some of my stuff, and she actually told me about the program. I kind of shrugged her off. And then, after summer school, I was placed into honors. And from there I've been in honors ever since, which is kind of a funny story since I flunked out of mainstream" (Rafael, interview, March 19, 2014). An inbound trajectory is not necessarily just a path into a particular type of literacy or into a particular literacy community; it may redirect a person's life in unexpected ways.

Insider Trajectories

As a community of practice grows and changes, possibilities for participation change as well. Etienne Wenger (1998) explains, "The formation of an identity does not end with full membership. The evolution of the practice continues—new events, new demands, new inventions, and new generations all create occasions for renegotiating one's identity" (154). In Metropoets, Jasmine and Nicole were insiders who participated fully and were deeply committed to the group. As Metropoets evolved, their participation in the group changed as well. Insider trajectories are not necessarily smooth, and changes in how one participates can be uncomfortable. Nicole talked about some of the tensions involved:

> I'm in a different position from where I was last year, so it's really weird. ... [Mark] always says that like, to be a master of something, you have to have ten thousand hours of experience.... I definitely have not put ten thousand hours into this. I feel like I'm not really a beginner, and maybe between intermediate and like almost advanced.... I feel really defined with my skills.... A lot of younger middle school poets, like they look up to me.... It's kind of weird because [Mark] and [Gabriel] kind of treat us like the same [as] ... when I was a sophomore in [Metropoets]. ... That's kind of like an unsure thing. Where am in [Metropoets]? Who am I? Do they really consider me ... professional? Or do they consider me

just another youth poet? So I'm not really sure, actually. It's kind of like on the fence of all these different statuses.... I've been in a phase that's kind of awkward, and I'm not really sure what's happening. (Nicole, interview, December 26, 2013)

Nicole acknowledged her changing status, yet she worried that Mark and Gabriel would always see her as "just another youth poet." Elizabeth Birr Moje suggests that "identities are always situated in relationships" (McCarthey and Moje 2002, 231). In this case, it was not enough that Nicole was participating differently; she was also looking for teaching artists to recognize her new identity in the group. She and Jasmine expressed frustration that Gabriel was telling them how to teach as they headed to the art museum event in July (i.e., as "ambassador poets" at that workshop they would be assigned to lead small groups). By this point, teachers at their high school had already trusted them to teach spoken word poetry to entire classes of their peers. Wenger (1998) points out that "it is not easy to become a radically new person in the same community of practice" (89). Being on an insider trajectory can be complicated.

Outbound Trajectories

Another way to understand a community of practice is to examine members' outbound trajectories. "Some trajectories lead out of a community, as when children grow up. What matters then is how a form of participation enables what comes next" (Wenger 1998, 155). Given that Metropoets is a spoken word poetry group for adolescents, what happens when poets go off to college or become too old for Brave New Voices? Gabriel said poets can only compete in BNV up to age nineteen. So what happens to these poets? Where do they go?

When I recruited Jorge to this study, I thought he would be an active member, yet throughout the 2013–2014 season, I saw him at interviews more often than I did at workshops and slams. A college student with unreliable transportation who lived across town from the library, Jorge had a hard time making it to Metropoets events. As his university coursework demanded more of him throughout the year, he attended events less frequently. He said he was having a hard time balancing school, work, and poetry. At the same time, his experience in the group seemed to be helping him as a college student. He said:

You have to shoulder all these new responsibilities being in college, and it's just so difficult to manage it.... You start to feel that sense of like, "Who am I really?" or "What am I really capable of?" And that's exactly when poetry comes into play. . . . That's when all those skills, all that training, all those things you developed through [Metropoets], that's when all that really comes out and helps you . . . I had a difficult time really connecting with a lot of the people . . . I'm really thinking about how am I going to combat [social problems], whereas a lot of these kids, the incoming freshmen that I've met, they were more concerned with [partying]. And you know, as great as that sounds, my mindset has matured [beyond theirs] because of [Metropoets]. (Jorge, interview, June 27, 2014)

Jorge had started writing a few poems in college, but he found he would get too busy to finish them. Although he does not intend to pursue a spoken word career, he still hoped to stay connected to this type of writing. He said that poetry is "an outlet," "a hobby," and "his friend." Also, Jorge said, "[I hope to keep writing] because it is a part of my identity, and it did help me out when I was younger. And you know, it doesn't feel right to not have the opportunity to write" (Jorge, interview, June 27, 2014). I asked him about his current role in Metropoets, and he said he sees himself as a "consistent supporter" (Jorge, interview, July 11, 2014).

Poets who did go off to college seemed to be greeted with open arms when they returned. They usually delivered a poem at the beginning or end of the slam, but they did not compete against the adolescent poets. Their role changed once they aged out of competition.

Near the end of the 2013–2014 season, another poet, Rafael, was getting ready to graduate from high school. Anticipating his shift out of Metropoets, he had already started attending adult open microphone events around town. Rafael said, "Now that I'm eighteen, I'm not going to have a lot of time left to do this [Metropoets] stuff. They concentrate on the youth. So once I get too old I'm going to have to start looking for a new place" (Rafael, interview, March 19, 2014). At the same time, he told me that he was hoping Metropoets would invite him back as a teaching artist.

Gabriel acknowledged this aging-out phenomenon. He said, "They can come back and perform, work as a teaching artist, [or] start [their] own club" (Gabriel, interview, June 5, 2014). Gabriel would like to employ the best poets as teaching artists once the group has more money. He explained, "The kids who come up in our program, who graduate, grow up and go off to college, who have been raised in our culture, those are our next teaching artists. The hard part is we don't have funding to be able to pay them yet" (Gabriel, interview, June 5, 2014).

Inbound, insider, and outbound trajectories reveal multiple paths for adolescent writers associated with this group. These paths are by no means fixed, however. Participants themselves shape trajectories, and as a group evolves, trajectories evolve as well (Wenger 1998). "In the end, it is members—by their very participation—who create the set of possibilities to which newcomers are exposed as they negotiate their own trajectories" (Wenger 1998, 156). In other words, as these poets forge their way into, within, and out of Metropoets, they are showing others possible paths.

Local-Global Connections

In a community of practice, "the local and the global are . . . related levels of participation that always coexist and shape each other" (Wenger 1998, 131). In Metropoets, global influences impact local practices. Specifically, members of this group connect to a larger network of spoken word poets through Brave New Voices. Throughout the 2013–2014 season, Mark and Gabriel mentioned the Brave New Voices event repeatedly, saying that poets were competing for a spot on the team. After Jasmine and Nicole performed a duo poem together at the Town Slam, Mark told the audience that the pair had competed in a BNV competition in Chicago, and he went on to say that all of the teenagers in the audience had a chance to make the team if they competed in slams at the library. In an interview, Mark told me that poets who compete in BNV undergo more rigorous training than those who stay behind. Once there, they become friends with poets from around the country and gain a deeper understanding of spoken word. Those on the BNV team come back changed.[2]

In January, Gabriel said the cost of taking a team to the competition would be about $15,000. As the season continued, the Metropoets group started to impose rules to prepare poets for competition. For example, poems could be no longer than three minutes. Gabriel also gave poets advice: "You need to work at your craft. You need to start memorizing your poems. You need to have at least three poems that you feel are ready. Study. Go on YouTube. Study other BNV poets" (observation, February 15, 2014).

Nicole talked about how much she enjoyed preparing for this competition. She said she would see the teaching artists in a new light as they transformed into slam coaches. Also, the training was rigorous, but it was worth it: "We're meeting twice a week, almost every day. . . . We're in crunch time. . . . It gets really intense. . . . We're writing group pieces especially for BNV. BNV just brings in a lot of things that aren't always there in the normal slam. . . . There are so many amazing poets. . . . I met people from Guam, Bermuda, Canada, England. . . . The team from Alaska was so awesome. Like

New Mexico kills it. It's crazy to see all the different communities of people" (Nicole, interview, July 21, 2014). Nicole believes that preparing for BNV is an incredible experience. She has met people from all over the world at this event, and some of these poets are still in touch with her. Through this larger network, Metropoets members come into contact with new poets, poems, and practices, which impacts how they engage with spoken word.

Boundaries and Brokering

Communities of practice are marked by boundaries, and members may engage in brokering, which involves interacting with groups outside of the community of practice (Wenger 1998). "Brokers are able to make new connections across communities of practice, enable coordination, and—if they are good brokers—open new possibilities for meaning" (Wenger 1998, 109). Gabriel engages in brokering often. He welcomes other groups into the Metropoets space and sends Metropoets members into the community. Throughout the season, Gabriel planned events in conjunction with other groups and institutions, including a public library, university departments, a religious organization, an art museum, and various arts centers. This work was in addition to sending teaching artists into approximately ten local schools and offering workshops and camps in conjunction with a local charity for youth.

It may well be that "joining a community of practice involves entering not only its internal configuration but also its relations with the rest of the world" (Wenger 1998, 103). Gabriel was open to working with people outside of the group, and he frequently invited adult guests, including poets and professors, into the Metropoets space. He explained his reasoning for this to the adolescent poets: "We want to give you guys different perspectives. There's tons of people in [the spoken word] community. So we're working really hard to get these people here" (observation, January 18, 2014). Gabriel is extremely resourceful and values a range of expertise, which seems to benefit members of this community.

A Safe Space for Storytelling

Gabriel and Mark carefully cultivate a safe space for storytelling in this community of practice. This section explores how they use language, ground rules, and supportive practices to create this atmosphere. Of course, Metropoets is not the first poetry group to create a safe space or to use the term. In fact, it seems that a safe space is an essential precondition for youth spoken word poetry to flourish.

When examining the elements of this safe space, it is essential to keep in mind the backdrop against which the group operates. As the introduction discussed, controversial legislation has upset many members of Metropoets. Ethnic studies courses have been banned from K-12 schools, racial profiling is a reality, and immigration is not just an abstract issue but something members understand through real experiences with loved ones. These Arizona poets respond to hostile conditions through poetic activism, speaking out against injustices and envisioning a better world.

Language
A Focus on "Safe Space"

The language used in Metropoets reinforces the idea that writers are in a safe space. The term "safe space" is in the group's mission statement, and members, both adults and adolescents, used the term often. For example, Gabriel has written that Metropoets creates "safe spaces for young people to find their voices" (online post, accessed November 6, 2013).

I asked the adolescent poets to discuss how the group creates a safe space. They said:

NICOLE: I think it's just the [teaching artists]. They have good energy, and they bring people together.... They make it clear this is a place where disrespect isn't going to be tolerated ...
JASMINE: It's just the atmosphere.
RAFAEL: Yeah, and you feel safe here. You feel like you can express yourself in a way that you won't be judged. (interview, focus group, March 22, 2014)

Teaching artists emphasize respect, and youth poets feel safe enough to be honest. Jorge told me the space is "free of judgments" and teaching artists "try to create as much positive energy as they can.... And you will feel it. You will feel happy. You just feel free. You feel like you have no worries in the world" (Jorge, interview, June 27, 2014). Stacey also mentioned freedom from judgment. She said, "To me, [Metropoets] is like an opportunity for people to express themselves without being judged for what they write, without worrying" (Stacey, interview, March 22, 2014). Several poets equated safety with freedom from judgment.

Gabriel said that if he and Mark create the right kind of space, young people will want to learn and grow. He said:

What we're doing is creating a space where you feel safe enough to make yourself a great writer and a great poet. . . . We're creating a space for empowerment to happen . . . In my personal experience, nobody made me a better speaker, a better writer, a better poet. The space that was created allowed me to develop those skills, or the desires to develop those skills, on my own. And now nobody can take them away from me because I own them because I got them myself, you know, with the help of people, but I made the decision. And that's the thing. When you turn homework in because you *have to* [versus when] you *want to,* the "want to" is always going to be better homework because you wanted to. So we create the space for them to want to grow. (Gabriel, interview, June 5, 2014)

According to Gabriel, when provided with the right conditions, young people will push themselves as writers and thrive. Rather than trying to create poets, he said he hopes to offer a space that motivates adolescents to take control of their learning.

A Focus on "Community"

Like "safe space," "community" is part of the rhetoric of this space. A query using the data management program NVivo revealed that the term "community" (including close variations) appeared 188 times in the data collected for this study. The adolescent poets described community in Metropoets:

RAFAEL: It's such a close-knit community that . . . it feels like you've been around for a while even though it's been like seven months or so.
NICOLE: Everybody feels like super welcome.
RAFAEL: You just kind of walk in, and you get absorbed into the culture.
NICOLE: [Metropoets is] a giant family. (interview, focus group, March 22, 2014)

Notice their use of words like "welcome" and "family." Similarly, Stacey described this community as a family. She said, "I'm finally a part of something that I fit in. Because I don't really fit in anywhere at my school, so I thought right here was really fun. I felt like I was in a family" (Stacey, interview, March 22, 2014).

Sharing poems builds community in this group. Gabriel said, "We are sharing our stories. . . . We are meeting new people. I bet there are at least five things in that last poem that you guys had no idea that's who I am. And now you know. And now we're closer because of that. And that's the beautiful thing about sharing our stories together in a community" (observation, July 19, 2014). Gabriel believes people bond through storytelling. And he is not alone. In related research, Marc Lamont Hill (2009) observed that when a student had the courage to share her story, she changed the atmosphere of the classroom. The moment "facilitated the formation of a classroom community in which students shared their own stories and responded to others" (69).

Members of this community are expected to treat each other well. At the Town Slam, Mark said, "All of you, realize that this little thing right here in the audience, this is a family unit. [*The crowd cheers.*] . . . [As] you go back to live your lives, . . . remember to make good decisions. You guys, this generation, the young people in this room, are the most at risk of anybody out there. So please take care of each other. Make smart decisions because stuff happens, man, and it's not a joke" (observation, November 8, 2013). Recognizing the dangers that adolescents face, Mark asked the youth poets to look out for each other.

While community is often emphasized in Metropoets, this does not mean that all members experience the group the same way. Etienne Wenger (1998) cautions, "Communities of practice should not be romanticized: they can reproduce counterproductive patterns, injustices, prejudices, racism, sexism, and abuses of all kinds" (132). Additionally, Javon Johnson (2010) has urged researchers to take a critical stance when looking at community in spoken word poetry groups.

It was in the final months of the study when some of the adolescent poets finally talked to me about tensions in the group:

WENDY: So I'm seeing the love and how it's all about family, but I'm not seeing the negativity?
JASMINE: Yeah, we try to hide that really well.
WENDY: So where is that hiding?
JASMINE: Sometimes during the events there is actual tension.
WENDY: I did actually catch something once. I think it was your poem about feminism. And you [said], "I'm tired of"—I'm paraphrasing—"these stupid poems about women hating men." And I felt like you were talking to some of the people in the room.
JASMINE: Yes. [*They laugh.*] Even in the last event that we went to, there was a little bit of tension just because we're wondering who [Gabriel] was going to announce next. And he has a preference.
RAFAEL: I'm here to place. When you go up on stage and you know you want to place, in your mind you're just like, "Oh, I better beat this person." [If] you don't get the scores you want, you kind of like get really upset. You'll see it on a poet's face when someone goes up right after them and they get a higher score. And I guess you can use it as motivation or you can just stay mad at the person for a long time. (interview, focus group, July 21, 2014)

In this exchange, the poets addressed several different types of conflicts. They admitted that their poems sometimes responded to other poets' works, which is in line with M. M. Bakhtin's (1986) notion that words shared are utterances in a larger chain. In other words, poems interact not just with the immediate people and context but also with what came before. Additionally, in this exchange, Jasmine suggests that the youth poets competed for Gabriel's attention. Although they worried that Gabriel favored certain poets above them, I observed that Jasmine and Nicole were both consistently valued in Metropoets. They received special privileges such as invitations to represent the group. If Gabriel paid attention to others, it was probably to try to even things out.

The exchange above is also interesting because Rafael highlights the competiveness some poets feel. Apparently he, Nicole, and Jasmine are in competition with each other, which can make things uncomfortable for these friends. Wenger (1998) warns, "A community of practice is neither a haven of togetherness nor an island of intimacy insulated from political and social relations. Disagreement, challenges, and competition can all be forms of participation" (77). Communities are complex, and they are certainly never perfect. Although Metropoets consistently felt like a warm, welcoming space to me, conflicts arise in any group of people who work together over time.

Ground Rules

Metropoets relied on three key ground rules to help foster a safe space for poets: (1) be brave; (2) be respectful; and (3) your voice matters. Gabriel had this to say about the first rule: "Being brave does not mean that you are not afraid. It means that you are scared as hell and you are still going to push through" (observation, January 18, 2014).

Regarding the second rule, Mark said poets must respect each other: "You might be like, 'Oh, dang. Yo, we grew up in the same neighborhood,' or 'Wow, my mom, too,' or 'My brother's locked up.' You might figure out that someone you don't think you have much in common with actually shares very similar stories with you. So being respectful requires you to listen to everyone, . . . [to] make sure that we are elevating each voice in the room" (observation, October 12, 2013). Mark highlighted the connection between respect and listening, and he suggested that listening to others' stories could uncover shared experiences.

Gabriel pointed out that the third rule is the most important. He said, "This space is created for you. . . . Oftentimes you are told to sit down and pay attention because we adults know what we are doing, and we're going to educate you. And in some situations, that's true, but in this particular situation, we want to hear what you have to say. And the sooner you can learn to articulate yourself in a powerful and empowering way, . . . there's no place that you can't go" (observation, January 18, 2014). Gabriel equated a strong voice with success. His comments also allude to other spaces where adults are in charge and adolescents are expected to remain silent (e.g., school). Rather than selecting ground rules that would control young people and silence them, in Metropoets they use rules that are focused on getting adolescents to speak (e.g., Be brave. Your voice matters.) and that value the stories of all (e.g., Be respectful). These ground rules foster a safe space for writing and sharing.

Supportive Practices

In this group, poets snap, give feedback, mentor each other, and offer encouragement. These supportive practices contribute to a safe space for storytelling.

Snapping

Poetry slam audiences snap in response to poems to show support for the performers and their words. Jasmine said she snaps because she understands how challenging it can be to get up in front of a crowd and share something personal. She enjoys when people snap for her because it means they appreciate her words. These responses energize her. Rafael added that if nobody responds to his poems, he feels unappreciated. He recalled a time when he performed and people were not responding. He said, "It crushes you a little. It hits you, and you're like, 'What am I doing up here?' And once you hear the one person snap or clap or cheer, you just kind of take that and you throw it right back at them. You take it in and you're just like, 'Okay, if you guys are going to make noise, I'm going to give you a little bit more emotion.' It's reassuring" (Rafael, interview, July 21, 2014). Snapping is an important practice in spoken word culture because it lets the poet know he or she is being heard, that the words are connecting with real listeners in that moment.

Giving Feedback

One of the key differences between Metropoets and some other youth spoken word groups is how members respond to poems. Whereas some groups encourage members to give each other focused feedback (Fisher 2007b; Weiss and Herndon 2001), Metropoets teaching artists consistently and intentionally gave minimal feedback to poets. Responses in writing workshops often took the following form:

MARK: So, who's going to be brave and share? All right.
[FIRST POEM READ.] Nice. Very good. All right. Who's next?
[SECOND POEM READ.] Nice. That cat is all over that red water. Crazy.
[THIRD POEM READ.] Nice. Who's next? . . .
[FOURTH POEM READ.] Nice. That's good. That's a good start. All right. Who's next?
[FIFTH POEM READ.] Oh. Dang. That's a cold-blooded woman in that. All right. Who's next?
[SIXTH POEM READ.] [*Group laughs.*] All right.
[SEVENTH POEM READ.] Nice. Nice . . .
[EIGHTH POEM READ.] W-w-wait. Read it loud so we can hear you. That was good. (observation, October 12, 2013)

When I asked Mark about this practice, he said, "I don't want to give kids license to be critical of other kids' poems" (Mark, interview, June 24, 2014). This approach varies from the "read and feed" practice that Fisher (2007b) observed in the Power Writers group, where "feeding had to be more than just affirming and complimentary; it had to be informed, critical, and specific" (21). The Power Writers used evidence as they responded to each other. They dug into texts. In contrast, the main goal in the Metropoets group was to get teenagers to speak up.

Occasionally Gabriel or Mark celebrated the writing process in their comments. In response to a poet who wrote her poem in a single day, Gabriel said, "She wrote that poem in our workshop. She didn't even have a poem, and she wrote it" (observation, March 15, 2014). He was impressed with this poet's speed and dedication. Mark said to another poet, "Look at you, making steps" (observation, September 20, 2014), honoring the progress he had seen her make.

Less often, teaching artists cited specific details from a poem in their feedback. They tended to do this with more advanced poets. When Jasmine performed a love poem at a slam, Gabriel responded by repeating a line ("For Halloween, I want to dress up like you when you loved yourself and show up on your doorstep"). He said he wished he had come up with that line himself (observation, July 19, 2014).

Sometimes teaching artists commented on issues the poems brought to light. In response to a poem about transgender challenges, Gabriel said, "One of the most beautiful things about this job is the many diverse stories and individuals . . . in one community. We share. We grow. And as an adult and as a teacher, it's an opportunity for me to sit back and be the student. And I really appreciate that" (observation, April 19, 2014). Comments like this one show intergenerational encounters (Fisher 2005) benefiting adults as well as adolescents. Gabriel's feedback focused on how a poem helped him to think more about a topic. In Metropoets, adolescent poets have knowledge that others, including adults, can learn from. The perspectives, experiences, and "funds of knowledge" (Moll et al. 1992) adolescents have gained in their lives outside of school are valued in this space.

Mentoring

Mentoring was used to support youth members of this group. It goes without saying that Mark and Gabriel did much of the mentoring in the Metropoets group. Jorge spoke of the importance of having access to poets like these two men. He said, "Sometimes it's difficult to relate to your own peers. They have no advice to really offer. Whereas somebody who's much older, somebody who has gone through what you're going through . . . they're able to give you advice" (Jorge, interview, June 27, 2014). Jorge appreciated their guidance.

While teaching artists typically gave advice and assistance to adolescent poets, mentoring was not always a top-down practice. There was a culture of mentoring in this group, and people stepped up to help each other. At one event, an adult teaching artist asked Nicole for feedback on a poem, and Nicole was thrilled to help. She recalled that the teaching artist had asked her for assistance with phrasing, and then he took her advice. She appreciated that he went to her for help because he had helped her many times. Nicole said, "It was really awesome for him to come to me and ask me for advice. I was like, 'Is this really happening?' . . . On the outside I was all cool and calm and collected, and on the inside I was like, 'Oh my god. I need to make sure I make the right decision'" (Nicole, interview, December 26, 2013).

In fact, at the same time Nicole was helping this teaching artist, Jasmine was in another corner of the same room working with Stacey. Jasmine had also started taking on more of a mentoring role at her school. Teachers had asked for her advice on teaching poetry. Jasmine reflected, "It's sort of funny and weird to know that we're role models because we feel like we are still in development, so it's really strange to like be a role model for someone else" (Jasmine, interview, December 26, 2013). Mentoring others can feel awkward when a poet is still growing so much herself.

Of course, despite one's best intentions, mentors are not always as effective as they would like to be. Mark admitted that he had unintentionally scared kids away. Sometimes new members will hear poets like Mark and Gabriel, they cannot imagine themselves ever being that good, and they quit. Therefore, Mark makes it a point to remind kids that even Michael Jordan did not become an expert basketball player without practice. If they want to become good spoken word poets, they need to stick around and practice. On a related note, Howard Gardner (1982) has acknowledged the tension adolescents may feel as they compare themselves to experts, a point at which some young artists give up. While writing alongside Mark may be intimidating because of his skill, I saw this poet go out of his way to be friendly and reassuring.

Offering Encouragement

I heard many supportive comments during my year with the Metropoets group. At poetry slams, the host would recognize poets, judges, the deejay, and audience members. "Keep that round of applause going for yourself. Come on. Love yourself," Gabriel would say to the crowd (observation, October 12, 2013). Teaching artists also encouraged writers. Mark would say things like, "I'm super proud of you guys for writing" (observation, October 12, 2013). Gabriel stressed that these shows of love were not acts. He told a poetry slam audience, "A lot of the emotion that you may see up here from me may look like a performance, but it's so real. . . . I'm so proud of anybody who explores their story through narrative because it's not an easy thing to do. It takes a lot of work, dedication, and then to share, it is just amazing" (observation, October 26, 2013). At events throughout the 2013–2014 season, teaching artists delivered an abundance of supportive comments, which helped build a positive climate for literacy learning.

In classrooms, teachers may offer positive reinforcement, and adolescents may support each other. However, it was fascinating to find that adolescents also supported adults in Metropoets. As readers may recall from chapter 3, when Mark lost his place while performing his poem, the audience encouraged him. They shouted out, "Keep going" (observation, October 12, 2013). That is, adolescent members immediately responded with the same kind of encouragement we might expect a teacher to give to students. It seems that Metropoets members are so used to practicing supportive behaviors that they kick in regardless of a poet's rank. Even adults need encouragement sometimes. It was moving to witness this reversal of traditional roles.

Conclusion

Nurturing a supportive writing community "dedicated to improving and applauding each other's work" takes effort (Weiss and Herndon 2001, 25), as this chapter shows. Gabriel and Mark have clear purposes for bringing people together, and they make use of routines and tools that connect with adolescents. Members participate to a degree that is comfortable, travel on various learning trajectories, and have opportunities to connect with a global community of poets. In addition, the language, ground rules, and supportive practices used in Metropoets help create a safe space for storytelling.

Corey Frost (2014) points out that spoken word communities are more egalitarian than some other groups of artists. Novices and experts "are relatively close in status," and group "borders are much less controlled than the borders of other artistic communities because spoken word aesthetics are so loosely defined in terms of style and level of refinement" (14–15). I see these features as strengths. Spoken word is not pretentious. It is written by everyday people and deals with everyday events and issues.

In Metropoets, few restrictions are placed on youth poets. Members come and go and participate to the extent that pleases them. They have access to teaching artists, who sit at eye level with them at workshops and who share their own writing at slams—even when the piece, or their performance of it, is not perfect. This is quite a different arrangement than we see in schools. Although Mark and Gabriel are clearly group leaders, their workshops and slams seem democratic. Also, kids are not penalized like they are in school. Even when judges give poems low scores, a host is quick to point out that the scores do not really matter. When it comes to nurturing a community of writers, there are many lessons that can be learned from the Metropoets group.

CHAPTER 5

WRITING AND AUTHORSHIP

I do consider myself a spoken word poet now. Before I was just like, "Yeah, I write poetry."
—Shawna

Writing is important to Shawna, Stacey, Rafael, Jasmine, Nicole, and Jorge. These poets voluntarily spend time writing and performing on their weekends, and they are valued members of the Metropoets community. This chapter examines writing and authorship in the lives of these young poets. The pages that follow look at their poems, their writing practices, and their understandings of various aspects of their writing lives. Investigating youth writers' out-of-school compositions, writing habits, and attitudes toward writing can suggest ways to make school-based writing instruction more useful, relevant, and engaging for today's secondary students.

Five Poets and Their Poems

As they wrote spoken word poems, the adolescents in the yearlong study drew on their "funds of knowledge" (Moll et al. 1992), bringing together various experiences, skills, and understandings to use poetry for their own purposes (Williams 2015). These writers have much to say about love, loss, family, culture, nature, school, bullying, racial profiling, and politics, as excerpts from their ten poems below will show. These poets also draw on their languages and ways of knowing in these works, as when Jorge integrates Spanish into his poems. In Metropoets, writers have a chance to tell their stories, and it is assumed that all teenagers have stories worth telling. Rather than taking a deficit approach (Valencia 1997) with urban youth, criticizing students or their families for different forms of knowledge or different "ways with words" (Heath 1983), the Metropoets group values the wealth of knowledge and understandings that young people possess. As their poems demonstrate, these youth poets are speaking about powerful experiences in their own ways.

Below are *excerpts* of the poems that five adolescents shared with me at our third interview.[1] Ellipses in brackets indicate omitted lines. Other than that, I have left the poems in their original, *unedited* form to retain poets' language, spelling, and punctuation choices. That is, I have not inserted or removed apostrophes, replaced homophones, changed spacing, adjusted capitalization, deleted repeated words, removed their ellipses, etc. My intent is to provide realistic samples of their writing.

Jorge

Jorge has written some emotional poems, and he believes that writing them has helped him mature. His adolescent years were difficult because he was still working through the death of his biological father, who was murdered when Jorge was an infant. This is the subject of Jorge's first spoken word poem. He writes:

> [...] I was three months old
> and getting no love from you papa
> Green paper was your only concern,
> I was the least of your worries
> or at least that's how it seemed.
> as your bags of money were stacking
> the hunger I yearned
> for a fathers love
> grew like a black hole with no boundaries.
> How the fuck
> Was I supposed to compete with this magical dank weed,
> and this snow white powder that made you so happy.
> By providing you with food,
> fancy clothing,
> and most of all
> females,
> to please your every sexual desire.
> All I was ever, able to give you were used diapers
> and time to waist on a baby you had no love for from the start.

> I was a burden to you,
> all I ever wanted was just a little bit of your love.
> Just a little bit of your time to show you that
> I'm worth making memories with,
> to show you, that I'll be someone
> with the life you blessed me with [. . .] (collected July 11, 2014)

This poem expresses Jorge's sadness, frustration, and anger at having to grow up without his father. When Jorge performs the piece, he imagines he is standing with his father, talking directly to him.

Jorge began writing this poem in his high school poetry club, and it took several months for him to finish the piece. He struggled with the idea that his family might hear the poem, and he also was not sure if he had all of the facts right, since the events took place when he was an infant. Mark, Gabriel, and poetry club members gave Jorge feedback. For example, Gabriel helped with some of the language in the poem.

Poetry "helped me to understand that I am not my dad. I am my own person. It really helped me to become a young man," he said (Jorge, interview, June 27, 2014). This poem made Jorge more comfortable with being open and emotionally vulnerable. Mark, who has known Jorge for several years, said, "It's his story, and I feel like having told it, it's easier for him to step into the world. Just like with any one of these kids' stories" (Mark, interview, June 24, 2014).

The other poem Jorge shared with me was the second poem he wrote. In fact, he wrote it all in one day and used his phone and a journal to compose the piece. In it, Jorge celebrates his stepfather. He embraces their different cultural customs. Jorge writes:

> You see, the man who raised me
> Is my pops, my step dad
> He's been by my side since I was two years old
> With his black hands he taught me to respect others
> and how to shoot a basketball
> he taught me the importance of responsibility
> and how to converse with girls [. . .]
> However, I remember how my grandmother
> would warn me as a boy
> To stay away from my stepfathers black children
> But those are my brothers and sisters [. . .]
> I love my grandmother
> And I forgive her for not seeing then
> That my pops is my

> my life mentor
> And I'm thankful for my mother
> For being so strong when my tios and tias would criticize her
> I'm grateful that she chose to marry my pops
> And even though the pain in my heart for never having really
>   known my biological father aches
> I'm blessed to have my pops in my life
> If only those who were drowned in racial ignorance could see
> How blessed I am
> To be able to dance banda at a quince while my brothers krump at a
>   cipher
> How fortunate I am to be able to rap while my primo's sing corridos
> I get to eat bean tostadas while my pops eats his chitlins
> I await for the day that my tio's and tia's will open their eyes and
>   realize
> that happiness comes from acceptance rather than rejection
>   (collected July 11, 2014)

Jorge said he wrote this piece "to illustrate the racism that goes on between Latino and African American communities," to "obliterate racism in [his] family," and to "show appreciation for [his] stepdad" (Jorge, interview, July 11, 2014). In fact, his stepfather and mother heard him perform this poem at a Metropoets event. Jorge recalled, "My dad, I think he's developed a sense of new respect for me because not only has he seen me as his son, but he's seen me as a young man. He's able to see what goes through my mind" (Jorge, interview, June 27, 2014).

Although this poet typically addresses social issues in his poems, these two works are more personal. Jorge said that the first poem is part one in his story and the second poem is part two. He said, "I've come around and realized . . . this is who I am now. This is what I had to go through in addition to my pain. This is the other side that I had to experience . . . before I began my life as a writer. It's one of those barriers that I had to overcome" (Jorge, interview, July 11, 2014). These poems have helped Jorge realize he is proud to be who he is today.

Nicole

Nicole is a thoughtful poet who spends time developing beautiful metaphors. In one poem, Nicole compares attending school to swimming, and the piece follows this metaphor through to the end as she compares graduating to being poured out of a pool for children:

> This is for Briana.
> This is for the girl in my speech class

> Who killed herself freshman year.
> This is for the kids who graduate with straight A's
> and the kids who won't
> even make it to graduation day.
> Swim the hallway [...]
> This is for the kids who eat lunch by themselves
> and hide out in the bathrooms.
> For the kids who leave the second the bell rings
> And the kids who stay on campus until the security kicks them off
>   because they're afraid of going home
> Swim the hallways [...]
> keep swimming those
> mystery liquid
> black foot marked
> Gum stained hallways
> For four years, five hundred and fifty-two days, and 33,120 seconds.
> Because if you can keep treading the water
> for four years, five hundred and fifty-two days and 33,120 seconds.
> Youll get dumped out of this kitty pool
> and released into the
> ocean full of
> Endless opportunity (collected July 21, 2014)

In this poem, Nicole demonstrates empathy as she considers multiple perspectives. She said, "All the little lines where I say, 'This is for ...' 'This is for ... ,' there's usually a person or a group of people that I've noticed from school.... I kind of just wanted to make sure that ... everyone was included" (Nicole, interview, July 21, 2014). She envisions multiple school cliques as the audience for this piece. Nicole said that when she performs this poem, she emphasizes the line, "Because they're afraid of going home." She explained her reasoning: "You need to realize that there are kids like that, and I feel like that's an important group of people that needs to be recognized because a lot of people forget" (Nicole, interview, July 21, 2014).

Nicole wrote this piece during a poetry workshop with Mark. They watched a video, did some brainstorming, and when she came up with the line, "Swim the hallway," the poem quickly fell into place. Nicole did find it challenging figuring out some of the phrasing and doing math calculations for the piece.

The second poem Nicole shared deals with love and emotional vulnerability. She uses the metaphor of a tower:

> [...] The foundation of this tower is now set in place
> And when you build a building you can't start at the top

> But I'm already looking at the blueprints for the end
> Where we are no longer lovers,
> And No longer friends,
> We will be back to where we started
> Stuck on the rooftop with the memories of us,
> In clouds of thoughts of us and what we had.
> We will be Trapped inside this skyscraper of mind
> This building finished earlier than expected,
> Some floors in the design are not included
> Trying to get out if it is virtually impossible,
> A long journey down flights of spiral wooden stairs is apparent to be the only way out.
> And sadly we weren't thinking about this even though we were the architects who designed it
> We were so anxious to get into this building and forgot possibly later we might want out.
> Each floor is a reminder of everything that happened [...]
> (collected July 21, 2014)

Nicole said she wrote this piece because she was feeling nervous about getting into another relationship, and the poem gave her a way to express her feelings. Both poems she shared contain extended metaphors, a device that works well in spoken word poetry.

When she was writing this second poem, Nicole did not worry about how her boyfriend would react. Instead, she wrote the poem for herself. As we talked about audience, Nicole said she had to consider which aspects of the story she felt comfortable sharing with others: "What parts of myself do I want to make vulnerable out of the situation, [do] I want to show to the audience?" (Nicole, interview, July 21, 2014). She pointed out that this kind of sharing, making oneself emotionally vulnerable in front of a group, is an important part of slam. Nicole said, "That's how you relate with people in the audience and you connect, and you bring people in, and all the good stuff of slam" (Nicole, interview, July 21, 2014).

When she started writing the piece, she had the idea for a building metaphor. After that, she was able to write the entire poem all at once. It took about a week for her to revise it. Writing directly on a computer meant Nicole could save work to her online drive and then revise later from her phone. During the revision stage, Jasmine, Mark, and a local professional poet helped her improve the work.

Comparing these two poems, Nicole said they are similar in how they use extended metaphor, line repetition, and emotion. She added, "They're not so serious or the political pieces that I typically try to write" (Nicole, interview, July 21, 2014). These two poems show different sides of this poet, while also revealing her skill in working with poetic devices.

Jasmine

Like Nicole, Jasmine has a compelling way with words. She is a philosophical poet who embraces contradictions and wordplay. Jasmine writes,

> I'm a walking contradiction [. . .]
> i say what i want but don't say what i mean
> i like smoking cigarettes on the rooftop
> because it makes me feel like a 1990s sitcoms bad girl
> and
> i like chocolate milk . . . . a lot
> i'm terrible at small talk but love conversation
> and if during our conversation i raise my hands above my head
>   just know
> that i'm internally yelling for you to understand my metaphors
> i'm a sucker for strangers with nice smiles and wandering eyes
> but i will always prefer the spines of novels then the arch of a human
>   being because novels
> are much more stable
> and less likely to fall apart in my hands [. . .]
> and I am always constantly wondering;
> if I sit long enough in a dark room
> will I develop like film
> or
> was this all just a waste
> of
> time? (collected July 21, 2014)

Jasmine thinks it is difficult to find the right degree of vulnerability in love: "To reveal so much of yourself to one person and then have that person not accept you . . . for them to leave. That's always been a really touchy subject with me" (Jasmine, interview, July 21, 2014). This is why she says in this poem that books are more reliable than people.

Although Jasmine did not imagine a particular audience while writing this poem, she said the poem gave her a way to show herself to others and reveal her insecurities. She wrote this "honesty" piece by fitting together a lot of ideas from her different notebooks. Even though a professional poet in the community has given Jasmine some feedback on this poem, Jasmine is not sure she is going to change it as much as that person would like.

In another poem, Jasmine tackles the theme of love. She writes:

> To the last person I will ever love. You are perfect.
> Or maybe not.
> Although I am still looking for that special someone who drinks
>   moonlight like wine
> I have learned that love is never what you imagine.
> and I know that one day we'll meet each other
> Breathless.
> We will both see our wandering eyes, tired.
> Our bodies' heavy with every heartbreak we carry.
> But we will ignore the obvious.
> And I know that we won't love each other at first sight because
>   let's face it. That only happens in fairy tales and
> this isn't a fairytale [. . .]
> We will be a beautiful catastrophe set in motion.
> Our love will be messy.
> We will have bruises between our knuckles for holding each other's
>   hands way too tightly.
> Sweat layered between our palms, wanting to melt into the pores
>   of each other's skin and
> Our first kisses will consist of us trying to piece each other just right
> So be ready for bumping noses and knocking teeth.
> But it's okay. We'll get better, I promise [. . .] (collected July 21, 2014)

Jasmine explained that real love is not like a fairy tale. People meet in unexpected and random ways. In this poem, she wanted to remind young people that probably their current relationship will not be their last. Before Jasmine composed this piece, she did some research, calling ex-boyfriends to get their perspectives on what had gone wrong in their relationships. She also researched the definition of love online.

As Jasmine thought about these two poems together, she said both poems deal with emotional vulnerability. "I think poetry is the art of letting go," Jasmine said. "Here's a chance [to] put it into a poem, [so I can let] go, sort of, so I can move on as a person" (Jasmine, interview, July 21, 2014). Jasmine's poetry tackles abstract ideas, but she grounds them in concrete, vivid details. Her writing seems mature beyond her age, and it is no wonder she placed first in the final slam of the 2013–2014 Metropoets season.

Rafael

Rafael is an activist whose poems tend to focus on social injustices, so I was surprised when he performed a poem about the open road:

> When I grow old, I want to see this world on an open road.
> I want to drive a beat-up RV from 1973.
> I want to discover what makes the United State a grand place [. . .]
> I want to take in the beauty of the open road. Every twist and turn, every crack and bump upon the blacktop road, I want to feel underneath my feet, as if I were reading braille and discovering an untold tale of what once was dirt roads.
> I want to visit every national park and stand there, pretending I'm Teddy Roosevelt, seeing everything for the first time.
> I want to see the Grand Canyon during snowfall and hope to God I don't fall in [. . .]
> I want to stop at every truck stop, rest stop, and gas station, just to talk to the old timers about simpler times [. . .]
> I want to lay on top of the hood and gaze at the stars I've not seen due to the city lights [. . .]
> I want to sit in front of Mount Rushmore and sip hot cocoa while I'm having an imaginary conversation with the founding fathers about society and the corruption of their image [. . .]
> When I grow old, I want to see this country on an open road and truly discover what makes the United States a grand place.
> (Rafael, interview, July 21, 2014)

When Rafael discussed this poem with me, he made it clear that this was not just a piece celebrating nature. Rafael explained, "A lot of people see the United States for capitalism, Walmart, McDonalds, these negative things. And when people say 'America,' they think New York, Boston, big cities, but they don't really think [about] what makes America great, the national parks, the things you can only see here. We concentrate on so many material items, and when you talk about a country and the only thing you can think about are material items or cities and not what the cities sit on, I think that's kind of a waste" (Rafael, interview, July 21, 2014).

Rafael originally wrote this poem because he needed a new piece for a slam, and he "always wanted to write a poem about things [he wants] to do when [he is] older, [a] retirement plan in a poem" (Rafael, interview, July 21, 2014). He said, "When I was writing it, the audience I viewed was me in a couple of years. I didn't want to slam the poem because it doesn't sound like a slam piece. It's not something that you would normally hear in a slam, so I guess the audience would be older me and whoever has enough time to listen" (Rafael, interview, July 21, 2014). Rafael is proud that he developed a plan for his future, and he feels that his love for exploration comes out in this work.

The RV in the television show *Breaking Bad* gave him the idea for this poem, which is a great example of how popular culture can make its way into students' writing (Dyson 1997). Rafael first wrote the middle of the poem, and then he added the beginning and ending. One of the challenges he had was researching national parks. When the poem was complete, he shared it with Nicole and Jasmine because he wanted to see their reactions.

In another poem, Rafael addresses a range of social issues, including hunger, poverty, and police brutality. He writes:

> It is said that history tends to repeat itself, but I'm sick and tired of reciting the same old lines: civilization, colonization, revolution, independence, recession, depression, and war.
> I feel like we live in a politician's America, where thugs don't hustle in the street, but make money off the poor in Wall Street.
> Where protect and serve becomes neglect and abuse [. . .]
> We live in a first world country, yet inner-city kids still go hungry.
> The big issues in this country like immigration, healthcare, and minimum wage are used as bases in political campaigns [. . .]
> So let's rewrite the lines of history.
> Civilization, colonization, revolution, independence, progress, wealth, and equality for all.
> Because once we start to see that the greatest magicians are on Capitol Hill, we remember that freedom is the greatest magical trick.
> Unless you see past the smoke and mirrors, revealing the people pulling the strings. (Rafael, interview, July 21, 2014)[2]

Rafael said he wrote this poem so "people [would] realize what's going on in their society and government" (Rafael, interview, July 21, 2014). He wanted to make people curious about the issues, so they would go and research answers for themselves. Rafael saw his audience as young people "because . . . , especially in Arizona, there are these old grumpy Republicans who only see one way. And it's our job as the next generation to see what is going on and what's going wrong, so we can take that in mind and actually try to correct the imbalance" (Rafael, interview, July 21, 2014). He added, "There [are] some cops, especially in Arizona. I see how it's unfair, and I've seen it firsthand with the whole racial profiling. Like, it's something that's actually happening and it's actually relevant" (Rafael, interview, July 21, 2014). Rafael uses poetry to speak out about injustices and seek change.

Rafael was at an open-mic event when he began writing this poem. He heard something that inspired him, took out his phone, and started writing. One of the challenges he encountered while composing the work was discussing race in a way that would not offend anybody. He typically does not seek feedback on his political pieces, he said.

When I asked Rafael to compare these two poems, he pointed out that they both show how he has grown as a writer. One is his retirement plan and the other is a call to action. These two works show Rafael's versatility as a poet.

Stacey

Stacey is the youngest poet in this study. In our interview, she shared a poem that opens with a series of questions. She writes:

> I wonder,
> did birds used to have fins and not float?
> Did grass hoppers used to skip on lava and ice?
> Would skies be on our right and seas on our left,
> and snakes on our mouths while our heads had turtles?
> Why do we have hands but we use them to hold weapons of war?
> Why do we have eyes if we don't want to see the truth hidden
>   within our lies?
> How can we have a heart and not love our enemies?
> Knees don't always support the burdens we carry on our backs,
> so why do our elders still keep their balance while we keep on
>   falling?
> I am grateful,
> that we do not hide in fear under our beds from the terrifying
>   sounds outside of gunshots and ticking bombs.
> To not have blood-stained hands and eyes full of regret and the
>   sound of children's cries for help ringing in our ears for as long as
>   our bodies haven't withered away [. . .] (collected July 26, 2014)

As we talked about this poem, Stacey said she was thinking about "how soldiers are out there like risking their lives . . . and sometimes they just come back and they're like haunted by everything they saw in the war. And they just wish they could disappear" (Stacey, interview, July 26, 2014). She wrote this poem to bring attention to this issue, and she imagined her audience as any person who has lost hope.

Her writing process for this piece was unusual. Stacey wrote part of the poem on a piece of paper and part on her leg. She then began to organize the poem, which was her greatest challenge in writing it. When the work was finished, she shared it with someone who really liked it, which made Stacey proud.

The second poem Stacey shared with me was one she wrote in fifth grade. It is focused on rhyme, and there is a change of tone at the end:

> Let me tell you a story............
> and if you're in a hurry
> it'll be short so don't you worry
> You've hurt us before
> and we will let you no more
> we've shed many tears
> and only blamed our peers.
> But i wont shed another tear
> for these eyes have dried since many years
> I wont become what I hate
> I am me so get used to it [. . .]
> I will be the blue rose
> blooming in the cold winter snow
> that has finally found a purpose in life
> before you strip me from my pride.
> I want to use my voice for good
> so that I could stay close to you
> So give me a call
> so we can hang with ya'll. (collected July 26, 2014)

In her commentary for this piece, Stacey said, "When you're a kid, every song or everything that you hear has to be in a rhyme" (Stacey, interview, July 26, 2014). She originally wrote this poem in her notebook, and then she transferred it to her laptop. Unlike other poets I talked to, Stacey generally did not receive help on her poems.

Stacey initially found it difficult to share this poem. It is about bullying, and she wrote it because she felt guilty about not standing up for someone who was being bullied. This poem warns against shedding tears because she is not comfortable crying in front of others. I asked her to compare these two works, and she said she had a specific person in mind while composing the bullying poem. Stacey hopes that both poems leave people feeling differently. She wants her writing to relieve suffering and lead to greater equality.

Distinct Writing Practices

This study found that the adolescent poets engaged in distinct writing practices. This section examines their prewriting strategies, their selection of topics and tools, their typical locations and schedules for writing, and whether they would write alone or with others. Many similarities can be seen across the six cases.

Prewriting

The poets used various methods of prewriting to generate ideas for poems. For example, Jasmine would begin by making lists of ideas related to a topic. Stacey would write a story before writing a poem. Rafael engaged in a very different form of prewriting, using "freestyle." He explained how his process works:

> When I freestyle, I sort of just shut off my mind. I let words flow. It's more about the idea than the word choice. . . . [It is] as if I'm talking to myself, and then it just starts flowing. Later I'll go back and see where I'm repeating myself too much or where I can use a rhyme or where I can strengthen the idea. A lot of the time I don't because it's weak, or . . . I was just venting. . . . When I freestyle, it's just to stop a restless mind. But when there's a topic that's bugging me, and I just have to write about it, I'll freestyle it, listen to it, write it down. And when I do a voice memo, it goes directly into my music library, so I'll just play it like a song and . . . write it down. . . . I keep writing and . . . editing it until I have like a rough draft. And from the rough draft I just delete the memo, and I continue with it. (Rafael, interview, March 19, 2014)

Rafael's use of voice memos is interesting. Out-of-school prewriting sometimes looks, and sounds, very different from the graphic organizers so often used in classrooms today (e.g., Venn diagrams, clusters, and outlines).

Although I have not observed Rafael's prewriting strategy used in schools, it does recall Shirley Brice Heath's (1983) point about supporting children's ways with words by having them audio-record their stories for later transcription. I wonder what would happen if secondary students were allowed to use audiorecorders or phones for oral brainstorming and drafting. Perhaps a class could spread out in a large room or outdoor space to experience this option. After all, it is important that students have access to a wide range of strategies, so they can discover what works best for them in particular writing situations.

Janet Emig (1971) has suggested that students engage in more prewriting in their out-of-school compositions. Although this study of Metropoets did not compare the adolescent writers' school and out-of-school writing, it did find that the poets took their spoken word prewriting seriously and certainly went about it in novel ways.

Topics

Metropoets writers take up a variety of topics in their spoken word poems. Shawna has written about beauty, the government, her stepdad, and kids who live in Child Protective Services. Jasmine enjoys recording stories others have told her in order to give the memories more permanence—in a sense, archiving her friends' experiences (Alim 2007). She has also written letters to her future self. Jasmine uses "writing at once for self-reflection and self-fashioning" (Herrington and Curtis 2000, 356).

Many poets address both personal and social topics in their works. Nicole enjoys writing about politics, love, and her life. She said, "I love doing satire and writing sarcastic poems, making fun of the government. . . . Like here in Arizona, I love making big jokes and making them look like a fool. . . . I also like to . . . write personal [narratives] about my life and things that I've gone through. . . . It's fun trying to not be cliché with love poems" (Nicole, interview, December 26, 2013). A good example of Nicole's political satire can be found in the duo poem, "Good Morning, America," which she wrote with Jasmine. This poem critiques various injustices, and the poets update it often to reflect current events.

Stacey tends to write about bullying and disability. She said, "I write [about] people who think nobody would understand them or people, like my sister, that were diagnosed with like a disability or illness" (Stacey, interview, January 18, 2014). Jorge frequently speaks out against discrimination in his poems. In addition, he writes about "personal experiences, difficult ones, sad ones generally that have really made it difficult . . . to move on and grow" (Jorge, interview, December 22, 2013). Similarly, Rafael said his works deal with "political activism . . . equal rights . . . immigration, gay rights, . . . [and] personal stuff" (Rafael, interview, March 19, 2014). Susan Weinstein (2009) found that adolescent poets in her study wrote about personal and social issues, and Korina Jocson (2011) has suggested that spoken word can be used to illuminate "social realities that are often steeped in the margins" (156). This sort of writing can help adolescents "work toward empowered identity development and social transformation" (Morrell 2005, 313).

It is important to note that Metropoets writers are free to select their own topics, which leads to meaningful and powerful writing. Too often teachers in schools dictate what students must write about, removing not only choice but also the chance for a student to care deeply about the writing he or she produces.

Tools

The poets used a variety of tools to write and store their poems. In fact, they often carried notebooks and phones around with them, so they had constant access to their works, a phenomenon Jabari Mahiri and Soraya Sablo (1996) observed as well in their study of voluntary writing. Etienne Wenger (1998) points out that "having a tool to perform an activity changes the nature of that activity" (59). Tools like cell phones, especially when used with online storage, can enable poets to stay connected to their writing even when they have left a journal behind. From the palm of a hand, a poet can write and edit a poem. Later, they can refer back to these texts, scrolling through them as they perform.

Nicole records her writing in a special notebook and sometimes composes poems on her phone. She explained her system:

> I usually always have a poetry notebook with me.... It has to be a composition book... college ruled. I have to fill out every page, and I can't skip pages. I keep everything chronological.... I write front and back [and] fill every single page... from the... first page all the way to the end.... I usually just write with a pencil, and I usually edit in different colored pens.... I also type on my phone and on my laptop on Google Drive. That's where all my poetry is. If I'm on the bus, I'll be typing on my phone, but if I'm at home, I'll just write in my notebook. (Nicole, interview, December 26, 2013)

This poet has definite preferences regarding writing tools, and she selects them depending on where she is when she writes.

Jasmine likes to get comfortable when she writes, and she enjoys having a tea packet, books, and music on hand. She keeps a notebook just for spoken word and another one where she records interesting words and sentences. Shawna also mentioned writing in multiple notebooks and on her phone, while Jorge writes in a special journal a girlfriend gave him. Stacey favors a certain pencil. She said, "I have this backpack, and I get my notebook, and I have this weird looking pencil with me. It's a little broken, with a little Band-Aid.... I always used that when I was in elementary school, so it helps me... be inspired with my writing" (Stacey, interview, January 18, 2014). Stacey is almost superstitious in regard to the power of this stubby pencil.

Rafael does not like to use paper. He said, "I don't write with pen and paper because... it's [not] fast enough to capture everything I'm saying, so I usually use my cell phone, my voice recorder, or the voice-to-text apps.... I have them on my phone and on my Google drive, so I'm very electronically connected with my poetry" (Rafael, interview, March 19, 2014). As technology evolves, new tools are becoming available to writers, offering new opportunities as well as new challenges. Unfortunately, Rafael ended up losing many of his poems during the study when he switched phones.

Schedules

All six adolescent poets reported that they prefer to write at night. Jorge explained, "Generally it happens at night, when I'm doing my little quest on what the world is about and what's going on in the world. My mind just starts really dozing off and going somewhere else, and that's generally when I start writing" (Jorge, interview, December 22, 2013). Rafael, who typically writes at 11:00 p.m. or later, responded in a similar way. He said, "When I'm trying to sleep and my mind is everywhere, I use it to get everything off my mind. And most of the time when I do that, I don't write anything down. I just kind of freestyle and let it all out so I can sleep. But if it's good enough, I'll write . . . a couple of key words to help me remember" (Rafael, interview, March 19, 2014).

Jasmine likes to write at night with background television noise. She said, "It gets my brain caught up with what I'm doing" (Jasmine, interview, December 26, 2013). Nicole also likes to write at night, but she will sometimes write in the morning as well. She said, "My yard is kind of bigger, and it's kind of like more secluded because we have fences, so I'll just sit in my front yard and listen to music and write. That's probably my favorite time to write, other than at night" (Nicole, interview, December 26, 2013).

The frequency of their writing varies. Jorge prefers to write two or three times a week, but being a busy college student means he only writes about once a week now. Rafael and Stacey said they try to write daily. Stacey explained: "I write basically every day. Like whatever pops into my mind, or whatever my sister says. . . . I just don't want to forget things" (Stacey, interview, January 18, 2014). Nicole also writes daily, sometimes multiple times per day. She said: "I usually try to write something at least once every day, but some days I'll feel really inspired, and I'll write a whole bunch, like I'll fill up five pages in a notebook. And then some days [I write] a few words" (Nicole, interview, December 26, 2013).

Shawna said, "It depends. Like, I have times when I'm writing a lot, and then I have times when I'm hardly writing. Um, so I don't know, I guess it just depends on the time period and how busy I am, what's going on, what's not going on, how much time I have, how much time I don't have" (Shawna, interview, December 27, 2013). Jasmine mentioned writing when inspiration strikes. She said, "I always have a notebook . . . with me. It doesn't matter if it's a line, or maybe a word I find interesting. . . . If it's at school and I can't get a notebook, I always have my phone, . . . I used to have pens with me to write . . . on my hands. [I'm] always just constantly writing" (Jasmine, interview, December 26, 2013).

These poets engage in deliberate practice as they work toward developing expertise (Chi, Glaser, and Farr 1988; Ericsson 1996, 2005, and 2008; Nandagopal and Ericsson 2012). They are passionate about their out-of-school writing and go to great lengths to do it, dropping everything to write when inspired and sometimes composing for hours.

Locations

The adolescent poets reported writing in a variety of places. Jorge likes to write in his dorm room when his roommate is not there. Stacey, who also has a roommate, waits for the opportunity to write. She said, "Well, I share my room with my sister, so I wait until it's like nighttime, and it's when she's asleep. And I go to my side of the room and stay as quiet as I can, and I start writing right there in my little corner" (Stacey, interview, January 18, 2014). In addition to writing in her yard, Nicole enjoys writing at school and in the library, as well as in the car or on the bus. Shawna also has a variety of places where she writes, including the charity where she works. She added, "And in my room. In my safest places, that's where I write. I wouldn't sit and write at my mom's house because I don't want anybody to pick it up and read it" (Shawna, interview, December 27, 2013). Jasmine tends to write in her room or in the park. Rafael prefers to write in his hallway. He said, "I don't know why, but walking up and down my hallway, it kind of just starts flowing. . . . I have to be up, and if my body isn't moving, I can't like get everything flowing" (Rafael, interview, March 19, 2014).

Except for Nicole, no one else said they enjoyed writing in a classroom. Privacy seems to be an important concern for these writers—not to mention, Rafael feels like he needs to be up and moving. These findings might explain why some students have such a hard time writing in classroom spaces. In classrooms, students typically lack privacy, space, and freedom of movement.

Writing with Others

The poets in this study write alone the majority of the time. Stacey and Shawna said they write by themselves, and Rafael feels he must be on his own because he uses voice memos. Nicole mentioned writing alongside others occasionally, as when she and Jasmine have collaborated on duo poems. Jorge emphatically declared, "I have to be alone" (Jorge, interview, December 22, 2013).

Several decades ago, Janet Emig (1971) made the following argument that is still very relevant today: "In most American high schools, . . . there is no time provided, and no place where a student can ever be alone, although all accounts of writers tell us a condition of solitude is requisite for certain kinds of encounters with words and concepts. (If teachers assume that the student will find elsewhere the solitude the school does not provide, let them visit the houses and apartments in which their students live)" (98–99). Consistent with Emig's argument, all six adolescent participants in this study mentioned a preference to write alone.

A Sense of Authorship

When I previously studied two rappers who had performed in a high school talent show (Williams 2013), I found they were proud of their songwriter personas and wanted to become famous for their raps. This motivated them to spend hours composing lyrics and making beats. "Writers see themselves to a greater or lesser extent as authors, and present themselves to a greater or lesser extent as authors" (Ivanic 1998, 26). Going public with writing can involve enacting an identity. The two songwriters I studied saw themselves as conscious rappers. They had a strong "authorial self," which is "the writer's sense of [himself/herself] as a writer" (Burgess and Ivanic 2010, 247).

As I embarked on this yearlong study of Metropoets, I wondered whether the adolescent members saw themselves as writers. As it turns out, they did. In fact, they specifically saw themselves as poets. Shawna said, "I do consider myself a spoken word poet now. Before I was just like, 'Yeah, I write poetry'" (Shawna, interview, December 27, 2013). These poets have not only learned to write in particular ways but they have also come to see themselves as particular kinds of writers. They take ownership of their work and go public with it, presenting their writerly selves to the world.

While some may argue that an "author" must have work published in a traditional sense to earn this title, I want to honor the multiple ways youth are going public with their works and taking on identities as writers. Adolescents' songs, comics, videos, and other types of texts can be as insightful, powerful, and artful as work that is formally published. Below I explore the youth poets' relationships to their writing by examining their writing histories, most powerful experiences, motivation to write, sponsors and role models, and experiences of "flow" while writing. In addition, I discuss their writing roadblocks, pet peeves, and predictions about the role of writing in their adult lives. Together, these findings demonstrate that writing is not just an isolated activity in these poets' lives; rather, it is an important part of who they are. They have developed a strong sense of authorship.

Writing Histories

The youth poets shared their writing histories, some going into much more depth than others. Some reached far back into the past to begin their writing histories, while one poet saw his writing life as beginning recently with spoken word poetry. Stacey recalled writing a short essay in first grade, which was a positive experience for her. Eventually, she started writing poems and stories and even preferred writing over going to recess. Rafael came to writing through drawing. He said he would draw a picture and then write a description of it. When he was in fifth grade, he wrote a short story that was twenty pages. As time went on and he entered middle school, he became interested in hip-hop and started writing raps.

Shawna said she started writing poetry in third grade, but it took time for her to improve. She recalled that on the first day of third grade, her teacher gave her a D on an assignment because she had not written enough in the allotted time. That night Shawna went home and wrote two full pages to make up the work, but the next day, her teacher told her it was not actually a graded assignment. Shawna characterizes her writing during that period as "horrible." She said, "I look at it and laugh at it, but it was a start" (Shawna, interview, December 27, 2013). In eighth grade, Shawna's English teacher taught poetry, which Shawna enjoyed. She recalled, "That's when I really started writing, and it actually made sense and was actually cool. And people would read it, and they were like, 'Oh, this is good!' . . . So I was like, 'Okay, cool. I have talent'" (Shawna, interview, December 27, 2013).

Nicole talked about sharing a poem about bubblegum with her third grade class. She recalled many successful writing experiences in school such as being placed in an advanced writing class, writing scary stories, and winning a $500 essay contest. Jasmine talked about writing poetry in second and third grade, and she composed stories for people when she was in middle school. Jorge saw his writing history as beginning at the point when he entered the poetry club in high school.

Powerful Experiences

I asked the youth poets to share their most powerful Metropoets experiences. Stacey remembered performing a poem about her sister who is autistic, and when Stacey looked up, her mother was there in the audience. Stacey immediately regretted performing the piece. Once they were home, her mother said, "Can you read that again, but can you read it in Spanish? I couldn't [understand] you, but I know it was about your sister." Stacey repeated the performance, and her mother cried. Stacey recalled, "I [thought] I hurt her. [My mother said], 'That's very beautiful. . . . If your sister could understand it, I would love for you to say that to her'" (Stacey, interview, January 18, 2014). Stacey's poem about her sister made her mother proud, which was a validating experience for the poet.

Shawna recalled performing and getting choked up: "I was starting to get emotional, and my voice began to shake. And that was the first time I had ever done that in public. . . . All the stuff that I've read for slams [is] heart wrenching. . . . I guess those were the first poems I ever wrote about my mom, expressing how she makes me feel. . . . It kind of threw me off. . . . Everybody got to see me bare my soul for a moment" (Shawna, interview, December 27, 2013). Although Shawna regularly shared emotional poems in Metropoets throughout the 2013–2014 season, some memories were still difficult for her to revisit. Losing control of her emotions and having the crowd respond with love was a reassuring and powerful experience for her.

Jasmine remembered the first time she performed for the group. She wrote a piece in about ten minutes, and Gabriel and the other teaching artists loved it. Jasmine recalled, "When they first heard it, they were just like, 'Wow, where have you been?' . . . So that was a big, powerful moment. [I thought], 'Oh, I have talent to do this. I can actually do this.' That . . . made a big impact on me" (Jasmine, interview, December 26, 2013). Jasmine realized she was good at spoken word poetry.

Nicole said the Town Slam was important to her. She bonded with people on her school team, and she enjoyed listening to the guest speaker. Also at this festival, she and Jasmine performed their "Good Morning, America" piece. She had been afraid she would forget the poem. Nicole recalled, "I closed my eyes, took a breath . . . and we just did it, and when we were walking off stage, I was like, 'Oh my god, we just finished that poem. That just happened.' [When they read the scores], I was like, 'Oh my gosh.' . . . So that was just a crazy moment" (Nicole, interview, December 26, 2013). As someone who attended that slam, I can confirm that this poem was impressive. They had good timing, earned several perfect scores, and the audience roared with approval.

Rafael also had a powerful Town Slam experience. He said, "It was the first time I was actually around people from outside our school doing the same thing I do. . . . I met a couple of people that I still talk to. . . . It was a [Metropoets] event, so I got in touch with mentors from other schools" (Rafael, interview, March 19, 2014). He enjoyed competing on a team with Nicole and Jasmine. Rafael also appreciated meeting poets from other schools. Although their team had many new members that year, they still managed to win. In addition, he made friends with a poet from another school. Rafael recalled, "It wasn't really about competition. [During the day of workshops, they] gave out lunch, and it was amazing to see that not everyone went back into their own teams. People sat with people from all around. It . . . shows you that even though you come from different schools, in the end, you're all one community" (Rafael, interview, March 19, 2014).

Jorge's most powerful experience was performing at Brave New Voices. He was afraid his poem was not good enough, and he felt intimidated by the other poets. At that time, Jorge had only been writing spoken word for a few months, whereas some competitors had years of experience. He recalled being surprised by the applause he received, and he discovered his scores were higher than he had anticipated. Jorge said, "It was a powerful experience because I had worked really hard, and I was always going to practices" (Jorge, interview, December 22, 2013). After Jorge performed, a poet from another state came up to him, crying. He told him that his dad had died under similar circumstances. Jorge appreciated that they came from different cities and different backgrounds ("He was African-American. I'm Mexican."), but they had similar stories. Jorge said, "It totally defeats the barriers that have been built. . . . He's hugging me, thanking me. . . . I had just told the story of our fathers. . . . Our story is not just our story. It's that guy's story, that lady's story. It encompasses a large group of people. Even though we come from different worlds, we really don't. . . . That's why it was so powerful for me" (Jorge, interview, December 22, 2013). Jorge's experience at Brave New Voices changed him.

Together, these stories provide insight into the power of youth spoken word poetry, revealing how members use the medium to heal, to build connections with others, and to test out their skills. It is significant that all six of these moments involved performance. More research is needed to understand the benefits of performance, especially in terms of learning and identity. As a relatively shy person myself, I find the poets' appreciation for performance fascinating.

Motivation

The poets in this study were motivated to write for a variety of reasons. Nicole said she writes because she is good at it, and she thinks it is fun. She likes getting on a microphone and performing for a crowd, and she appreciates the freedom to speak her mind. She added, "When I go on the microphone at [Metropoets], I know that there is at least one person in the crowd that's listening to me.... It's nice... to know that someone's listening. That's one of the biggest reasons I write" (Nicole, interview, December 26, 2013). Even before she has written a poem, Nicole knows there will be an audience to hear her words.

Stacey writes to help others who are struggling. She said, "I wanted to write poetry to save someone, like how [Mark] did to me" (Stacey, interview, January 18, 2014). In addition, Stacey talked about her sister's autism. She said, "When she was younger, she didn't speak at all. She couldn't speak anything. And then I started writing, and she started pronouncing the words I would write. It felt very beautiful to see her talk for the first time" (Stacey, interview, January 18, 2014). Stacey hopes to eventually write a poem that is so great her sister will understand it: "I just want her to know how grateful I am for her, so that's my goal, to make the most memorable poem before I die" (Stacey, interview, January 18, 2014). Stacey's writing motivation is strongly tied to her desire to communicate with her sister.

Shawna is motivated to write because it helps her deal with things that have happened to her. However, these days, writing does not offer the same relief it used to. She said, "I used to be able to write, and whatever was bothering me, ... I was fine after awhile. But now it's not so much. I'll write about it. A little bit later, it's still on the brain.... I've met some really cool kids that have been through some pretty hard stuff. It kind of reminds me of myself, so I write a lot of poems about stuff like that, too" (Shawna, interview, December 27, 2013).

Jorge writes to vent. He said, "I have anger issues, and it's a great way for me to express myself without turning to drugs. It's a great avenue to go down, you know. Writing is perfect. It improves you as a person. It helps you reflect. The more you express yourself, the less you have to bottle up" (Jorge, interview, December 22, 2013). Similarly, Rafael is motivated by the therapeutic benefits of writing. He said, "I see it as therapy because I'm too broke to afford therapy" (Rafael, interview, March 19, 2014). Rafael added that poetry helps him vent and get through difficult times.

Rafael also writes to speak out about important issues. He sees himself as an activist. He said:

> I feel like there's not enough outlets for youth to express themselves. What motivates me to write a lot is the problems going on. I recently wrote a poem based on one of my friends who ... [said], "You heard about the new law [allowing discrimination against gays and lesbians, SB1062]?" ... He was really upset [because] he's gay.... For the first time, I saw from a

different [viewpoint].... He doesn't even have the chance to marry the person he loves. So I guess it's just a way to like vent and get my message out there because there are a lot of kids who are too afraid to do what a lot of us do, so it's just a way to give people ... a voice. My brother was my father figure [because] I grew up without a father. [He] always showed me that everyone's equal and that there's nothing you can't stand up to.... Even if they are the government, we the people have the power to change anything that's unjust.... That activist side of me ... feels like if I'm not writing something to help someone out through tough times or to give someone a voice, then I'm not really using the opportunity that I was given to be here in this moment and ... send a message out into the world. (Rafael, interview, March 19, 2014)

Rafael pays attention to current issues and their effects on people, and he engages in poetic activism. Similarly, Jasmine wants to persuade people to think differently about important topics, such as race. She writes to connect with people and let them know there is someone else out there who feels the same way.

Sponsors and Role Models

The poets were able to identify important literacy sponsors and writing role models in their lives. Literacy sponsors include "the figures who [turn] up most typically in people's memories of literacy learning: older relatives, teachers, religious leaders, supervisors, military officers, librarians, friends, editors, [and] influential authors" (Brandt 2001, 19). Deborah Brandt (1998) explains that these sponsors "affect literacy learning in two powerful ways. They help to organize and administer stratified systems of opportunity and access, and they raise the literacy stakes in struggles for competitive advantage" (178). In Metropoets, Mark and Gabriel are sponsors who offer workshops and slams, as well as assistance and encouragement.

Jasmine mentioned feeling supported by poets both inside and outside of Metropoets. She looks to several poet role models. She said, "Sierra DeMulder and Andrea Gibson use very heavy metaphors, and they layer them and layer them. And I am obsessed with the metaphors they use, even though it sometimes takes a while to fully understand" (Jasmine, interview, December 26, 2013).

Jorge's sponsors include family members, the poetry club president at his former high school, and teachers who have invited him to speak to their classes. He said Gabriel and Mark have also influenced him in important ways: "If not for them, I wouldn't know who to go to. I don't have anybody to go to. My family's not very artistic. [Gabriel] and [Mark], ... they opened that door for me.... They attracted me to the writing community, to the poetry community, so they definitely have had a huge impact on my life in terms of writing and in general" (Jorge, interview, December 22, 2013). Jorge added that he looks up to several nationally prominent spoken word poets including G. Yamazawa, Willie Perdomo, and B. Yung.

Nicole talked about her family. Even though she does not invite them to slams, her mom drives her to events, and her aunts and cousins ask about her poetry. Other supporters include her friends (especially Jasmine), her school poetry club, and Metropoets. Nicole spoke of Mark and Gabriel, saying, "I see them do a poem, and I'm like, 'Okay, let's see what they're working on, maybe see what they're doing, what new style they're bringing'" (Nicole, interview, December 26, 2013). She also mentioned being influenced by authors such as Henry David Thoreau, Edgar Allan Poe, Roald Dahl, Suzanne Collins, and Ellen Hopkins.

One of Shawna's high school teachers was an important literacy sponsor. When the teacher noticed she was writing poetry in class, he encouraged her to enter a poetry contest and even took her to hear Maya Angelou speak. Furthermore, the people at the charity where Shawna works have supported her, turning her volunteer work into a paid internship, helping her with GED preparation, and coming out to support her at Metropoets slams. For writing role models, Shawna looks to authors including Robert Frost, Langston Hughes, and Maya Angelou. In addition, she talked about how Gabriel and Mark have influenced her. She had this to say about Gabriel:

> I like how he slams, how his style is, like how he commands the whole room. That's so dope, and I want to be able to do that. So, every time I see him, I'm taking mental notes. It's in my head. But it's cool to be able to see it like in the flesh [because] all these other [authors], I mean, they're dead or going to die, or you get stuff in books, which I mean is really cool, to see how like they put stuff together, but to see it in the flesh, it's like mind-blowing. (Shawna, interview, December 27, 2013)

Shawna appreciates that she can interact with Gabriel. He is accessible and teaches her new things all the time.

Rafael referred to supporters such as poetry club teachers, his friends at school, and his family. His sister drives him to poetry events and will ask him how he did. Also, Rafael has an older brother who has influenced his poetry in various ways. He explained, "I get a lot of stuff from my older brother. He was an activist. [When SB1070] was going to come into effect, he would take me to rallies and protests and you can really tell in my writing because I write a lot of political pieces. I really like the works of Martin Luther King Jr. and Caesar

Chavez. When I do my pieces, I kind of envision myself as if I'm them, an activist, so when I perform the political pieces, it's like a speech" (Rafael, interview, March 19, 2014). Rafael appreciates the writing of Pablo Neruda, William Wordsworth, Eminem, Ice Cube, Grand Master Flash, and Barack Obama. This diverse list of writing role models includes poets, rappers, and even a president.

I noticed that the poets in the yearlong study tended to keep their families away from Metropoets events. Jasmine, Rafael, and Nicole said their families did not really understand what they were up to, and these adolescents were fine with that. Nicole's family has seen recordings of her performances, but she said they do not understand that she sometimes performs for hundreds of people. On the other hand, Stacey cited her family (especially her mom, dad, and brother) and friends as important supporters of her work. Stacey recalled how her mom went to a slam and was impressed with her: "[My mom said], 'This is the first time I've seen you say stuff in front of crowds. . . . I just like how there's all these people, and they're all writing, and they're doing something with their lives'" (Stacey, interview, March 22, 2014). Her mom was impressed to see these adolescents turn to writing rather than drugs to deal with their problems, an observation Jabari Mahiri and Soraya Sablo (1996) have commented on as well.

These poets feel supported by friends, family members, and Gabriel and Mark. They also look to other teaching artists, famous spoken word poets, published authors, and songwriters as role models. I found that the adolescents in this study were able to identify many people who contributed to their development as writers and poets.

Experiencing a "Flow" State

The adolescents in this study suggested they had experienced a flow state while composing poetry. Mihaly Csikszentmihalyi (1990) defines "flow" as "the state in which people are so involved in an activity that nothing else seems to matter; the experience itself is so enjoyable that people will do it even at great cost, for the sheer sake of doing it" (4). In a flow state, the world around the person fades as the task at hand becomes the focus. Csikszentmihalyi (1990) describes some of the conditions for flow: "Self-consciousness disappears, and the sense of time becomes distorted. An activity that produces such experiences is so gratifying that people are willing to do it for its own sake, with little concern for what they will get out of it, even when it is difficult, or dangerous" (71).

All of the youth poets in this study reported being consumed by their writing and losing track of time. This section considers some representative examples. To start with, Nicole said:

> Usually I try not to write whenever I'm in like crucial time periods. Like say I have like ten minutes before I have to go somewhere. . . . I hate having to worry about that time frame. . . . Sometimes I'll write for thirty minutes, and it will feel like four hours, or sometimes I'll actually write for four hours, and it will only feel like thirty minutes. I usually do get lost in the time. I'll just be so focused on writing, and then I'll look up at the clock, and I'm like, "Crap, it's like 5:00 in the afternoon. I was supposed to do a whole bunch of stuff! Oops!" (Nicole, interview, December 26, 2013)

Similarly, Stacey talked about time passing unnoticed: "I was once writing when I was really mad. It was like 8:00 p.m., and once I stopped, I was going to go to sleep, but I couldn't. And then I looked at the time, and it was like 5:00 a.m. I was like, 'Oh my goodness! I was this mad?'" (Stacey, interview, January 18, 2014). For Stacey, writing served as a release that required more time than she had anticipated.

Shawna's story about working in a flow state is humorous because she did not notice the day turn to night, and a friend seemed to appear out of nowhere. This poet recalled, "It was light outside when I was writing. And I plugged in my Christmas lights, so. . . . I guess I wasn't really paying attention to time, but the sun faded out and the Christmas lights were the brightness that were going on. I was in the kitchen, and somebody had knocked on my window, and I was like, 'It's dark outside?' And they were like, 'Where have you been? Like your window's open.' And I was like, 'I don't know. I don't know where I've been'" (Shawna, interview, December 27, 2013). Her description probably resonates with anyone who has lost themselves in their work. Prematurely coming out of a state of intense focus can be disorienting.

As they lose themselves in their writing, these poets seem to enjoy the work and commit to it in a highly focused way. I wonder, by contrast, how often adolescents tend to experience a flow state while completing work for school, losing themselves in their in-class writing.

Overcoming Challenges

Each adolescent poet was able to think back to a writing obstacle he or she had encountered. For example, Stacey recalled the challenge of having to read an essay out loud in third grade. In response to this challenge, she cut a lot of her essay, so she would have less to read aloud. As she shared the work, she realized she had cut out everything interesting about the piece. Her solution turned out to be a mistake she did not want to repeat.

Nicole talked about writer's block. She said that with each new Metropoets season, it was challenging to figure out what to write about and what to say. To prevent herself from getting stuck, she now keeps a notebook listing ideas for future poems. Jorge also mentioned struggling with writer's block. These days, he listens to music for inspiration. He said, "The music is like grabbing my brain with the tandem, like squeezing the juice, the words out of it, so I definitely have to listen to music. That's something that I've learned, ... my writing habits, the ones that make me feel comfortable when I'm writing.... That's how I dealt with that in terms of finishing that poem" (Jorge, interview, December 22, 2013).

When Jasmine was writing "Good Morning, America" with Nicole, she struggled because they have different writing styles, and they had to get used to writing together. By checking with each other that the changes they were making were okay, the two began to feel more comfortable working together.

Shawna remembered not having a poem for the Town Slam. She recalled, "That morning I was like, 'I have to write my poem because I don't have anything new, and I don't want to read anything old.' So I took a poem and then these two half poems that I hadn't finished, and I put them all together" (Shawna, interview, December 27, 2013). Shawna acted quickly so she would have something for the performance.

Rafael talked about the challenge of finding his voice. He ended up listening "to Caesar Chavez and Martin Luther King [to see] how they give their speeches and ... [then he] took on that speech-type way of performing" (Rafael, interview, March 19, 2014). These influences are discernible in Rafael's performances.

Some have argued that both opportunities and obstacles are important in forming adolescents' identities (Csikszentmihalyi and Larson 1984), and the obstacles these writers faced did seem to shape them in significant ways. In addition, these examples show how the writers self-regulated (Zimmerman and Labuhn 2012). They not only came up with solutions to challenges but also altered their habits so they could avoid encountering the same challenge a second time.

Pet Peeves

Not everything is wonderful in the world of writing for these poets. They have writing pet peeves that annoy them. Shawna abhors essay writing, Jorge dislikes grammar, and Jasmine struggles to stay on topic. Rafael hates writer's block and memorizing poems. Nicole is annoyed when writers tell rather than show. She also hates it when a performer delivers a long preface before starting a piece, as this shows a lack of editing.

While the poets in this study discussed a range of issues, the similarity running through their responses is a sense of definite preference. Only Stacey, the youngest writer in the study, was not concrete in stating specific writing dislikes. All of the others were adamant about their pet peeves, showing what they value in writing through discussions of what irritates them.

Writing Futures

I asked the poets to speculate on the role writing would have for them in the future. I wanted to get a sense of how important they thought writing would be later on in their lives. Jasmine said she thought it would be very important because she wants to study spoken word poetry when she goes to college. Jorge believes he will still be a poet in future years, but it will not be a focus for him to the extent that it is for Mark and Gabriel. Shawna talked about becoming a teaching artist for a school, something she would prepare for by shadowing Gabriel soon. Stacey talked about someday becoming a book editor. Nicole said she is probably going to be an English or education major when she goes to college, and she would like to teach spoken word and one day publish a book. Rafael also wants to be a teacher, either in history or English, and he said that writing will always be important to him: "I'm going to have more essays ahead of me, more late nights. And hopefully I don't stop writing poetry. I think writing in general is going to be in my life for the rest of my life. It's something that I'm not going to give up for anyone. It's something I hope I never have to give up" (Rafael, interview, March 19, 2014). All of these poets envisioned writing as something that would matter to their future selves, which may not be that surprising because it is an important part of who they are today.

Conclusion

In Metropoets, youth writers share their experiences and speak out about problems they see in the world around them. They write poems on a variety of topics, reflect deeply on their work, have distinct writing habits and preferences, and see writing as an important part of who they are and will be.

There are many ways to support young people's writing practices and preferences in the classroom. Teachers can encourage youth writers to make choices of various kinds. Writers could use their preferred forms of prewriting and write on topics that matter to them. Perhaps they could have the option to orally compose drafts, listen to music while writing, or perform their works. The possibilities for accommodating students are endless. While the findings in this chapter suggest many ways writing instruction could be tailored to students, probably a teacher's best bet is to talk to the actual students in the room to learn about their writing practices and preferences and then design writing assignments in collaboration with them.

Like Ernest Morrell (2008), I am concerned that schools are not providing the tools and time for more personal forms of writing. Those who engage in more personal forms of writing on their own time, like the participants in this study, must compartmentalize school writing from the meaningful writing they compose voluntarily, as if these different works were composed by separate selves. To support authentic writing and authorship in the classroom, teachers can build choice into assignments, connect students to larger networks of writers, offer opportunities to share, and see students as writers with important things to say.

CHAPTER 6
WEIGHING BENEFITS AND CHALLENGES

I can read a passage without having an anxiety attack and running out of the classroom.
—Rafael

Youth poets in the yearlong study reported many benefits from writing and performing in Metropoets, including academic, writing, and personal changes. These findings make a powerful case about the value of this youth spoken word poetry group. At the same time, this group is not without its challenges. Throughout the 2013–2014 season, Metropoets faced several administrative-level challenges regarding growth, space, and funding. It may seem odd to bring together individual benefits and group challenges in the same chapter, but as I take all of the data from the yearlong study into consideration, I feel it is necessary to show what is at stake if Metropoets is unable to address its most serious challenges, especially if the group does not overcome its funding issues. Literacy groups like Metropoets must not be taken for granted, as they do not exist by default but require a great deal of time and energy to sustain.

Perceived Benefits

The adolescent poets reported several benefits related to their participation in Metropoets. These benefits have immediate, as well as future, use as poets navigate their worlds, build relationships with others, and pursue college and careers.

Changes to Their Writing

According to the youth poets in this study, participating in Metropoets has improved their writing, especially their use of poetic devices. Jasmine said she uses metaphors in her writing more frequently as a result of participating in Metropoets. Nicole also uses more metaphors now, and she believes this enables her to express herself better. Rafael talked about using fewer rhymes in his poems. (Generally, rhyme is used more in rap than in spoken word, so rappers who are also spoken word poets may need time to sort out differences between the types of writing.) Nicole told Rafael, "You'd be so focused on the rhyme that you would lose track of the actual meaning of the words. Once you broke out of that, you just bloomed" (Nicole, interview, March 22, 2014).

Jorge talked about being able to put poetic devices to use in other writing situations. He said:

> I didn't learn anything [in school] until second semester when I started going to poetry [club]. . . . If you don't practice it, you're not going to retain the information. I started . . . practicing all this stuff about onomatopoeia. I was practicing similes, metaphors. I was able to better incorporate them into my writing. Something big [Mark] taught us was to show rather than tell, so that was a big helping point when filling out scholarships because they ask you, "Tell me about an experience when you helped somebody and it paid off." . . . If you're really able to not just tell them, but you're actually able to show them, like put them in the moment, I feel like that helped me a lot more with winning scholarships. (Jorge, interview, December 22, 2013)

In the excerpt above, Jorge hints at the difference between "just in case" and "just in time" instruction (Gee 2004). He suggests that studying poetic devices in school was not as useful as practicing them right away in club. Using poetic devices in an authentic writing situation helped him remember them. He was also able to transfer new writing techniques to other rhetorical situations, such as scholarship applications, which literally paid off.

Participating in Metropoets expanded the range of topics these adolescents wrote about and allowed them to achieve more depth in their writing. They talked about learning to address emotional topics and social issues in their poetry. On his participant information form, Jorge wrote, "Through my involvement with [Metropoets] I have developed awareness for societal issues that I otherwise would have never known about. [Metropoets] has shown me that the world is bigger than I am."

Some of the poets believe that participating in Metropoets has helped them with organization and conventions in their writing. Jorge talked about learning to better organize his thoughts, and he said this change required time and assistance from others. Mark said he led revision sessions with Jorge, helping him move stanzas around and tighten up his poems. Mark said, "That level, that sophistication of writing [we see in Jorge's poems today], is something that [he] fought for" (Mark, interview, June 24, 2014). In addition, Nicole has found that her editing skills have improved through her involvement in Metropoets.

Jorge believes that young people grow as writers in Metropoets because the group does not use "[textbook] definitions and examples. They just involve us. . . . They just make us do it. We do it. And when you just do it, that's when it happens. You're able to really learn it. You're able to soak in the information. It becomes second nature after a while" (Jorge, interview, June 27, 2014). Jorge's comments are interesting because he is highlighting the way learning works in a community of practice—that is, through authentic participation (Wenger 1998).

Changes as Students

Participating in Metropoets seems to help adolescent writers in school. Rafael talked about experiencing several academic-related changes. He explained:

> It's really helped me open up in class. I used to not want to read passages, and I still don't, but if I get called on, it's not that big of a hassle for me anymore. I can read a passage without having an anxiety attack and running out of the classroom. I'm more comfortable going up to the board and doing math problems or presenting . . . or reading my essay out loud to the class. So it helps you a lot. Especially in my English class, I've got to do peer-review where we talk one-on-one with a person, and even that can be a little stressful. So it really helps a lot with breaking out of your [comfort zone]. (Rafael, interview, March 22, 2014)

It sounds as if spoken word has helped Rafael feel more comfortable participating in school activities, including reading aloud, going in front of the class, and working with peers. Stacey also reported feeling more comfortable at school, and she believes this is why her grades have improved. She reported raising her hand more often to speak, not being afraid to write, and not being afraid to share her writing with others or to say her words out loud. Talking to new people and sharing her work at Metropoets events has helped her in school.

Jorge also talked about how his attitude toward school has changed. He said, "I wasn't much of a writer. I wasn't much of a reader. I was just another student in the school, you know. I wasn't really anybody. I didn't really have any goals. I was just there. And junior year, that's really when my life started to change, especially when I got into poetry" (Jorge, interview, December 22, 2013). When Jorge continued on to college, he found that Metropoets had put him on a different level. He said that he talks to his professors and cares about learning what they have to teach him. Anything might end up in a poem, so he wants to learn all he can.

Personal Changes
Social Skills, Self-Confidence, and Leadership Skills

Poets reported growing as people through their participation in Metropoets. Writing and performing spoken word seems to have helped them with social skills and self-confidence. Rafael said he is more willing to talk to people, and Jasmine and Nicole mentioned seeing each other become more comfortable talking to people and performing. Likewise, Stacey believes her involvement in Metropoets has changed her. She said:

> Before going to [Metropoets], I was very antisocial. I really did not speak to anyone. Like even now, it's hard for me to make eye contact. . . . And then I went to [Metropoets] and I [heard Mark say], "Okay, stand up and talk to random people." And I'm like, "Um, no." And I sat down. My friends told me, "You need to go talk to people." And there's actually like people who talked to me, and I was just like, "Oh my gosh. How are they not embarrassed? How can they do this?" And after a while, like now, after going to slams, I actually am the one to tell my friends, "I want to talk to people." (Stacey, interview, March 22, 2014)

The practice of meeting new people after slams made Stacey become more confident in her interactions with people elsewhere. These observations are in line with Susan Weinstein's (2010) findings that spoken word can help adolescents increase their confidence and become less shy.

Some poets seem to gain leadership skills through Metropoets. Gabriel noted that Jorge had become a "leader" and "a mentor for the younger kids" (Gabriel, interview, June 5, 2014). Mark added, "One of the really strong things about kids like [Jorge] and [Jasmine] . . . is they're super supportive of other kids" (Mark, interview, June 24, 2014). According to Jasmine, Nicole also has improved her leadership skills and seeks out opportunities to assist others. Rafael said, "[Nicole] was always the president of poetry club. She kind of ran it from behind the curtains, and now she's like, 'I'm here. This is what we're doing.' I guess poetry's really helped her to find her inner dictator" (Rafael, interview, March 22, 2014). It is worth pointing out that Nicole, Jasmine, and Jorge have all participated in Brave New Voices competitions. It may be that preparing for and participating in this international competition fosters leadership skills.

Empathy, Healing, and Emotional Vulnerability

Another personal change these poets mentioned was increased empathy. It makes sense that poets would develop empathy as they share their stories and learn from others. After all, every poem at a slam is a window into someone else's experiences. Poetry has helped Jorge see his stepfather in a new light and see issues from multiple points of view.

Participating in this spoken word group has also helped many poets heal. Gabriel said of Shawna, "[Shawna] comes from . . . this submarginalized group of individuals. [She] has had a very rough life in many ways. I've seen [her] begin the healing process . . . through her art" (Gabriel, interview, June 5, 2014). Mark has also observed this change in her. He said:

> I can look at someone like [Shawna] and know . . . how she's like risen above it, [becacuse] she's like hilarious and full of good energy, like witty. But I think writing and poetry [have] really led her to have more power to reflect about who she is. And that's the thing about writing. You are using this notion of semipermanence to write who you are. And when you go back and read it, you can revise it. You can go, "Okay, who am I?" So when you come into that juncture, you come into that place and the revision process of someone like [Shawna], you go, "Okay, well do you believe this, or do you want to believe this?" And then they usually choose the one that feels the best. (Mark, interview, June 24, 2014)

Shawna uses poetry to work through past abuse and write herself a new future.

Jorge has also used poetry to heal. Gabriel said, "[Jorge] has an interesting life. We all have interesting stories. [Jorge]'s father, his biological father, was murdered when [Jorge] was a baby, and his first series of poems really spoke to that. I remember [Jorge] crying one time on the mic, which I think was huge for him, you know, because he definitely needed to talk about something that was important" (Gabriel, interview, June 5, 2014). Sharing stories with members of this community can be incredibly therapeutic. As Gabriel said at a Metropoets event, "Poetry is healing ourselves. And . . . the first step to healing is to put it out there" (observation, February 15, 2014). In Metropoets, young people confront the pain they have experienced in their lives.

This finding supports Ernest Morrell's (2008) point that youth literacies can help adolescents heal. As Jabari Mahiri and Soraya Sablo (1996) have found, "rather than keeping . . . pain bottled up for years and then retrospectively writing about the problems of doing so, [participants] were expressing themselves more immediately in their voluntary writing during their adolescent years" (175). Metropoets members were similarly trying to deal with their pain instead of suppressing it.

Participating in Metropoets helps some writers become more trusting and open to emotional vulnerability. Gabriel has noticed that "[Shawna has] become more trusting [and] loving . . . through this community" (Gabriel, interview, June 5, 2014). Also, Nicole believes that participating in Metropoets has helped her become more comfortable with her feelings. At first, she had a hard time writing emotional poems because her family tends to be more reserved. Nicole wondered, "How do I connect with people? What is connecting with people? How do I write something that's going to touch these people's hearts? Like how do I do that?" (Nicole, interview, July 21, 2014). Apparently Mark told her to make a connection with audience members through eye contact. Over time, performing like this has changed her. Nicole said, "When I started having a relationship with people, I was actually able to be honest with how I felt. . . . Now I'm actually really big on being honest because I'm always honest on paper, so why don't I be honest all of the time? It just made me be more true to who I am" (Nicole, interview, July 21, 2014). As Nicole has explored her own feelings, she has learned how to be herself around other people. Similarly, Soraya Sablo Sutton (2008) found that poets assumed "that if people can get closer to their own sense of 'truth' by finding their voice, they can learn to deal with each other more truthfully" (217).

Mark believes that kids pick up on the teaching artists' openness to emotional vulnerability. He explained: "[Gabriel] and I . . . exhibit masculinity. I mean, we're men. We have beards and shit, whatever, but we're also vulnerable. And our vulnerability does not make us weak. I think [Rafael] observes that and is interested in it" (Mark, interview, June 24, 2014). Mark and Gabriel are role models who demonstrate that it is okay to write poems about emotional material and to even become emotional themselves.

While embracing emotional vulnerability is an important aspect of participation in this group, this does not mean that poets always feel comfortable with their vulnerability. For example, on her participant information form, Jasmine wrote the following note at the end of the study: "I feel like my poetry right now is in a vulnerable stage. I am now giving my blood and sweat (literally and figuratively). I am giving what is left of me." Mark has noticed that Jasmine does not share drafts of her poems anymore and does not seem to want feedback. It may be that learning to embrace emotional vulnerability is not a linear process, but a recursive one involving growing and pausing, moving forward and moving backward. Participants may be more open with their feelings, or less so, at different times.

Challenges Facing the Group

Any group is going to face challenges. How it responds will determine its success or failure over time. Because groups are not static, the challenges a group faces today could very well be different than those it faces later. During the 2013–2014 season, Metropoets was struggling with growth, space, and funding.

Dealing with Growth

As membership increased during the 2013–2014 season, the Metropoets group had to make some adjustments. Mark and Gabriel realized they needed to host functions less often, so after the two events they hosted in October 2013, they switched to offering one monthly event. With so many participants, they also had to change how they selected their Brave New Voices team. For the first time, they needed to hold a preliminary slam before the final slam-off. Gabriel said, "It's because we've grown so much that we can't do the slam-off in one day" (observation, March 15, 2014).

This growth also led to some confusion and inconsistency at times. As the slam in chapter 3 shows, Gabriel had laid out a whole system for earning points at the beginning of the season. Poets would get a point for performing in a slam. In addition, placing first would earn the poet three points, placing second would earn two points, and placing third would earn one point. At the end of the season, the person with the most points would go last, the coveted spot due to "score creep." However, this system was abandoned without notice. At the preliminary slam in April, all poets participating that day were asked to draw numbers from a hat to determine their order between one and twenty. The poets who had shown up every month, slammed at every event, and even placed multiple times throughout the season were subject to the same luck of the draw as a poet who had just walked in for the first time that day. Based on Nicole's record of placing throughout the year, she should have been one of the last performers. However, she drew the slip to perform first. She was the "shotgun poet" of the preliminary slam.

Gabriel admitted his mistake:

> Had we done it the way where we calculated points, [Nicole] would never have gone first in the slam off. When you're first of twenty kids, you're not going to make it. . . . So technically [Nicole] kind of got a shittier deal. It was really, really difficult because we kept having so many new people. Like if you notice, at the beginning of the season, we went from maybe like six to ten to fifteen to eighteen to twenty [performers], and I wanted to encourage everybody to continue to be a part of it, and so, and it's really difficult because we do really deemphasize the slam, and I'm managing it all on my own. It was tough for me. I didn't have that system in place [because] we've never had this problem. The group has always been much smaller. (Gabriel, interview, June 5, 2014)

Nicole did not advance to the final slam. Mark expressed his disappointment over what had happened: "We failed [Nicole]. Traditionally in slam culture, you're supposed to give points for how much you participate, and how many times you win that season, and that dictates your place in the draw. And she didn't get that padding that she should have gotten. So that will be different next year" (Mark, interview, June 24, 2014). The group's growth was more than Gabriel could manage on his own, and Nicole suffered as a result.

Nicole was not the only poet who was affected by the group's growing size. It became harder to make the Brave New Voices team with so many members. Also, Gabriel created rules to limit the number of people who could compete in the preliminary slam. He announced to the group through social media, "Poet sign up will begin at 1:00 pm and will close promptly at 1:45 pm. Only the first twenty poets will be entered into the competition. [The slam] will begin at 2 pm and will only be one round. The top ten poets will move on to the final slam off on May 3rd" (online post, accessed May 23, 2014). Poets were told to show up early. Only twenty of them would be allowed to compete, and if they showed up after 1:45 p.m., they would not be added to the list. Gabriel adhered to this policy even when Shawna arrived late that day. She was barred from the competition and was heartbroken. This probably would not have been an issue in previous years, when there were fewer people vying for the same four slots.

Securing Space for Events

Another challenge Metropoets faced was securing space for events. The library did provide free space to the group, but these rooms were not guaranteed. For example, the group was going to hold a slam in December, but they had to cancel it because an arts festival was going to be held in the library. In

November, the group was having a workshop in a large room, and they had to relocate for a class that needed the computers in one corner of that room.

The group's growing size contributed to space issues as well. Sometimes an event would have to be moved. For example, the preliminary slam brought in so many people that the group had to find another location for the final slam. As Gabriel explained through social media:

> The turn out at yesterday's [Metropoets] Slam Championship qualifier was incredible. It was standing room only. . . . I am so blessed to be [a] part of such a beautiful community. In just one year[']s time we have doubled our number of youth participants! . . . These youth want and need a place to let their voice be heard. Thank you all for your blessings and support. Championship will [be] May 3rd! I will send out details as soon as the venue is confirmed. We can't break fire code . . . so we will have to host it somewhere else! Good problem to have! (online post, accessed May 23, 2014)

The final slam was ultimately scheduled outdoors at an arts center. This new venue was not ideal, however, as May evenings in Arizona can hit one hundred degrees or more, and the deejay had issues accessing online songs outside.

Achieving Financial Sustainability

As it turned out, Metropoets did not end up sending anybody to the Brave New Voices competition at the end of its 2013–2014 season. It was not until my June interview with Gabriel that I heard Metropoets would not be sending a team to this competition after all. He explained what happened. Basically, the group ended up getting less funding than expected from a university partner. In addition, Gabriel received the BNV dates after he had already committed to doing a camp in Arizona that week. Since Gabriel could not go, the group's fiscal agent was nervous about sending somebody else in his place and not being insured. (The additional insurance would be $1,500 on top of at least a $10,000 trip, he said.[1]) Gabriel tried to stay upbeat about all of this and said staying home would give them a chance to reflect on where they were as an organization and what they needed to do to improve. Still, the hype all season long about getting on the BNV team was all for nothing.

As my interview questions show (see appendix A), I had not planned to discuss funding with the teaching artists in our interviews. However, when I met with Gabriel, he vented his frustrations about the lack of funding, taking our interview to a place I had not anticipated. He revealed that the issue of funding was the most serious challenge Metropoets was facing. Gabriel said he had conversations with various arts and cultural groups in Arizona, but they were not financing Metropoets to the extent that Gabriel needed. He said, "[Our] name is circulating all throughout . . . these different arts agencies, but nobody's stepping up to help us fund or manage our program, and I think that needs to stop. They're just getting a free program. At the end of the day, when I'm the only one who doesn't mind donating their services, I'm stretched very thin" (Gabriel, interview, June 5, 2014).

To support their residency program, which brings teaching artists into school poetry clubs, Metropoets received funding from a few programs and institutions. In total, that tended to bring in about $30,000 to split among Gabriel, Mark, and another teaching artist. Gabriel commented, "It's about $10,000 for an entire year's worth of work. And, I mean, it's a lot of work. I use that for paying myself for going into schools but also to do all of the administrative stuff. It's not a sustainable system right now" (Gabriel, interview, June 5, 2014).

Gabriel has had some training in arts funding as part of his degree program. In his arts entrepreneurship class, he developed a business plan for Metropoets. He also has plans to raise money, but putting on a gala and developing promotional materials for sponsors takes time that he does not have right now as a college student. By the time he graduates, he would like to get enough in donations to pay himself a $30,000 salary or to pay himself half of that and use the other half to hire someone to manage tax forms and other paperwork. Gabriel said the way the tax system is set up, the group cannot afford to be a nonprofit, so they work through a fiscal agent, an agency that takes a small cut for administrative costs.

As Gabriel and Mark work on building a financially sustainable organization, they also have to balance funding concerns with their desire to remain autonomous. Mark explained that when he takes money from an organization, he has "to do their programming . . . or at least interpret what they want" (Mark, interview, June 24, 2014). Similarly, Gabriel spoke about his desire to protect the group's autonomy. He said, "Now I'm faced with the reality of developing sustainable business practices and not being co-opted by institutions, you know, and maintaining the integrity of our program. And so there are a lot of challenges that come with it now" (Gabriel, interview, June 5, 2014).

Supporting Youth Literacy Groups

Readers may be wondering what they can do to support literacy groups like Metropoets in their own communities. Various types of assistance are needed, beginning with the most obvious one, individual donations.

In addition, universities could offer internships in arts entrepreneurship, business, writing, or education to get students volunteering in these groups. This would enable college students to give back to the community while also cultivating useful skills for careers. Universities could host poetry slams, which can have the dual benefit of funding poet-hosts and deejays and showing youth poets that college is not a scary place. (I have started offering an annual poetry slam at my university in response to this research.) Schools, libraries, and community centers are important partners for youth literacy groups. They can offer free and reliable space for workshops and slams. Also, funding agencies can offer grants toward the salaries of teaching artists like Mark and Gabriel. So often it seems that grants will not allow funds to be used for salaries, which puts groups like Metropoets at a disadvantage.

It is worth mentioning that moving to a pay-to-slam system is not a viable option for Metropoets because some youth members live in shelters or group homes. Many families do not have money to spare. One of the hallmarks of Metropoets is that the group is open and free to all kids. Perhaps adults could pay a small entrance fee at slams. Another option is that organizations could sponsor an event or a poet for a season (i.e., a fair teaching artist wage for all events in the season divided by the average number of youth typically present). More research is needed to understand the financial practices of successful youth literacy groups.

Conclusion

As Metropoets members write and perform spoken word poetry, they experience various personal, academic, and writing-related benefits. Poets may become more honest with themselves and others, develop empathy, grow more confident, and learn leadership skills. They may use poetic devices more intentionally in their writing and pay more attention to editing and organization. In school, these writers may participate more seriously and be less intimidated when it comes to sharing ideas or working with others. Although the perceived benefits varied for each poet in the study,[2] all of them associated their Metropoets participation with multiple improvements to their lives.

The Metropoets group provides a safe space for diverse youth to write, speak, perform, and listen. Poets are encouraged to be brave, and they learn that their voices matter. The resistance literacies practiced in the Metropoets group are both timely and necessary, especially in a setting like Arizona. This makes it all the more serious that Metropoets is struggling financially. This research shows that community literacy groups may need assistance with funding, space, and growth management. Those of us at universities may be well positioned to support such groups by assisting with grants, internships, and events. However, assistance from multiple reliable funding sources will better ensure the sustainability of these groups.

Without enough support, the danger is that groups like Metropoets could quickly go quiet like a microphone unplugged. And the silencing of the voices of urban youth would be a terrible injustice.

CHAPTER 7

EXPLORING A HIGH SCHOOL POETRY CLUB

[The club is] where the magic happens...
—*Jorge*

When I began the yearlong study discussed in the previous chapters, I was under the impression that Metropoets was a writing group that met on weekends in a public library, and it was no bigger than that. However, over the course of that study, participants talked about their high school poetry clubs, which have assigned Metropoets teaching artists. I began to see that the Saturday group was only one community of practice located at the center of a much larger network consisting of multiple communities of practice all over town. Once I finished my yearlong study of the Metropoets group, I designed a follow-up study to investigate one of these high school poetry clubs.

Etienne Wenger (1998) uses the term "constellation" to refer to communities "sharing historical roots, having related enterprises, serving a cause or belonging to an institution, facing similar conditions, having members in common, sharing artifacts, having geographical relations of proximity or interaction, having overlapping styles or discourses, [or] competing for the same resources" (127). As it turns out, the communities of practice within the Metropoets network are "related enterprises" that share "overlapping styles or discourses" and "artifacts." They have "members in common" who go back and forth between Metropoets events at the library and meetings at their school clubs. These clubs have "geographical relations of proximity," operating within a landscape of about thirty miles. They "[share] historical roots" with other communities of practice in this spoken word network, "[face] similar conditions," and "[compete] for the same resources." For example, poets from across the network compete for a spot on the Brave New Voices team and to win first place at the Town Slam.

I use the term "network" to describe the Metropoets constellation because it emphasizes the interconnectedness of people and clubs. That is, a poet in a school club might form connections with fellow club members, members of other clubs in the district, and poets around the state. District poetry events and the annual Metropoets Town Slam bring these different groups together. Clubs also put members in touch with multiple experts over time as teaching artists rotate through different school assignments. These teaching artists bring Metropoets goals, practices, language, and tools with them into school spaces, building continuity across the network.

The first section of this chapter serves as a bridge between my studies of the Metropoets group and Palo Brea Poets Club,[1] a high school poetry club in the Metropoets network. I share what participants in the yearlong study told me about their school clubs, findings that prompted me to design this follow-up study. In the second part of this chapter, I describe the study of Palo Brea Poets Club and share findings about the club's features and practices. This chapter concludes by comparing Palo Brea Poets Club to the Metropoets group. Comparing these after-school and out-of-school groups reveals possibilities and limitations of literacy learning in different types of contexts.

School Poetry Clubs

Adolescents in the yearlong study spoke highly of their school clubs, saying these clubs introduced them to spoken word and nurtured their growth as poets. Recall that Rafael, Nicole, and Jasmine attended the same high school poetry club, and Jorge attended a poetry club at another high school in the same district. Shawna and Stacey did not have poetry clubs at their schools.

Jorge talked about what makes school poetry clubs special. He said:

> On Saturdays, that's . . . a public event and . . . more of a showcase/get-together, kind of event. Whereas in the school, it's more of a practice, more of a harnessing [of] newly developed skills. And I believe one of the most beautiful things that [Metropoets] does is it connects students that otherwise never would have known each other, would have never met, would have never had something in common. And in that classroom where they practice and train is where the relationships are really being strengthened. . . . It's in the classroom where they tell the other students, "Look, I'm your friend. I'm here for you." And at the Saturday event is where the results of that appear, you know, the results of all that friendship

> strengthening. That's one of the more beautiful things that I've seen. [Metropoets] creates that sense of community. And I mean, on Saturdays, it does as well because of the, "What time is it?" or those little things that they do. That stuff definitely helps create a sense of community, but not like the sense of community it creates in the classroom. (Jorge, interview, June 27, 2014)

While the sense of community at Saturday events seemed strong, Jorge suggested that the community in his high school poetry club was even stronger. Saturday events may give writers opportunities to present their poems, but much of the hard work leading up to these performances seems to happen in school poetry clubs.

Rafael said that the feedback process works differently in clubs than it does in the Metropoets group. Poets receive more detailed feedback in their school clubs, and they work closely with a Metropoets teaching artist. Rafael explained:

> There's about fifteen of us. And [Mark] is the main guy who comes in. He's like the team's mentor. But he has that one-to-one approach. We'll do a workshop, . . . and like he'll ask for volunteers to read [their poems]. And if I read, he'll directly look at me, tell me one-on-one what the strengths are and what the weaknesses are. I read a message poem. It was a minority in the 1950's speaking to a police officer, and he told me to research . . . it, to [get] the facts straight because it's a strong poem, and it would be even stronger with facts. He's the type of mentor that kind of like calls you on your stuff but also gives you feedback. (Rafael, interview, March 19, 2014)

As readers saw in chapter 4, in the Metropoets group, teaching artists tended to take an "Okay. Who's next?" approach when it came to giving feedback to poets at the library. However, Rafael describes a more in-depth and text-based response to his work in the club setting. It may be that the greater frequency of club meetings, the consistency in membership from week to week, and the smaller size of clubs create better conditions for more in-depth feedback on students' poems.

According to Gabriel, going into schools makes up the bulk of the work done by Metropoets. He said, "The slam is a monthly event, but on a weekly and daily basis we are in about ten different schools consistently, developing new workshops, new programs" (Gabriel, interview, June 5, 2014). He added that the Saturday events give poets from the school clubs a chance to "[come] together to formalize one community" (Gabriel, interview, June 5, 2014).

In these clubs, a teaching artist from Metropoets visits regularly (usually weekly) to lead the group through writing activities. If the group is preparing for an event, the teaching artist may visit more often. Mark said each school club should plan an event each semester (e.g., a play, a slam, a performance at a shelter), which can vary depending on the club members' interests. These events connect club members to larger audiences, and different student groups from around the school (e.g., dancers, musicians) can get involved. Friends, family members, teachers, and other community members attend to celebrate students' voices. While school poetry clubs have their advantages, these groups are not without their challenges, as this chapter demonstrates.

Studying Palo Brea Poets Club

I conducted a semester-long (January-May 2015) qualitative case study (Hancock and Algozzine 2011; Merriam 2009; Yin 2006) of Palo Brea Poets Club. I wanted to understand the club's features and practices, especially in relation to the Metropoets group. This study focused on the adults who oversaw this high school club, and participants included Ms. Sanderson and Mr. Casale (club cosponsors who teach English at Palo Brea High School) and Brian (the teaching artist assigned by Metropoets to this club). Data sources included observations, interviews, and artifacts. Below, I describe the study in more detail.

Gaining Access

I selected Palo Brea Poets Club for my follow-up study based on the recommendations of adolescent members of Metropoets. I was aware of Palo Brea High School already, having encountered its faculty at various conferences for English teachers over the years. The teachers I have met from this school have seemed invested in their professional development, and according to the school website, nearly three-quarters of Palo Brea teachers have at least a master's degree.

Gaining access to this school required institutional review board (IRB) approval from my university; fingerprinting and a background check by the school district; and district, principal, and teacher approval of my study. Six months after first sending in my materials, I thought I had been cleared to begin my study. It was January 21, 2015, when I drove toward Palo Brea High School. The school has a fence around its enormous lot, so I circled the block, going deep into the surrounding neighborhood as I tried to find a way inside. Finally I spotted the only entrance to the school. As soon as I pulled into the lot, a parking attendant stopped my car. He recorded my name and destination on his clipboard, and then I proceeded to search for a parking spot. I saw in my rearview mirror that he was writing down my license plate number. I parked, signed in at the front office, showed identification, and received a sticker with Ms. Sanderson's room number. Before I could head there, however, I was asked to check in upstairs with the person on site assigned to deal with research. She looked over my materials and said I could not enter the classroom until she received a signed work order from the sponsoring teachers of the club. I would have to come back another day.

I told her that Ms. Sanderson had invited me to this club meeting. Reaching into my bag, I pulled out district paperwork, as well as emails from the club teachers and principal. She eyed a signature on one of the district forms and asked whose name it was, saying she did not recognize the signature. I showed her my current Arizona secondary English teaching certificate and state-issued fingerprint clearance card, along with my university credentials. She still seemed suspicious, and my trip appeared to be a waste of time.

Eventually, she decided I could attend the meeting after all. (I am not sure what changed her mind.) By this point, I was very late. I hurried outside and looked at the campus map, trying to locate Ms. Sanderson's building. School was already out for the day, but some students were still hanging around. A group of three students saw that I was lost, and they offered to escort me to Ms. Sanderson's room. We made our way through hallways lined with lockers.

At last, we arrived. I opened the door to the classroom and found that a student was right in the middle of performing a poem, so I awkwardly froze in the doorway. After the poem ended, the teacher sitting behind the desk asked me who I was. Then she said I should introduce myself to the students.

Taking a seat, I surveyed Ms. Sanderson's room and saw eight students were attending club that day. After each poem, Ms. Sanderson provided feedback, praising the poet or asking for clarification. The other sponsoring teacher, Mr. Casale, was not present at this meeting, and apparently it was the first time he had missed a club meeting without a phone call in five years. Brian, the Metropoets teaching artist assigned to this club, was also not present.

I noticed that Ms. Sanderson's classroom was divided into rows of desks that faced each other. A walkway ran down the middle of the room. Posters on the classroom walls addressed the writing process, reading strategies, and writing jobs. A school banner was posted as well. Each desk had a copy of Chinua Achebe's *Things Fall Apart* on it. Looking around at the club members present, I recognized some faces from Metropoets events I had attended during the previous school year.[2]

As their meeting was coming to an end, Ms. Sanderson asked the poets why their club was shrinking each year, and they speculated that perhaps people did not understand what they did in this club. Tired and ready to go home to do her grading, Ms. Sanderson ended the session at approximately 4:20 p.m. Some students lingered and chatted with her. I heard her recall, half to herself, how a poet had said he would come back to visit her after graduating, yet he had not done so. I stayed for a few moments, and we talked about this club's performance at the last Town Slam. We also talked about the four events that Palo Brea Poets Club members participate in during the school year: two school slams, a Poetry Out Loud contest, and a district-wide slam. As we talked, Ms. Sanderson lamented that her school had done away with her literary journal and speech class. The school's goal of reading informational texts fifty percent of the time in English (what was then a common misreading of the Common Core State Standards) had resulted in cuts to creative writing. This teacher struck me as someone who would speak frankly about what was on her mind.

On my way out, Ms. Sanderson told me I looked like an English teacher, which made me smile as the door closed behind me. After signing out at the front office, I walked toward my car. I passed a sign in the parking lot that reminded students to have their identification badges visible at all times. Another sign informed me that I could not make a left turn out of the parking lot, so I drove away from the school, temporarily headed in the wrong direction (observation, January 21, 2015).

Site

Palo Brea High School is a public school serving grades nine through twelve. It is located in an urban area in Arizona. The school was built during the first half of the twentieth century. A metal fence separates the school from the adjacent busy street, and a modern electronic marquee communicates school-related announcements to the traffic zooming by. This high school is part of a large, ethnically and linguistically diverse district, and the majority of students in this district speak a language other than English at home. This particular high school serves between two thousand and three thousand students. According to figures released by the school, the student population was approximately seventy-five percent Hispanic, ten percent African American, ten percent Caucasian, and five percent Native American at the time of this study. The four-year graduation rate was approximately seventy-five percent, and the number of students on free and reduced lunch was also around seventy-five percent. About one-tenth of students participated in the International Baccalaureate (IB) program offered at the school.

Throughout the semester, the club typically met in Ms. Sanderson's classroom. Sometimes the name of the club and the ground rules were posted on her whiteboard. Outside her room, fliers announcing club meetings were posted in hallways. These walkways were generally quiet by the time the club started, except for those days when the guitar club practiced across the hall, and amplified strumming echoed throughout the building. Once during the study, the club met in Mr. Casale's room. I noticed that his whiteboard announced the date of the next Metropoets slam at the library. He was offering his students extra credit to attend.

Participants

Participants in this study included Ms. Sanderson and Mr. Casale, who are Palo Brea English teachers and club cosponsors, and Brian, a Metropoets teaching artist. I originally had plans to include students as well, but when only one poetry club member returned consent documents, I decided to drop that part of the study and focus on the adult leadership.

Ms. Sanderson

Ms. Sanderson, who had been teaching for sixteen years at the time of this study, founded Palo Brea Poets Club. Before transferring to Palo Brea, she worked at another school in the district for eight years, where she taught English as a second language. During this study, Ms. Sanderson was teaching sophomore English. She has National Board Certification and a master's degree in education.

She reflected on the club's beginnings:

> I have always wanted to be a poet myself. . . . In the beginning there were four members, and three of them were not even writers. They were just kids who liked hanging out with me and each other. But I met [Mark in] 2001 . . . at [our district poetry event]. . . . And then I came [to this school] and started the club. I found out that [Mr. Casale] and another teacher were paying [Mark] out of their own pockets to teach their kids. [Mr. Casale] has always done this poetry unit, so after a couple years of being here, I asked [Mr. Casale] if he would be my cosponsor because I knew that he was a good teacher of poetry. . . . I can teach poetry, too, but because I'm rusty, I just decided that he would be good. Plus I knew that he was beloved, and he is, so that was how I started the club. (Ms. Sanderson, interview, May 7, 2015)

Ms. Sanderson told me that the Metropoets teaching artists who have visited over the years have taught her a lot about spoken word. In reflecting on the state of the club, she said she would like to see more camaraderie among members. She explained, "Kids come in, one sits there, one sits there, you know. It's really not a group of people that even know each other" (Ms. Sanderson, interview, May 7, 2015). In the semester when I observed this club, some of its most active members were cycling out. The club appeared to be in a state of transition.

Mr. Casale

Mr. Casale is the other sponsor of this club. A teacher of ten years (the majority of that time at Palo Brea High School), Mr. Casale was assigned to teach junior English during this study. He holds a master's degree in the teaching of English and was working toward getting certification to teach English language learners. He talked about his path to this club:

> Well I knew [Ms. Sanderson] because we were colleagues in the English department . . . before she was the department chair. . . . When she came here, she did the poetry club and [the district poetry event], and . . . [my colleagues] told the department that I do a poetry slam. There's a fairly sizable unit leading up to it, and I think the one thing that she was missing in poetry club was new, exciting, interesting curriculum for them to work on, just new ways of teaching poems. This was all before we got any slam coaching from [Mark] and [Gabriel] and their team. (Mr. Casale, interview, May 6, 2015)

Mr. Casale became involved with this school poetry club sometime around 2008. He did not previously have special training in teaching spoken word. Mr. Casale said, "I don't write a lot of poetry, other than models for students in classes. I definitely have never slammed a poem out loud" (Mr. Casale, interview, May 6, 2015). He enjoys teaching his poetry unit, and he likes to build bridges between contemporary works and traditional canonical texts.

This club cosponsor appreciates that teenagers are willing to come in and "sit around for two hours after school and think about poetry" (Mr. Casale, interview, May 6, 2015). Mr. Casale acknowledged the range of skill in the group. Some members have competed in national slams, while others were writing "because they were hurt, and they gotta get it on paper" (Mr. Casale, interview, May 6, 2015). He said the purpose of the club is for students to be heard. Mr. Casale added, "And for some of the students, that's everything, right there. It's not about the brilliance of the finer points of language. It's like, 'I have something to say, and this is a safe space for me to be able to say it'" (Mr. Casale, interview, May 6, 2015).

When their Metropoets teaching artist does not come to the club, Mr. Casale is the one who plans the lessons. Ms. Sanderson takes care of the club's paperwork. This division of labor seems to serve these two teachers well. Ms. Sanderson said, "We split up the work, and we're really good together" (Ms. Sanderson, interview, May 7, 2015).

Brian

Brian was the Metropoets teaching artist assigned to Palo Brea Poets Club during the semester of this study. He has a bachelor's degree in communication and radio, and he worked for thirteen years in radio. Brian grew up playing around with technology and recording his voice. His father did radio in Vietnam, and his mother was a special education teacher.

When Brian was nine, he had a bike accident that resulted in a serious head injury. He told me that with the learning disabilities that resulted from that accident and his knowledge of poetry, he is uniquely positioned to help students with learning disabilities express themselves through poetry. At the time of this study, he was working as a substitute teacher in the district and earning a master's degree in education.

This teaching artist has been doing open mics for more than a decade, which is how he met Mark of Metropoets. Brian talked about their relationship:

> I was already up on stage, but I was at a point where I felt like I needed further development, so [Mark] was my rock in terms of that development, and I valued his feedback. I still do. And I think in me, he saw a deejay for these events but also someone who is a little bit older who could serve as a mentor to the kiddos, and things just seemed to click. . . . I'm still active in the community. I'm doing radio and also deejaying, and that sets me up pretty well as a teaching artist at [Palo Brea High School] because the kids can see me perform, and it's easy for them to kind of buy into whatever I'm selling as a teacher there. (Brian, interview, March 21, 2015)

Brian has been a teaching artist for this club since 2013 and has worked with other school clubs since 2012. As Metropoets has expanded, Brian has been asked to take on more work in its residency program. He said that these school poetry clubs nurture writers, and club members trust each other to a greater degree than is typical at Saturday events at the library.

Brian talked about the responsibilities involved with being a teaching artist for a club. He said that all of the Metropoets teaching artists get together over the summer to go over the residency curriculum with Mark, and Mark makes sure the curriculum is aligned to Common Core State Standards. Brian said, "We've got a strict curriculum in terms of my time being spoken for. I've got an hour, so sixty minutes, and each minute has something attached to it" (Brian, interview, March 21, 2015). Mark gives teaching artists "the lesson plan [and poems] . . . so [they] go into it with a whole arsenal of tools under [their] belt. That pretty much sets [them] up for the whole semester" (Brian, interview, March 21, 2015).

These lessons follow a basic structure. They begin with a five-minute warm-up. Brian said, this "can . . . be a poem of mine that I read, and that's where I show my vulnerability. Empathy is a big part of this effort" (Brian, interview, March 21, 2015). Then they read a model poem aloud and discuss it for approximately ten minutes, examining the poem's meaning and techniques. After writing for about twenty minutes, the students share their works and receive feedback in the time that is left. It is interesting that Brian mentioned vulnerability and empathy when discussing this lesson plan format. It seems that there is a lot more at work in these lessons than reading, writing, speaking, and listening. Although lessons follow a basic structure, teaching artists do have some leeway as far as bringing in their own ideas. Of the twelve visits a teaching artist will do, Brian said that Mark only provides plans for eight.

It is important that the teaching artist arrives prepared. Brian explained, "[This] includes writing my own poems so I can try those out on students" (Brian, interview, March 21, 2015). Brian feels that an essential component of preparing for this club is preparing as a poet. Another responsibility he mentioned is being in touch with students' needs. He said:

> [I try to] give these kids the best opportunities in terms of their progress [so I need to be] in tune with where each individual student is [and] where they see themselves. Is it just someone who comes to class and wants to write poems? Is it someone who wants to bring it to the stage? Is it just someone who wants to observe? So that's part of my job, too—not only being prepared but also sussing out these kids' interests. And what plays into that is deejaying because that's what you do as a deejay is you read the room. Well, who's dancing and to what songs, right? And so again that kind of speaks to my background. (Brian, interview, March 21, 2015)

Brian sees similarities between his work as a teaching artist and his work as a deejay. He has to "read the room" in both cases, quickly determining what people need from him.

Data Collection and Analysis

Data sources for this case study consisted of observations, interviews, and artifacts. Over the course of the semester, I observed thirteen club sessions at the high school, typically club meetings that ran from about 3:45 to 4:30

p.m. I also attended three public Metropoets events at the library during the study. I wrote ethnographic field notes (Emerson, Fretz, and Shaw 1995) during observations. Also, I used audiorecording at five of the club sessions, transcribing selectively and omitting nonparticipants at the point of transcription. I interviewed each adult participant once. These audiorecorded interviews averaged forty-five minutes, and I transcribed them in full. The semistructured interviews (Merriam 2009) contained similar questions for the sponsoring teachers and the teaching artist. (All interview questions can be found in appendix A.) In addition to conducting interviews and observing events, I collected artifacts, mostly handouts used at meetings, such as model poems and writing guides that Brian distributed.

As in the yearlong study of Metropoets, I used grounded theory and a constant comparative method (Charmaz 1983; Corbin and Strauss 2007; Glaser and Strauss 1967; Sowell 2001) to make sense of the data. I found that open coding resulted in many codes that overlapped with those used in the yearlong study (e.g., poem feedback, ground rules, model texts). This is not a surprise, as teaching artists in the school clubs use many tools and practices they have picked up from Mark and Gabriel. Combining and collapsing the codes into categories resulted in several findings about the club, as explained below.

Palo Brea Poets Club Findings

This study found that Palo Brea Poets Club is a community of practice within the Metropoets network that has distinct practices, benefits, and challenges. This club has also changed over time.

Club Practices

Many of the club's practices were similar to those I observed in the Metropoets group. This section examines the club's writing workshop structure, sharing in the group, poem feedback, advice, and ground rules. Club events and connections to the Metropoets group are discussed as well.

Writing Workshop Structure

When Brian was present for club meetings, the sessions tended to run like a Metropoets writing workshop. That is, Brian focused on learning students' names and began with low-risk sharing, such as asking them to name their favorite breakfast foods. He often shared his own poetry in these sessions and brought copies of mentor texts to read and discuss with students. Sessions typically provided time for writing and sharing. Despite the influence of Metropoets, the club had practices of its own that reflected the school setting. For example, an attendance sheet would sometimes be sent around the room for members to fill out, a practice I never observed in the Metropoets group.

Discussing mentor texts was central to almost every club meeting. Over the course of the semester, Brian led the group in discussing "Things That Make Hearts Break" and "Cupid's Smile II" by Tupac, "Humanity I Love You" by E. E. Cummings, and "Where I'm From" by Willie Perdomo. Ms. Sanderson read "My Friend" by W. S. Merwin, and Mr. Casale shared "Diving into the Wreck" by Adrienne Rich. As adults discussed texts with students, they drew on specialized language as needed. For example, Brian taught students about concrete nouns, abstract nouns, list poems, lyrical poems, narrative poems, haikus, persona poems, and the turn of a poem. Mr. Casale discussed enjambment and connotation, and he pointed out differences between words with Latinate and Germanic origins.

A lot of the writing exercises these poets engaged in were similar to those I observed in the Metropoets group. At one workshop, students made lists to describe high school and summer in Arizona, and then they built poems out of these. In another workshop, members were asked to list things they loved and hated about cameras. Another time, members wrote about a place they both loved and hated. In February, they wrote about Valentine's Day. Reading a poem, watching a video clip, or listening to a song would lead into a writing activity.

Sometimes these sessions varied from Metropoets writing workshops. For example, one session focused on elaboration, and students revised their poems using a guide. Brian went around the room during this workshop and checked on the poets, asking, "What are you working on?" (observation, April 1, 2015). In a session focused on performance, Brian distributed a handout about overcoming stage fright. In another session, Mr. Casale asked members to draw topic cards out of a box and then write poems that incorporated all of the words. He said activities like this one can help poets step outside of themselves, which he feels is necessary because so much of their poetry is autobiographical.

Sharing Writing

People in this club were expected to share their writing, and poems typically addressed themes like love, home, and family. A poet might read a piece in the club and later perform the work at a Saturday Metropoets slam at the library. I enjoyed seeing how poems would evolve between the two spaces (e.g., moved stanzas, the addition of vivid details, the cutting of repetitive lines, etc.). If poets did not have their pieces memorized, they could read them from phones, journals, or school laptops.

Brian regularly shared his poems with members of the poetry club. Once he performed a wonderful piece about the students he had encountered while subbing. Another time he shared a short piece about a sad fence. When I asked the sponsoring teachers about performing their poetry for students, Mr. Casale said:

> Really it's not that I'm in any way intimidated with putting something out there. It's, I don't think it is. Maybe it is. But I think a lot of it has to do with I know what it would take for me to be proud of a poem. I feel like I could, but [there is] the dedication to time. It's really just a matter of like can I prioritize the five [or] ten hours of my life to actually build something that I'd be willing to memorize and then do in front of a group of people.... There's that weird sense of ... if you're a wrestling coach but you don't wrestle. I've always had a strange relationship with the poetry club because of that. It's like the slam coaches come in and they're in the trenches. So [this] is a very legitimate question because I feel like I should. I very much feel like I should. As a sponsor, I feel like it would make, I don't know. When I say stuff like, "Poetry is fun," there's a certain ... gravitas to it if I'd been there.... You gotta go to war to say war stories. One of these days I'll do it. (Mr. Casale, interview, May 6, 2015)

Brian joined me in encouraging the sponsoring teachers to share a piece, and they considered writing a duo poem. Ms. Sanderson said, "We are what we tell our students not to be.... [*turning to Mr. Casale*] I think we should do it together ..., so it would be less stressful and less scary" (observation, April 15, 2015). They brainstormed some ideas for poems but had not performed by the time my study ended a few weeks later.

This brings up an interesting question about whether sponsoring teachers should write and perform in club spaces. I understand what it feels like to be a teacher who has no extra time. With English papers piling up and hours of grading ahead, taking the time to write a poem may seem like an impossible luxury. Another concern is that if teachers do participate, students may feel that adults are co-opting their special space for writing. However, studies like Maisha Fisher's (2007b) have shown the value in having a teacher write and perform poems alongside students. Also, sharing stories and exploring one's emotional vulnerability through poetry can be incredibly rewarding, as I discuss in the afterword. Perhaps teachers who host poetry clubs could use some of the time in the club to craft their own poems and occasionally share these works with students. If the writing is about something real and is from the heart, most students will appreciate the effort, even if the poem is not perfect. I have found that sharing my writing with my college students has freed them to tell powerful stories of their own (Williams "Exploring").

Poem Feedback

Poem feedback in Palo Brea Poets Club was more specific and detailed than in the Metropoets group. Adults commented on each poem. For example, Brian once told a poet not to sacrifice meaning for rhyme, saying the person should "use rhyme sparingly, like cooking with pepper" (observation, February 11, 2015). He sometimes asked a poet to repeat a line, or he commented on a poem's details, setting, or mood. Once he reminded a poet, "Again, the 'who, what, where, when, why, how.' Think about the nightly news. They nail all that in the first two sentences, so bring this in, all those details, as soon as possible" (observation, April 8, 2015). Other comments addressed moving sections around, perhaps putting the "turn of the poem" in a particular place or making a conclusion the hook. Brian told one poet to double the length of a poem and another to forefront an important detail that was buried in the piece.

Club members occasionally asked Brian for feedback on poems they had written outside of the club. When a poet wanted feedback but had to leave, Brian told the person to take a picture of the poem and e-mail it to him. Overall, poems received more feedback in this club than in the Metropoets group. In fact, the feedback process was closer to the "read and feed" described by Maisha Fisher (2007b) or the "detail-hunting" described by Jen Weiss and Scott Herndon (2001).

Sometimes Brian's feedback addressed performance. For example, he told a poet, "Slow down and articulate every one of those words. Your mouth is your instrument" (observation, April 8, 2015). Brian also praised a poet for not depending on the printout of a poem. He said, "Trust in what you know.... We want you to get to the point where you are off the page.... We really want to get you guys to the point where you're facing your audience members and you're talking and telling your story using blocking, using body movements" (observation, April 8, 2015). I even saw Brian stop a poet briefly to remind the group to "center ourselves when we start. Understand the content of our poem and how we want to present it" (observation, April 8, 2015). Then he had the person begin again.

As in the Metropoets group, feedback in Palo Brea Poets Club did not necessarily travel in one direction, from adult to adolescent. After Brian read his poem about students he had met while subbing, he received praise about specific parts from a club member. Brian also told me how an adolescent member of the Metropoets group had once given him feedback on one of his poems at a Saturday event at the library. The poet told him to move the second half of his poem to the top. Brian remembered the poet had been "tickled at the fact that I, as her teacher, would ask her for [feedback] and that I would [listen to it], ... the same way that she's applied it when she's come to me" (Brian, interview, March 21, 2015).

Advice

Adults in Palo Brea Poets Club offered the young writers advice of various kinds. For example, Brian said, "Hang onto these poems. These are your poetic history.... Every great poem starts with a first draft" (observation, February 11, 2015). Also, Mr. Casale acknowledged that beginning a poem is sometimes the hardest part of writing. He recommended they start by making a list of three to five topics.

Brian gave the poets advice about performing. He said they should stand with their feet shoulder-width apart, lean slightly back, rock slightly forward, and then find the comfortable space in the middle. Before beginning their poems, they should take a couple of deep breaths. With his background working in radio and as a deejay, Brian understands how to use a microphone. He told the students to imagine they are speaking into the back of the microphone. "If you are this silent, no one's going to hear" (observation, April 8, 2015). Brian also suggested that poets listen to recordings of themselves, so they can hear how they sound, and he recommended they practice in front of a mirror. This teaching artist even led adolescents through vocal warm-ups and had them practice saying vowels in an exaggerated way.

Brian recommended that the poets work on memorization for at least ten minutes per day, and he told them they would need to review a piece at least eighteen times before it would be in their heads. He taught them memorization techniques, suggesting that they take a poem, break it into thirds, and focus on memorizing one section at a time while walking around the house. Having Brian in the space gave students an opportunity to interact with an expert poet and performer. He brought professional insights about performance and memorization into this school club.

Ground Rules

Palo Brea Poets Club adhered to the same three ground rules that the Metropoets group used during the yearlong study: (1) be brave; (2) be respectful; and (3) your voice matters. Brian would often remind club members about these rules, and they would sometimes be posted on the board. As club members were preparing to perform in their school slam, Brian stated each rule and applied it to the context of the upcoming school poetry slam. He said:

> What is our first rule, please? . . . Be brave. Good. I'm going to call on you guys to be brave next week. . . . Some of you guys have [performed before] and are seasoned veterans; others, not so much. . . . We're one whole, so I invite you to feed off of each other's energy next Wednesday. . . . It's going to be a lot of fun. You guys have worked really hard. This is your reward. Let's celebrate your poems. . . . Second rule of poetry club. . . . Be respectful. . . . You have to earn it. But you have to give it. Cool. Third rule of poetry club? . . . Your voice matters. Again, on Wednesday of next week, you guys are going to kill it on stage." (observation, April 8, 2015)

As Brian addressed the group and reminded them of the ground rules, he also acknowledged that the poets were probably feeling anxious about performing, a natural response.

Events

Palo Brea Poets Club was involved with several special events during the semester, including the district slam, which is an all-day poetry event for clubs in this district. At the district slam, Mark would typically lead a writing workshop and perform, everybody would eat pizza, and then the students would read their writing. During this study, twenty Palo Brea Poets Club members signed up to go to the district event; however, the van would hold only fifteen people, so Ms. Sanderson told the poets that those who returned their signed permission slips first would be able to go. As the event neared, only six club members had returned permission slips.

Palo Brea Poets Club also held its own school slams. Near the end of this study, the club performed for the school. Members prepared for this event for several weeks, and the club paid Brian to serve as the host of this slam. On the day of the event, a banner with the club name hung outside of the auditorium, and classes filled the very large space inside.

Sometimes the club had special meetings. For example, they had a pizza party for their final meeting of the year, and members were encouraged to bring a guest. Ms. Sanderson organized the event to attract more members to the club. At least fifteen people dropped by that day, but many left immediately after eating. Earlier in the year, a musical group performed during a club meeting. Brian paid the musicians himself. Ms. Sanderson remarked, "That's how we roll around here. We pay for a lot of things out of our own pockets" (observation, April 1, 2015). The way that Brian brought another group into the club space was similar to the brokering practices Gabriel engaged in with the Metropoets group. Teaching artists seemed to recognize the value of connecting youth poets to outside groups, and they worked hard to bring in expertise that would benefit the adolescents.

Connecting to Metropoets

The adults in Palo Brea Poets Club encouraged club members to participate in Metropoets slams at the library on Saturdays. Three times during the semester-long study I attended Metropoets events, and I noticed club members in attendance. Poets seemed to work on pieces in their school clubs and then perform polished versions at Metropoets slams. Brian attended Metropoets events frequently, and I once saw Ms. Sanderson and Mr. Casale at a Saturday slam. We commiserated when one of the club members did not earn a spot on the Brave New Voices team.

One interesting observation I made when moving between these two groups was seeing a brand new Palo Brea Poets Club member eventually make his way to a Metropoets slam. As he went from new club member to new Metropoets member, I realized that poets who come to their first Metropoets event at the library may not be new to the Metropoets network at all. They may have previously been working with Metropoets teaching artists at their schools for several weeks or months before making it to the library.

Some poets move back and forth between their school clubs and the Metropoets group. Ms. Sanderson pointed out that those who participate in both communities may eventually value their participation in the Metropoets group over their participation in their high school club. Placing in Metropoets slams and participating on a Brave New Voices team may take priority over fulfilling leadership responsibilities for a school club. This is a good example of how different communities of practice within a constellation are "competing for the same resources" (Wenger 1998, 127). A young poet's leadership skills may be valued by multiple communities of practice within a network, yet there is only so much of a person's time and energy to go around.

Perceived Benefits

The adults associated with Palo Brea Poets Club believe this club benefits young people. Brian said the club encourages adolescents to explore their interests and be creative. He thinks poetry is a great tool for students who are English language learners or in special education programs because it allows students "to experiment . . . [and] have fun with the language and also incorporate their own language" (Brian, interview, March 21, 2015). He added that as students share their stories through spoken word, teachers get to know them.

Mr. Casale said that the poetry club is a place where members can "celebrate language." He went on to say:

> We don't have a creative writing program at [Palo Brea High School] anymore. There's no class that you can take [that says,] "Let's write because writing is awesome and [we can] tell stories that people want to hear." We have [club, the] one spot where people can find that energy and do something, but I wish more people knew that. Poetry has this weird stigma. The word "poetry" is just awkward and goofy and reminds us of things that were in the back of textbooks and written by people that died a long time ago. And it's so far from the truth. . . . There's a catharsis [like] a psychology session. . . . Everybody's strongest poem is almost universally their most personal. (Mr. Casale, interview, May 6, 2015)

Mr. Casale pointed out that the club supports creative writing at a time when these electives are being eliminated from many schools. Such cuts are unfortunate because writing, and spoken word in particular, can be therapeutic for adolescents.

Brian loves being a teaching artist because he enjoys watching students grow. He told me, "It's the breakthrough moments that keep me coming back. When you see a kid *hear* themselves for the first time and get feedback, you see that growth. It's really special" (Brian, interview, March 21, 2015). He has seen students become more confident. Similarly, Mr. Casale told me, "The coolest, most obvious growth is watching people who take a microphone and speak in public for . . . the very first time and discover their voice. . . . And I would say that's the biggest growth, seeing really shy people not be shy" (Mr. Casale, interview, May 6, 2015).

It appears that this club may be changing school culture as well. Mr. Casale said the poets have shown fellow students that spoken word can be "exciting and entertaining" (Mr. Casale, interview, May 6, 2015). Ms. Sanderson said, "People want to go" to school slams, and they have fewer empty seats at these assemblies each year (Ms. Sanderson, interview, May 7, 2015).

This club seemed to be influencing the sponsoring teachers' own classrooms, as well. Occasionally Brian would introduce a poem that the sponsoring teachers would want to use in their English classes. Mr. Casale commented, "This year I'm doing one or two activities [in my class] that the slam coaches have done that I thought were cool" (Mr. Casale, interview, May 6, 2015).

Encounters with a Metropoets teaching artist exposed these teachers to new activities and materials. Similarly, Korina Jocson (2008) found that classroom teachers discovered useful teaching ideas when they partnered with university student-teacher-poets.

The classroom-club exchange works in both directions. Teachers would also reach into their own materials for club activities. For example, Mr. Casale's poetry unit has been a useful resource for this club. He said, "My favorite part of my year as an English teacher is the poetry unit. And then I get to come to poetry club and distill out the best, most interesting lessons from that unit and do it with people who voluntarily show up and usually have a lot of writing skill. So it's a great way to spend a Wednesday afternoon" (Mr. Casale, interview, May 6, 2015).

Challenges

Size and Nature of the Club

Palo Brea Poets Club was facing several challenges during this study. To begin with, the club struggled to increase membership throughout the semester. Typically a handful of students attended meetings. The club had an end-of-the-year pizza party to attract new members. However, it was disappointing to see friends of members come in, eat pizza, and immediately leave without expressing any interest in actually joining the club. "I don't know how we can corral people and make them sit in a chair," Ms. Sanderson said (observation, April 29, 2015).

Many members were seniors, so by second semester, when this study took place, those students were only attending club meetings sporadically. They were on outbound trajectories (Wenger 1998) from the group, accepting the reality that their time in high school was almost over. I saw some of these seniors more frequently at Saturday Metropoets events than I did at club meetings at their high school. Ms. Sanderson said, "It's been really hard having seniors, and [Brian] and even [Mark] told me, 'This is just a transitional period for these kids.' And I'm like, 'I don't care. If I'm at a job, and I'm working until June 1, I'm going to work until June 1" (Ms. Sanderson, interview, May 7, 2015). She found their inconsistent attendance frustrating, especially because some of the graduating poets held elected positions in the club.

In addition to their need to grow, Ms. Sanderson pointed to the need for a more defined purpose for the club. She said, "These kids are like, 'I'm not going to be a poet. I don't even want to be a writer necessarily.' . . . That's one of the big challenges" (Ms. Sanderson, interview, May 7, 2015). Ms.

Sanderson continued: "What is the purpose of this club? What do we actually want kids to know how to do? If we just want them to be slam poets, then that's a hard goal. If we also want them to write other kinds of poetry or read all kinds of poetry and discuss poetry, you know, that's a whole different thing, too. Maybe we want to be an adjunct to their English class and help them to analyze poetry. It's on almost every standardized test" (Ms. Sanderson, interview, May 7, 2015).

For those who are interested in starting clubs at their schools, Ms. Sanderson suggests that club sponsors talk to club members to find out what they want to get out of their participation in the club. That way, sponsors can better tailor the club to fit students' interests. (I have created a list of possible planning questions with this concern in mind, and it can be found in appendix B.)

Resources

A scarcity of resources, including a lack of funding and demands on teachers' time, impacted this group. In regard to funding, Brian said he wished being a teaching artist was a full-time job. He explained, "It's underfunded, and it's something that's really important. It should have a lot more attention and funding. But as far as the job and my position there and teaching the kids, I love that. I don't like that these kinds of classes and services are being cut" (Brian, interview, March 21, 2015). Palo Brea Poets Club paid Brian $100 to host the school slam from funds that Mr. Casale had donated to the club. As far as I could tell, the school district was not paying the sponsoring teachers or the teaching artist anything for their work in the club.

Brian did receive some money from Metropoets. In an email, he said he made $50 per class for the twelve classes he taught during the 2014–2015 school year, so $600 total that year. He confirmed that he paid $100 to bring in a musical group to perform for this club. Brian added, "I pay for gas and poetry books. The school makes copies" (email, July 22, 2015). I asked him what amount would be appropriate for a school to pay a teaching artist like himself. He responded, "$50 for the hour is okay, but $100 is better. Ten classes [per] semester at $75 . . . is great. There is a lot of time put into preparation, writing, researching, memorizing, practicing reads, etc." (email, July 22, 2015).

For busy teachers, sponsoring a club can be a challenge because of the demands already being made on their time. For example, during the pizza party, Ms. Sanderson was called to the front office to interview a teacher for an English position for the following school year. By the time she returned to the event, she found that the pizza—along with most of the students—had vanished. In addition, she sometimes had grading to do after the club ended around 4:30–5:00 p.m., which made for a very long day of work. Mr. Casale said that on poetry club Wednesdays he is at school from 7:00 a.m. until 5:00 p.m. While setting aside an hour for a club each week may not seem like a big time commitment, it adds up over the course of a school year. On top of other responsibilities, hosting a poetry club can be a burden.

Throughout my semester with Palo Brea Poets Club, I wondered why the sponsoring teachers and teaching artist were not paid a stipend by the school district for their work coaching student writers. While spoken word may not bring in ticket sales and merchandising profits like athletics can, teachers are often paid stipends for other sorts of activities like running a community newsletter or a school poetry contest. These adults deserve compensation for their work in this club.

Bureaucracy

This club faced school and district bureaucracy. Brian talked about how red tape kept him out of Palo Brea Poets Club for several months. He said:

> I was out of the loop for three and a half, four months because of volunteer paperwork. I mean, I get it. The safety of the kids. I totally get it, but they really sidelined my efforts. I was already in the district, a certified substitute with my badge and everything, and now I've gotta wait three months for this other volunteer paperwork to go through? And I'm like, "You guys know me. I've been here for the past year and a half. How come now?" So that's a pain in the ass. . . . I said . . . , "You called me to sub on Friday. Today is Wednesday and you're telling me that I can't come to teach poetry because you don't have my paperwork? I'll be here on Friday teaching kids. You called me." Again, I get it. Safety of the kids. I get it. (Brian, interview, March 21, 2015)

My experience gaining access to this club was similarly frustrating. And the bureaucracy we faced was not limited to adult visitors. Students not only needed permission forms from parents and teachers to leave campus for the district poetry event, but they also needed permission from their teachers to participate in the school slam. The default answer to "Can I __?" seemed to be "No." Even with various signed forms in my hands, I was still met with suspicion, which was humiliating. I wonder how many students did not end up participating in the school slam or the district poetry event simply because they did not want to go through the bother of asking so many adults if they could.

Testing

Testing is affecting schools across the country, taking time away from instruction and narrowing the curriculum. Since this study only ventured into the school day once (for the school slam; all other club activities occurred after school), I did not see the many ways testing was affecting the students and teachers of Palo Brea High School. That being said, testing still did manage to influence this after-school club in a couple of ways during the study.

In February, I showed up to a club meeting and found that it had been cancelled. Apparently, during a week of testing, students at Palo Brea discovered that the Arizona Instrument for Measuring Standards (AIMS) test would no longer be required for graduation, yet the school was still required to administer the exams. As word of this spread among students at the school, they stopped coming to school on these AIMS days. As I wrote in my field notes, "It is the week of state testing. The kids found out on Monday that the test is not required for graduation. Fewer attended school on Tuesday and even fewer came to school today. There were just not enough kids around to make it worth it. While I talked to Ms. Sanderson, three kids came in, and she told them club was cancelled."

A few weeks later, Ms. Sanderson was trying to schedule the school poetry slam for an upcoming school day. However, she kept running into conflicts with the dates of a new standardized assessment, AZ Merit, which was spread over a large testing window. Ms. Sanderson and I had the following exchange:

MS. SANDERSON: I can't believe I made that mistake. We don't have a seventh hour on the fifteenth. We have a third hour because of the [state assessment].
WENDY: They are starting that test already?
MS. SANDERSON: The thirteenth through the twenty-first.
WENDY: I thought they were starting it next year.
MS. SANDERSON: No. The kids are going to be the guinea pigs. They're establishing a benchmark. (observation, April 1, 2015)

These tests, neither of which seemed to matter for students' graduation, both interfered with poetry club activities to some degree.

Poem Content

Sometimes poem content was an issue in this club. Occasionally there were concerns about what was appropriate for the school setting. For example, when a poet delivered a piece that made an obvious reference to sex, Brian looked to Ms. Sanderson for guidance. She immediately turned to the group of students to ask if they thought it was appropriate. The group determined that the poet needed to tone down that section, and Brian offered to work with the poet one-on-one to smooth out the piece and add figurative language to explore ideas with nuance.

At the school slam, one of the poets swore multiple times. Brian addressed this after the slam, reminding the poets that they always needed to keep their audience in mind:

> [Respect] also means . . . being aware of your surroundings and the situation in which you have the opportunity to tell your stories. Right? . . . As poets, we have to be aware of who our audience is, right? So if I'm going to . . . a coffee shop or like kindergarten, right, it would behoove me in terms of being welcomed back, as well as the organization I'm representing, whether it be [Metropoets] or [Palo Brea High School] or just your family name or whatever, to kind of be aware and be sensitive toward the age of the audience, right? . . . Being specific about today on campus, what we should really keep in mind is that there are folks in the audience who can unfortunately pull the rug out from underneath us for future opportunities. So this goes for everybody, . . . myself included. . . . We want to be heard. We have stories. They are important. Our voices are important. To best put ourselves in the position to be heard more than once, invited back to places, we need to, again, be respectful. (observation, April 15, 2015)

He suggested that what is appropriate for an adult slam is not necessarily appropriate for school.

Ms. Sanderson followed up by sending out an email of apology to the faculty. In it, she thanked the teachers for attending, commented on the success of the event, and reminded teachers that their support mattered to the poets. She then complimented the work that Metropoets teaching artists had done with club members over the years, emphasizing that students had learned about language and audience: "While keeping suitability in the forefront of their mind as they write to perform, they have been encouraged to only use curse words sparingly, if at all. They have been taught they are not often needed in order to compose a poem that grips their audience" (email, forwarded to me on May 3, 2015). In this email, Ms. Sanderson acknowledged the problem and said this had not happened before in the many years Palo Brea Poets Club had held this event. She recognized that some teachers might say it is okay to swear on stage because this is art; however, she expects students to use appropriate language. Ms. Sanderson concluded by apologizing and asking for their continued support.

In addition to issues with language use in students' poems, sometimes there were concerns about personal content. Mr. Casale addressed the difficulty involved with going public with personal stories:

> [Poems get] into some pretty personal stuff, so that's something that's surprised me, . . . the burden that I end up with, carrying other people's stories with me, hearing things that they maybe have never told anybody else before, and then being a part of something that is all of a sudden a very public thing. . . . So that's always been a challenge for me is making sure that what moves from the intensely personal to the completely public is handled appropriately. . . . As a teacher there are certain expectations that I have to legally follow. For instance, in my classroom if any of my students [discussed] instances of physical or emotional or sexual abuse, . . . even if they mentioned that my mom locked me in my closet when I was seven because whatever, well mom did something that was evil and there is a route to punishment for that. (Mr. Casale, interview, May 6, 2015)

When stories of abuse are told, club sponsors will need to get involved to protect students. Before starting a club, teachers should get clarification from administrators and social workers about what they are required to report, as well as what to do when this information comes out in a club meeting and the office is already closed for the day. Going along with this, teachers should be upfront with club members about the kinds of stories they are required to report.

Tension

One last challenge I witnessed in this group was tension between the sponsoring teachers and the teaching artist. This tension was evident when the term "class" (instead of "club") was used. Brian referred to the group as a class, and Ms. Sanderson corrected him, saying, "Club! We don't consider it a class" (observation, March 4, 2015). This distinction mattered to Ms. Sanderson, who likely did not want students to feel they were extending their school day with yet another class. "Club" implies that the activity is optional and people participate in it because they have a real interest.

In addition, the sponsoring teachers sometimes felt unnecessary when Brian was teaching. Mr. Casale remarked that he felt "a little redundant" at times because the teaching artist was taking care of the curriculum. Mr. Casale said, "This year . . . I've been in a weird spot. Other than tutoring people and participating in the activities, this has been kind of a backseat job for me as a curriculum person" (Mr. Casale, interview, May 6, 2015). Similarly, Ms. Sanderson said, "We've . . . been observers the last three or four years, rather than the teachers." She continued, "I would like for it to not be that way in the future because I can show a YouTube video of a performance artist. I can critique it. I can say what's good and what's bad about it. I'm experienced now with this stuff, so I'm hoping that next year . . . [Mr. Casale] and I really do take a role and teach more" (Ms. Sanderson, interview, May 7, 2015). They feel they have learned enough from Metropoets teaching artists.

In contrast, Brian talked about how much he enjoyed working with Palo Brea Poets Club precisely because its two sponsoring teachers are so involved. He said he appreciated that the teachers would stay for the whole time, contribute, and give kids support. Brian said, "[If I] have a brain fart, [Mr. Casale] will jump right in and get things back on track, and I appreciate that" (Brian, interview, March 21, 2015). In some of the other school clubs, the sponsoring teachers would leave the room as soon as Brian arrived, saying "Great, you're here. . . . I'll see you later. If you need anything, I'm down the hall" (Brian, interview, March 21, 2015). Brian appreciates having Palo Brea teachers in the room who already know the kids. If anything were to get out of hand, they would be there to assist him.

The teachers would occasionally nudge Brian in particular directions. For example, when Brian asked if any other poets wanted to read, Ms. Sanderson insisted that all of the poets should read because the school slam was right around the corner. Brian was receptive to this suggestion and said, "Yeah, let's do it" (observation, April 8, 2015). He never appeared threatened to have two more experienced teachers present. He only talked about the benefits. Brian said, "Collaborative efforts are more advantageous because you have more ideas coming in. . . . I really like the balance at [Palo Brea]. I feel like I have room to do my thing, and I can support the teachers" (Brian, interview, March 21, 2015). It seems that having multiple adult leaders present created issues primarily for the certified teachers, who were used to handling writing instruction alone. Perhaps this club could address this challenge by asking each adult to take over on a different day. A club calendar could identify the adult in charge that day, the topic or focus of the workshop, and planned activities.

Changes over Time

According to the sponsoring teachers, Palo Brea Poets Club had changed a great deal over the years. Prior to its affiliation with Metropoets, the club had fewer members, and students would come to meetings mostly to visit with each other. They had club T-shirts, and members sold valentine grams to raise money. Before Metropoets came into the picture, Mr. Casale oversaw club activities and curriculum for up to forty meetings per year.

Palo Brea Poets Club became affiliated with Metropoets when Mark received a grant to do outreach in schools. Mark already knew Mr. Casale from visiting his classes, so he asked him if Palo Brea Poets Club would like to have a Metropoets teaching artist assigned to work with them. By the time of my yearlong study, Metropoets had been sending teaching artists to Palo Brea High School for several years.

As Palo Brea Poets Club moves forward, the sponsoring teachers would like to see some changes. For example, Ms. Sanderson thinks the club should host monthly slams and encourage members to attend poetry slams at coffee shops. She said, "Whoever comes next year [their assigned teaching artist] is going to have to get on board with that" (Ms. Sanderson, interview, May 7, 2015). Ms. Sanderson would also like the students to take a more active role in the running of the club. Mr. Casale agreed. He said, "You see other clubs . . . the teacher unlocks the door, but the students basically take over at that point" (Mr. Casale, interview, May 6, 2015).

These teachers would like to see changes made to their meetings. Ms. Sanderson wants to integrate "poems from [her] poetry shelf"; she sees value in these canonical texts and said, "I miss my books" (observation, April 29, 2015). She remembered how the club was before Metropoets teaching artists arrived. They addressed poetry in general, not just spoken word. Ms. Sanderson also talked about the need for greater organization. She would like the club to keep a calendar of events, and she wants to be able to text important club announcements to members. She said that club officers should attend every meeting and take responsibility for club records and announcements.

When club members perform, Ms. Sanderson wants them to have their pieces memorized. She said, "Nobody can get up on the stage with paper or their little phone. A poem they just wrote. Oh, please. That would be like me getting up in front of a class and saying, 'Okay, I'm going to teach you something, but I'm not sure exactly what it is yet'" (Ms. Sanderson, interview, May 7, 2015). She wants poets to be better prepared for school slams.

Mr. Casale talked about ways they could give poets more focused feedback. He mentioned that each poet could "bring six copies of a poem [so members could] tear it to pieces [and] give honest feedback" (Mr. Casale, interview, May 6, 2015). While they recognized that they had learned a lot from working with the Metropoets teaching artists over the years, they seemed eager to take back their club.

During the semester I spent with Palo Brea Poets Club, they were definitely going through a shift. Of course, communities of practice are not static. They can change from year to year, depending on who is present and what their goals are. "Because the world is in flux and conditions always change, any practice must constantly be reinvented, even as it remains 'the same practice'" (Wenger 1998, 94). This club seemed poised to redefine itself in the coming year.

Spoken Word in After-School vs. Out-of-School Contexts

There are interesting similarities and differences between Palo Brea Poets Club and the Metropoets group. Examining spoken word in these two communities of practice, one after-school and one out-of-school, can be useful for considering the possibilities and limitations of literacy learning in different contexts.

These studies found that both groups engaged in similar practices, which suggests that the Metropoets writing workshop format can work in both after-school and out-of-school settings. In both settings, the teaching artist focused on learning names and used some kind of low-risk sharing to encourage all poets to talk. These workshops also involved the study of mentor texts of various kinds, including the teaching artists' own works. Adolescents had time to write and share in these spaces. They followed the Metropoets ground rules and received encouragement and advice from the teaching artists. In both settings, the poets participated in slams. Although the school slams happened less often (twice a year rather than once a month), they took place in an auditorium filled with hundreds of students. In comparison, the slams that Metropoets held at the library tended to attract between fifty and eighty people.

In the club setting, poets seemed to receive more text-based and in-depth feedback. Also, the teaching artist, Brian, added his own twist on things when he taught in Palo Brea Poets Club. Because of his background in radio, he taught poets how to speak into a microphone and compared poems to news stories. He also made time in the club to really teach performance and memorization techniques.

Whereas the Metropoets group struggled to deal with its growing numbers, Palo Brea Poets Club was struggling all semester to attract new members. Outbound trajectories were in play in both settings, but the club seemed to have a tougher time when influential members cycled out as seniors. While the Metropoets group sometimes had problems securing free, reliable, and convenient space large enough to handle its events, this was never an issue for Palo Brea Poets Club, with its many classrooms and enormous auditorium on site. Both of these communities of practice demanded a great deal of effort from the adult leaders, and much of their work was unpaid.

The school club faced several challenges that the out-of-school group did not. Because Palo Brea Poets Club was situated within a school space, there were sometimes concerns about whether the content of a poem was appropriate. Youth poets were therefore not able to speak as freely in the club as they could in the Metropoets group. Palo Brea Poets Club was also subject to school and district bureaucracy, which kept Brian out for a few months and limited what students were able to do in terms of district trips and school performances during the school day. There were also interferences related to standardized testing. These school-specific challenges restricted youth poets.

The two sponsoring teachers seemed eager to take back their club from the assigned Metropoets teaching artist. While teachers like Ms. Sanderson and Mr. Casale may understand how to lead poetry workshops themselves, a teaching artist does represent an important connection between adolescents and a larger spoken word community. If this connection were severed, club members would miss out on the chance to build a relationship with a professional poet, and they would lose access to a much larger network of poets. The teaching artist's importance as a role model and literacy sponsor (Brandt 2001) for youth poets must not be overlooked. As readers saw in chapter 5, adolescent poets in the yearlong study very much saw Gabriel and Mark as role models, and they looked to these older poets to see what new writing they were doing. Contact with experts can lead to meaningful learning opportunities that may even change how students see their writing and themselves as writers. The challenge is making these partnerships between schools and local experts sustainable, so teachers are willing to sponsor these clubs in the first place and all adults working in the space receive fair compensation for their labor.

Conclusion

Despite the many challenges that come with running a school poetry club, Ms. Sanderson and Mr. Casale continue to cosponsor Palo Brea Poets Club year after year, investing their time and their own money into the group. Brian and previous teaching artists have worked tirelessly on behalf of this school club, creating an important link between students and a larger community of writers.

Some youth poets who have participated in school clubs like Palo Brea Poets Club have gone on to become active members of Metropoets and have competed in Brave New Voices. Some former club members have also blossomed into magnificent writers and spoken word poets who take great pride in their authorship—thanks to the opportunities they first received in high school poetry clubs like the one described in this chapter.

CONCLUSION
RETHINKING WRITING INSTRUCTION

We have English teachers who are so involved with our poetry that they'll ask if we've written anything new.
—*Jasmine*

Recently I was having lunch out, and I ran into an adult poet, a friend of Mark's and Gabriel's, who had performed for the Metropoets group during the year that I was studying them. Almost three years had passed, but I still remembered her and her moving poem. While I may not be the best listener in the world or have the greatest memory, I was able to remember her story because she had spoken from the heart and revealed a part of her life that was real and meaningful and painful. I had been a witness to her testimony, and that moment had stayed with me for years.

I first began studying spoken word poetry groups because I wanted to see what schools could learn about writing from those who write on their own time with great interest and dedication. Coming face to face with this poet again, the answer was clearer than ever. Sharing stories in a supportive community is incredibly powerful.

For thousands of years, people have shared stories about the human condition. Stories are "fundamental to the human search for meaning" (Munro 1998, 66), and they help us "make sense of [our] worlds" (Ellis 2003, 32). In contrast, secondary writing education often focuses on preparing students for formal writing situations they *might* encounter later. The logic goes something like this: students need to learn to write essays so they can write even more essays later in college, and students need to learn to compose professional documents so they can compose even more professional documents later in careers. All of this writing is future-focused—not to mention, sanitized. What about the writing that will benefit students personally *right now* as adolescents? This may be the most important "real-world" writing that students learn, the writing that will help them work through abuse, disappointment, loss, regret, fear, anger, and sadness, the writing that will help adolescents make it *to* their futures (Morrell 2008).

The fact that expressive and personal forms of writing, including the writing of poetry, are largely ignored in the Common Core State Standards is problematic. In short, we are missing opportunities to teach writing that can change lives. Students should not have to go outside of school walls to finally find a form of writing that is meaningful to them, to finally be allowed to say something that matters, to finally discover an audience of listeners. It is no wonder that some students disengage in secondary English classrooms. What is in it for them right now?

In the sections below, I offer some suggestions for rethinking school-based writing instruction inspired by the innovative ways Metropoets approaches writing, performance, community, and authorship. In line with the book's theme of listening to the poets, this chapter closes with advice from Metropoets writers themselves about how to best improve schools.

Writing

We have seen that spoken word can be an empowering form of writing for young people. Fortunately for readers who are interested in using this medium with students, there are many ways to incorporate it into curriculum. Teachers can start small, perhaps by bringing in videos of a couple of spoken word poems and asking students to define spoken word poetry as a class. I have shown works by Prince Ea and Sarah Kay, for example, but there are numerous poems available online, including poetry by young people themselves. Some teachers show the full-length documentary *Louder Than a Bomb,* which follows several teams of adolescents as they prepare to compete in an annual youth poetry slam. There is even an accompanying teaching guide available online that pairs poems from the movie with extension activities.

Teachers can spend a few days or several weeks on spoken word. For those who only have a few hours, they could introduce students to this form, invite them to write about an injustice they have witnessed or a life event they have experienced, and provide time for sharing with partners. Other teachers might launch a full unit, complete with explorations of historical, cultural, and political aspects of spoken word, as well as a culminating class or school-wide poetry slam. Spoken word can expand to fit the time available, and it can be returned to several times throughout the school year.

When I teach spoken word to preservice teachers at Arizona State University, I need at least six hours, typically spread out over three class meetings. I begin by performing a poem I wrote (see the afterword). Then I show a few videos of poets performing, we define spoken word together, I provide some historical and cultural background, and we start brainstorming and drafting. At the second class, students give each other feedback on their drafts. Then, at the third class, students share final drafts in small groups, and we have an optional poetry slam for anyone who would like to perform for the whole class. (See Williams, "Exploring," for a full description of this unit and accompanying handouts.)

The Metropoets writing workshop described in the introduction and analyzed in chapter 4 is an instructional model that teachers could implement in their classrooms. Mentor texts could consist of lyrics, songs, published poems, videos of poems, or even live performances. Students will need some freedom to pursue the topics that matter to them. Also, frequent low-risk opportunities to write and share can help students feel more confident about their writing. Adolescents appreciate having the chance to write without always being corrected. When students are granted little agency in school settings, they learn over time that their voices do not matter. It is no wonder that some students are disengaged or scared or embarrassed by the time they arrive in secondary and college classrooms. Therefore, when using spoken word in the classroom, the focus should be on correcting this imbalance—that is, empowering students through writing and sharing. We need to put the red pen away and listen.

What is innovative about the Metropoets approach to teaching writing is the focus on writing as a tool of empowerment. As young people write and speak and receive praise for sharing in Metropoets, their voices grow stronger and louder and clearer. As Mark said at the beginning of this book, "We are not approaching young people as if they're lacking" (Mark, interview, June 24, 2014). In some ways, the entire Metropoets philosophy derives from this single idea. Young people have stories worth telling. Their ideas and experiences matter. So we should encourage young people to write. And we should listen to what they have to say.

The Fear of Losing Instructional Time

Some teachers may be concerned that asking students to write spoken word in the secondary English classroom will take time away from everything else they have to accomplish. After all, standards must be met, and isn't spoken word an add-on?

Actually, spoken word is a form that many adolescents appreciate and find engaging, so the better question is why wouldn't we make an effort to include it? This medium brings writing to life. Students can also meet a variety of Common Core State Standards through spoken word. Indeed, it is difficult to do any kind of spoken word activity in the English classroom without addressing multiple writing, reading, language, speaking, and listening standards. When students analyze text structure or point of view in poems, examine an author's use of figurative language or nuances in language, interpret texts in different formats and media, or use research in their writing of poetry, they are meeting specific standards (Common Core Standards Initiative 2014).

The *Framework for Success in Postsecondary Writing* (Council of Writing Program Administrators et al. 2011) recommends that students cultivate a variety of skills throughout their education. As it turns out, spoken word can be used to support all of the "habits of mind" outlined in the *Framework*, including curiosity, openness, engagement, creativity, persistence, responsibility, flexibility, and metacognition. Also, when students write spoken word poems, they gain experience thinking critically, writing for different audiences, and working through various aspects of the writing process. Spoken word can help students now and prepare them for future writing situations.

Supporting Creativity

It is worth acknowledging that spoken word is a form that encourages creative thinking and decision-making at every step of the way, something that students of all ages and academic levels need for our fast-changing world. Students deserve to have access to activities that help them exercise their creativity (Amabile 1989; Dewey 1934; Eisner 2002; Greene 1995; Robinson 2009 and 2011). Spoken word, which involves both creative writing and performance, supports arts-based pedagogies (Emert, Macro, and Schmidt 2016).

Valerie Kinloch (2005b) has argued for "a creative pedagogy that does not resemble constant testing drills," one that encourages "imaginative explorations, freedom of idea expression and generation, and the journeys of the creative writing process" (111). Unlike the formulaic writing many students are asked to undertake throughout their school years, spoken word is an exciting medium that motivates adolescents to tap into their creativity. Through this medium, young people are inspired to reflect, critique, and imagine.

Performance

Performers of all levels can get something out of the performance experience. Advanced poets may have their poems memorized and use accompanying vocalization and movement to bring an additional dimension to their poems, and they may be focused on competing in national competitions. On the other hand, less advanced students may read from a paper and hardly look up from it, yet when the experience is over, they may be proud that they had been brave enough to share. Although poets may be at different performance levels, this does not matter much in a space where everyone is working to improve at their own pace.

In the classroom, spoken word could be used to explore how blocking and other performance choices impact a message. After all, spoken word poems are multimodal compositions that use sound and movement. A useful exercise would be to give students copies of the same poem, and in groups, ask them to decide how to use their voices and bodies to best communicate the poem. After the groups have performed, the class could talk about the effects of different choices.

Students could also have opportunities to share their writing with authentic audiences. Kelly Gallagher (2006) has argued, "One reason students don't write well is that they do not care what they are writing about" (90). In contrast, youth spoken word poets know ahead of time their writing will be heard by others, so they put a lot of time and effort into this writing. During the years I taught high school English, I found the writing that students prepared for performance was some of the best they composed in my class. Students tend to be excited to write when they know they will have an opportunity to share their work beyond a teacher. This can be accomplished through regular writers' circles (Williams 2013) or open-mic events with students sharing their writing once a month, quarter, or semester.

In Metropoets, there is a lot of time set aside for adolescents to share and perform their writing, which is an innovative way to structure writing instruction. Teachers interested in incorporating more performance could examine their own curriculum and look for opportunities for students to share their work with peers, with others in the school, and with authentic audiences outside of the school. Are opportunities to perform built into the year? Perhaps students could even select their own audiences. For example, after completing a research project, students could select another format and audience to further disseminate their findings. This could take the form of a spoken word performance at a school assembly, a letter to a legislator, or a public service announcement on social media. There are many ways to go public with one's work beyond a poetry slam, and other types of literacy performances can also be rewarding.

Poetry Slams

The Metropoets poetry slam shown in chapter 3 and discussed further in chapter 4 is a useful model for those who are wondering how to run a youth poetry slam. Notice that the host uses a lot of encouragement, and audience members are reminded to show love to the poets through snaps and supportive utterances. While poems are scored, the host reminds everyone that the scores do not really matter. Ultimately, a youth poetry slam should be exciting and interactive, and performers should feel accepted and supported.

A poetry slam can take various forms on school campuses, involving just one class, an entire school, or a whole district. Regardless of the format, I cannot stress enough how important it is for performing to be optional. Students should never be compelled by teachers (those who hold power over them) to be made emotionally vulnerable.

Community

Sharing stories can bring people together and strengthen community in a group. In a supportive writing community where there is an "atmosphere of acceptance," adolescents may even come to "[take] themselves seriously as writers" (Ruday 2011, 191). This relationship between performing in a supportive community and writers' attitudes toward their writing and themselves as writers needs further investigation in future research.

When young people share their experiences, critique unjust systems, laugh and cry together, and applaud and reassure each other in the Metropoets community, they may experience "wounded healing." Marc Lamont Hill (2009) explains, "By wounded healing, I refer not only to the therapeutic dimensions of personal and collective storytelling, but also a critical engagement with majoritarian narratives that exposes and produces new possibilities. Through this practice, students formed a storytelling community in which membership was predicated upon an individual's ability and willingness to 'expose their wounds' (share their stories) to the remainder of the group" (65–66). In writing communities like Metropoets, youth poets learn that they are not alone in their feelings and experiences. Writing is "a means of connecting with and understanding others" (Lauscher 2007, 102). Poetry used in this way facilitates bonding between people.

Because Metropoets teaching artists understand the importance of writing in a supportive community, they approach community building as seriously as they approach the teaching of writing. This is an innovative take on writing instruction that seems to inspire literacy learning. Building community takes effort, and Mark and Gabriel engage in the "work of 'community maintenance'" (Wenger 1998, 74). Since these groups are complex and changing, keeping the right tone requires constant attention from leaders. Mark and Gabriel nurture the Metropoets community by encouraging frequent low-risk sharing in workshops, and they do not criticize students. Slams are structured so poets know to support each other through snaps, claps, cheers, and comments. The poets can choose to participate in this community in a way that is comfortable to them, participating peripherally or more centrally. Furthermore, teaching artists influence the community through the language they use, emphasizing community, love, family, and safety. Rather than using rules that would reinforce the teacher's authority and silence students, they use ground rules focused on encouraging adolescents to speak. Teaching artists actively work to bring people together, and they are largely responsible for the kind of community that results. In this community, literacy learning is relevant and exciting for adolescents.

Teachers may notice that some of these practices could be used to foster writing communities in school. Learning names immediately, observing rules that amplify students' voices, using language that emphasizes community, and writing alongside students are all effective strategies, for example. In their guide to teaching spoken word poetry, Jen Weiss and Scott Herndon (2001) recommend moving desks into a semicircle. They also acknowledge the vulnerability students may feel in these spaces, especially when a classroom has been transformed into a spoken word space. These authors write, "Achieving comfort in a classroom is a difficult task" (6).

Spoken word can be used on school campuses to help build inclusive communities. This medium also supports many of the goals of culturally relevant pedagogy (Ladson-Billings 1995). Schools must ensure that "ethnically diverse students feel recognized, respected, valued, seen, and heard" (Gay 2010, 51). We need more spaces that honor all students' cultures, languages, and experiences.

School Poetry Clubs

One way teachers can build community on campus is through spoken word poetry clubs. These clubs bring together writers of different levels, ages, and experiences from across the school. As we have seen in chapter 7, a club may face various challenges, but it can also offer many benefits.

In light of the Palo Brea Poets Club findings, it seems prudent for club sponsors and members to do some planning together (see appendix B for a poetry club planning guide). Clubs also need the support of the schools and districts where they operate. District administrators can support poetry clubs by offering events that bring together poets from different schools, like the annual poetry celebration held in Palo Brea's district. Local school administrators can make sure clubs get the funding they need.

Communities of Practice in the Classroom

These studies have me wondering whether it is possible to foster micro communities of practice within a single classroom space. Perhaps students could meet in small groups to engage in a form of writing that they care about (e.g., raps, plays, films, spoken word, novels, graphic novels, blogs, journalism, etc.). These groups could locate mentor texts and tools, make contact with experts, and share their work in ways that make sense for their chosen form. These small writing-focused, simultaneously meeting communities of practice might work if they offer students opportunities to gather around a form of writing they enjoy, support learning through participation, and give students a chance to identify with their writing. I intend to investigate such an instructional model in future research.

Authorship

As we have seen, the adolescent poets in Metropoets do not just write. They favor particular writing practices, have strong feelings about their writing lives, and have developed a sense of authorship. They see themselves as writers, an identity that has likely solidified through multiple performances of their work over time in a supportive community. While these poets have faced challenges when writing, they have also developed strategies for overcoming obstacles. Furthermore, they are able to reflect on their writing histories, identify important literacy sponsors and role models, and explain their motivation for writing. It is probably no wonder that all of the adolescent poets in the yearlong study predicted that writing would play an important role in their adult lives.

Writing and performing for authentic audiences can influence how adolescents feel about their writing and about themselves as writers. Jorge described the difference between writing and being a writer when he said, "[In the club] I could actually claim to be a writer. 'I wrote two poems, you guys. I'm a writer.' Whereas, [in English class], I would have just been like,

'Yeah, I wrote three English papers, but nobody read them other than the teacher. Nobody cares'" (Jorge, interview, June 27, 2014).

G. Lynn Nelson (2004) points out, "To talk about writing apart from the people who do it, apart from their being, is to put writing in a small box and remove the wonder and the magic and the power from it" (xii). Adolescents need opportunities in their writing to explore who they are and what they care about, whether that means thinking through relationships (as Nicole and Jasmine did), reflecting on painful experiences (as Jorge and Shawna did), or speaking out about injustices (as Rafael and Stacey did). Whether the form is spoken word poetry or something else, it seems key that teachers offer choice in topic and that they encourage writers to draw on their life experiences and "funds of knowledge" (Moll et al. 1992).

In addition, trusting writers to make choices can encourage them to apply their learning in creative and meaningful ways. For example, something as basic as a narrative assignment could take many forms, such as a short story, spoken word poem, illuminated text (Williams 2014), or short film. In the world of writing outside of school, deciding on the appropriate medium for the task is actually an important part of the writing process.

Adolescents need experiences working with multiple forms of writing, including those that offer personal satisfaction and those that offer training for careers in writing fields. "Students must be enabled to explore who they are, who they are not, [and] who they could be. They must be able to understand where they come from and where they can go" (Wenger 1998, 272). When students are taken seriously as writers and as practitioners of other disciplines, they come to see themselves in new ways. Gerald Reyes (2006) suggests that teachers think about the ways they address learners: "It matters how we speak to our students. It matters what we call them. So let's call them Poets. Let's call them Writers. Let's give them the titles that have traditionally seemed to be reserved for the professional adults" (14–15). Respecting students includes acknowledging their roles as young writers, scientists, mathematicians, historians, artists, and athletes.

Asking students to reflect on their writing practices and identities can impact the writing they do (Worthington 2008). Teachers might ask students to describe their writing practices and attitudes in a survey, perhaps using some of the categories in chapter 5 (e.g., What kinds of prewriting do you prefer to use? What topics do you like to write about? What tools do you use when you write outside of school?). Also, students could write author statements to accompany their works or include explanatory annotations or marginalia. They could even compose a writing autobiography, a paper that invites metacognitive reflection as students consider their writing histories and attitudes toward writing. For example, I have asked secondary and college-level students to write about a significant moment in their lives that had to do with writing. From these papers, I have learned about traumatic moments that turned students off from writing, positive experiences that were still lifting their spirits years later, and various forms of writing I had no idea they were engaging in outside of our class.

Young people deserve to have opportunities to engage in learning that matters to them and to identify with the work they do. Teaching artists in Metropoets understand this, and I would argue that their most innovative approach to writing instruction is taking adolescents seriously as real writers. This is not difficult to replicate in schools, but it does require a shift from focusing on errors and problems to valuing the assets that each writer brings to the table.

Teachers as Writers

It is significant that Metropoets teaching artists do not just encourage young people to write and share in this group. They participate, too, performing their own poems. As these teaching artists model how to be emotionally vulnerable, they encourage young writers to make this leap as well.

Teaching artists like Gabriel, Mark, and Brian have a close relationship with their writing, which is noticed by the adolescents they serve. Susan Weinstein (2009) explains how this process works: "the learner takes an active role by observing the work of a skilled practitioner, asking questions, and practicing with the skilled other's guidance. In this model, the novice is not required to take on faith the teacher's expertise; instead, she actually gets to observe the expert's craft firsthand—something that is often not the case in the standard classroom, where students may be taught writing by a teacher whose own writing they've never seen" (141). In Metropoets, the teaching artists are poets first and teachers second—as compared to teachers in schools who may not write or identify as writers. Recall that when Brian outlined the responsibilities of being a teaching artist, he mentioned preparing original writing to share with students. In contrast, many teachers focus on their lesson plans first and their mentor texts second, some finding examples elsewhere rather than writing them from scratch. While this is understandable given all of the pressures on teachers, it is also unfortunate because these moments are opportunities for teachers to embrace their authorship and connect with students as fellow writers.

The National Writing Project offers summer institutes that help teachers develop as writers. In addition, many venues such as the *English Journal* will publish teachers' writing. Districts should encourage English teachers to pursue their own writing and provide teachers with time to write. Schools and districts could even offer contests or forums for teachers to share their work. Opportunities like these could inspire teachers to focus on their writing lives. When is the last time a high school English department allocated professional development hours for its teachers to write for their own purposes? This is a change in education that I would like to see.

Janet Emig (1971) is critical of teachers who teach writing and do not write themselves. She states, "many teachers of composition, at least below the college level, themselves do not write. They have no recent, direct experience of a process they purport to present to others. . . . Partially because they have no direct experience of composing, teachers of English err in important ways. They underconceptualize and oversimplify the process of composing. Planning degenerates into outlining; reformulating becomes the correction of minor infelicities. They truncate the process of composing" (98). Emig claims that writers relate to their art in very different ways than nonwriters do, and she recommends that teachers at least write in journals to express themselves.

There is much to be gained when teachers write with students. Valerie Kinloch (2005b) found that writing alongside students "allowed them to witness [her] participation in the writing process, day after day. . . . [She revealed her] vulnerabilities and uneasiness with both the process and act of writing" (103). Students could see her writing and how she responded at various stages of the writing process. Etienne Wenger (1998) points out that "teachers need to 'represent' their communities of practice in educational settings" (276). He stresses the need for "lived authenticity" and claims that "being an active practitioner with an authentic form of participation might be one of the most deeply essential requirements of teaching" (276–77). In high school English classrooms, this means that teachers should be practitioners themselves. It may be that the most important implication of the research presented in *Listen to the Poet* is that teachers should engage in authentic writing alongside students.

Teaching artists in the Metropoets group write, perform, and identify as writers. Similarly, the adolescents in the yearlong study write, perform, and identify as writers. This is no accident. Role models are right there in front of them. As readers saw in chapter 5, adolescents look up to these adult poets and learn from them. Recall that Shawna called Gabriel's poems "mind-blowing," and Nicole said she looked to Mark and Gabriel to see "what new style they're bringing." While it is true that out-of-school and after-school groups are voluntary while school is not, students will never connect with teachers as writers if we do not open up and share our writing with them.

The Poets Offer Advice

A discussion of the implications for education would not be complete without the adolescent poets' perspectives. We need to know how they would like to see schools change to better meet the needs of writers like themselves.

Rafael said he would like to see contemporary poetry and political speeches used in the English classroom. He would also like more choice and less routine. He is tired of writing one essay after another. Rafael also believes students should be able to choose the books they read from an assigned era, rather than everyone reading the same title. In addition, he would like to see library days in which students choose a book and spend the whole period reading.

Jorge would like teachers to explain the purpose for each assignment. He wants to know, "How does this assignment help students in life?" While Jorge acknowledged the value of structured papers, he thinks creative projects should be used more frequently in English classes. He talked about wanting fewer restrictions and more choice. Additionally, Jorge thinks teachers need to focus on building community in classrooms.

Nicole said she would have liked more exposure to literature in school. She found the reading they did in class too narrow, and they read too few books. Nicole would also like to see a more diversified curriculum that includes contemporary poetry like spoken word. She does value canonical literature, but she believes young people connect to spoken word.

Jasmine recommends that schools offer poetry clubs to students. She said, "In our school we've actually been kind of blessed because we really don't have to go through so much struggle. We have English teachers who are so involved with our poetry that they'll ask if we've written anything new. We have a dedicated poetry club" (Jasmine, interview, July 21, 2014).

Stacey also talked about poetry clubs. Her school did not have one, but she wished it did. In fact, she thinks there should be multiple reading and writing clubs on school campuses. She also said that students should be able to write in their classes without always having to worry about whether it is perfect.

Shawna would like to see less formulaic writing in schools. Like Stacey, she said that her school did not have a poetry club, and she would have appreciated one. Attending the Town Slam made her realize what she had missed out on. She said, "I was watching all the schools go up there. I was like, 'Man, I would have totally been all over this if I would have known that it was allowed at high school.' Like if this was something that we could take, you know. Man, I would have been all over it!" (Shawna, interview, December 27, 2013).

Conclusion

Metropoets approaches writing, performance, community, and authorship in ways that benefit youth writers. In particular:

- Writing is a tool for personal empowerment and growth.
- Significant time is set aside for performance and the sharing of writing.
- Group leaders cultivate community.
- Adolescents are taken seriously as real writers.

These principles can be used in school settings as well. After all, we can show students the power of their words, encourage sharing and listening, focus on community building, and acknowledge that students are writers with something to say.

In Metropoets, youth writers regularly speak up, listen, applaud each other, and laugh together. They spend hours writing, and they are incredibly devoted to their craft.

Anger. Loss. Hurt. Love. Family. Friends.

Youth poets come together to make sense of it all, growing stronger through their self-expression. The power of their writing is evident at every Metropoets event, and it is beautiful to behold.

AFTERWORD
The Paradox of Emotional Vulnerability

You don't die. It feels like you're going to die, but then afterwards you're like, "Oh my god. I'm still alive, and that was amazing! When can I do it again?"
—*Gabriel (on performing for the first time)*

When I began studying Metropoets in September 2013, I expected to keep to myself in the back of the room, recording events and writing observation notes. I was there to gather data on the group's characteristics and practices, as well as learn about the youth poets' attitudes toward their writing and themselves as writers. I was not there to write spoken word poetry.

When the poets had time to work on their pieces, I typically wrote field notes. One day, however, I recorded two lines that were dancing around in my head, dreaming of becoming poems: "My mom is in a jar somewhere in my dad's house" and "For the poets baring their souls, what do I have to give you?" I suppose I realized that the most upsetting experience I had lived through was the death of my mother (hence the jar of her ashes). The second line revealed the guilt I was feeling because the poets were sharing their stories, and it seemed wrong for me to listen without giving them a story of my own. As the months went on, nothing came of either line. I concluded that I had no business dreaming of poems. After all, I was there as a researcher, not a poet.

In the summer when I interviewed Gabriel, something changed. I can pinpoint the moment in our interview transcript from June 5, 2014. We were talking about the poets and how they had changed through their participation in the group. When we arrived at the subject of Stacey, I said, "She showed up to a workshop. That was the change I saw in her over the course of the school year. It was her first workshop she said she'd ever [been] to, and it happened right at the end of the season. . . . She sat in the back right next to me."

Gabriel responded, "The success of our program has everything to do with the community. Like I think you have been able to reach [Stacey] and [Nicole] and [Jasmine] in ways that we can't. You know, we're just, we don't have enough time or resources to do it, you know what I mean? So like to see changes in them has everything to do with the entire community, you, being there."

"Oh!" I said, surprised.

Gabriel continued, "You know, for reals. . . . What I've just learned in youth development is it's not necessarily your educational background. It's your commitment to consistency. . . . That's what allows these kids to feel safe. And they get to know you. And then they start to like absorb whatever it is that you're putting out into the world, you know, as an adult mentor. . . . With [Stacey] it's weird for me because I don't know her super well outside of the slam. And she's a young female. I don't have much in common with an eighth-grade[1] young woman, so I always try to be encouraging to her, a little high five, 'Hey, how's it going? Nice to see you.' But other than that, you know, it's going to be somebody like you who breaks through to [Stacey]. So there you go. You saw her show up to a workshop. That has everything to do with you."

On an objective level, I know that Stacey showing up to a workshop has absolutely nothing to do with me, but hearing Gabriel say that I mattered to the group made me feel like I was more than an outsider. Suddenly, I felt like I could write a poem for them. Over the next twelve days as I went about my daily activities, I began to do some prewriting in my head based on the two lines I had come up with before. The ideas were awake and bouncing around now. When I did finally sit down to write, the words spilled quickly onto the paper. I had a draft and some editing done in just two hours.

My mother had died almost three years before I wrote this poem about her, and I believed I was finished grieving. Not true. The tears streamed down my face while writing. Everything I had pushed deep down inside of myself, too horrible to deal with, appeared there on the page. By the time I put my pen down, I felt like something heavy I was carrying was gone. Revisiting the most upsetting memories was cathartic.

Over the next several weeks, I read through the poem out loud again and again, adjusting a word here, a phrase there. Without fail, I would pause and get choked up on the most painful part of the poem for me: "I was in the room when her breath stopped." That memory was horrible. I imagined someday performing the poem, breaking down, and being unable to continue. I could not remember any of the poets abandoning a poem in the middle or having to be carted off the stage, but perhaps I would be the first.

Eventually, I tried out the poem on my husband. Reading the words to someone else for the first time was extremely difficult, but I pushed through and felt stronger afterwards. In fact, each reading became easier than the one before it. Not only was I mastering the lines, but I was also mastering the memory. This may explain why adolescents are so drawn to spoken word; they can use it to work through pain.

The kickoff Metropoets event of the 2014–2015 season, a workshop and slam to be held on September 20, 2014, was announced through social media. This would be my last visit of the yearlong study. As the event neared, I practiced my poem with more focus. I decided not to attempt to memorize the piece because I was sure that I would get nervous and forget the whole thing. Instead, I would take my poem up to the microphone like so many of the youth poets in the group do.

At the beginning of the slam, Gabriel announced:

> We also have a couple of adults who are going to read poems. One of them is Ms. Wendy Williams. Everybody say hello. For those of you who do not know, Wendy . . . has kindly selected [Metropoets] to . . . research. And through this process, she is not just coming as an outsider like looking in and doing research. She has become a part of the family. A lot of you guys know Wendy. And Wendy wrote a poem about her experience, and it's so beautiful because she's nervous. And that's what's really dope about it, that she's like, "I'm nervous to read that poem." And that's the point. That's what this is, right? You're nervous, you get up, you share your story, and that's beautiful. So I'm excited. (observation, September 20, 2014)

The crowd was generous in their cheering as I approached the stage. I hoped I would not let them down. I took a deep breath and launched into my poem:

A Poem for the Poets
Poets, you have faced fear head on,
Cut out tumors, brought them out into the light, and turned them over in your hands, examining them.
Like philosophers, you have contemplated their meaning.

I have watched you banish demons like priests,
    heal wounds like miracle workers,
    forgive like saints,
    and rally for change as activists.

Poets, you have schooled this teacher,
had this researcher investigate herself.
And now I stand before you, at your altar, ready to shed my blood.

I present my mom to you.
In a jar.
She sits on a shelf at my dad's house.

My mother lived in this desert back when crop dust fell from the sky.
Next to fields, the cupboards of her home were hungry.
Memories of an abusive father rattled the girl even into adulthood.

But my mother grew up to be joyful and kind.
And I have heard stories about her singing in bars in South Phoenix in Spanish.
(She didn't know Spanish.)
And I remember the way she approached big bearded bikers in Ziggie's Music and asked for the stories behind their tattoos. And they smiled and told her everything.

Those memories—all her memories—are now on the shelf.
Ashes of mystery.
Thousands of stories locked away forever.

For twenty years my mom died of cancer.
With each tumor removed, two more would appear. It was a losing battle.
She grew thinner, more confused.

I spent many hours with her at the end, when she was delirious about a crooked car salesman stealing a novel she had never written.
I didn't want to remember her like that,
My poor sweet mother who built a safe, happy home for two girls and a husband who did not hit us, or drink, or cheat on her.
She broke the cycle.

She was a homeroom mother.
And she packed little notes in my lunches and made shapes out of the sandwiches.

When her cancer came, I was a teenager.
My world did not just stop. Planets paused mid-rotation. The universe held its breath in a twenty-year gasp.

> And when she died, I no longer had to be afraid of the phone ringing because the worst thing that could happen had already happened.
>
> I was in the room when her breath stopped.
>
> Two men in suits collected her.
> They put on latex gloves and hoisted her into one of two vans making nightly pickup rounds.
> I wondered how many bodies were piled inside.
>
> Life is precious. Limited. Fleeting.
> We encapsulate stories.
> We are vessels transporting volumes.
>
> Poets, you have helped me shake the dust off this thirty-eight-year-old body and speak, embracing the vulnerability that comes with honesty, ready to rise from the ashes in a blaze like a phoenix.
> Thank you.
>
> And for the record, poets, I see you.
> This
> isn't about the search for the perfect word or extended metaphor.
> Listener by listener, you are changing lives.
> Line by line, you are re-writing a world in desperate need of revision.
> Thank you. (September 20, 2014)

As I performed, the paper I held was shaking and my knees were trembling. Strangely, though, I did not feel scared standing up there. Rather, I felt energized, excited, pumped full of adrenaline. My voice was steady throughout, and I had control over the lines, delivering them with the volume and emphasis I had practiced at home. This experience brought to mind Stacey, who always performed with shaking hands. Maybe I truly had been witnessing something besides fear in her performances. After all, many people enjoy the rush they get from performing. Susan Weinstein (2009) found the experience of performing for her students in a public venue exhilarating. She writes, "I left the stage wanting to do it again and again. . . . I enjoyed the individual writing of my poem, but even more, I liked the performance, the response, and the thrill of jumping in" (12). It can be rewarding to perform our own words.

Back at the microphone, Gabriel said, "Give it up for Wendy. [*Cheering.*] We always say it. The point is the poetry not the score; the point is the community. And that, shit, that was dope. What was that last line? I was like, 'What? She's been researching! 'The world needs revision.' Yes. Definitely. Thank you so much. We really appreciate you, and we appreciate you coming up here and sharing" (observation, September 20, 2014). After the slam, I talked to Stacey and Jasmine. They said they could see my paper shaking, and we laughed about it. I have concluded that understanding the vulnerability of being up on stage and exposing one's soul to a room full of audience members requires experiencing that sensation firsthand.

This experience helped me to reflect on participation in Metropoets from a different vantage point. Specifically, writing and performing "A Poem for the Poets" helped me better understand what it means to belong to this community, to write for an authentic audience, to heal through writing, and to learn through peripheral participation. I elaborate on each of these aspects below.

To start, feeling like I was a part of this community gave me confidence and inspired me to write. It was only after I heard that I mattered to the group that I began to feel I had a story worth sharing with the poets. Second, knowing there was an authentic audience to hear my words encouraged me to invest time in the piece. Participants had mentioned during the study that it was nice to know that someone would be listening to their poems. Knowing ahead of time that I would perform on September 20 meant I could imagine the event long before the actual day. I practiced saying the words and planned my gestures. I visualized myself on stage and imagined ways the audience might react to different parts of the poem. Because real people would hear my words, I wanted to make sure the piece was as good as I could make it. This is in line with Ann Marie Smith's (2010) finding that "writing for oral performances persuades [poets] to think about their readers or listeners during the writing process" (206).

Third, composing and performing a spoken word poem helped me to work through a painful experience. I thought I had finished grieving my mother's death, but I was wrong. Writing about her helped me confront the most troubling aspects of her death. Saying the words out loud gave me power over the memory. This is the paradox of emotional vulnerability: strength can come out of exposing, and grappling with, deep personal wounds.

Finally, I realized I had experienced a form of "legitimate peripheral participation" (Lave and Wenger 1991). As a researcher in the space, and someone much too old to be a member of this youth group, I generally saw myself as a "transactional participant" (Wenger-Trayner and Wenger-Trayner 2011) located beyond the periphery that is an access point for many newcomers. What is interesting is that resting that far on the outskirts of this group had prepared me for deeper participation later. During my time studying Metropoets, I had been learning about writing and performing spoken word poetry, absorbing more than I had realized about gesturing and vocalization. I had also learned to weave together two ideas in a poem. Jorge addressed this technique in an interview that took place after I had drafted my poem. He said, "[Spoken word poetry] jumps. The topics [jump], but there's a . . . definite relationship established between one topic [and] the other. It's just a matter of how you connect those dots. Without ever listening or going or attending on a regular basis, you won't understand connections. Even though there is no structure, there is" (Jorge, interview, June 27, 2014). Strangely enough, the two ideas I had worked out months before I sat down to write my poem were like the double helix twisting through the entire structure.

Of course, there are clear limits to my experience writing and sharing in the Metropoets space. To begin with, I performed only one poem in this group. While that experience was meaningful, I have not developed a distinct set of practices or preferences in regard to this medium. I also do not identify as a spoken word poet, as identities develop over time (Holland et al. 1998). Nonetheless, these poets did teach me about spoken word and changed my attitude toward emotional vulnerability. They showed me how powerful it can be for a writer to share the stories that really matter. Also, they helped me understand that as a teacher I need to be open to the sharing of wounds in the classroom (Dutro 2011). There is value in vulnerability and "courageous truth-telling" (Rivera 2013, 115). Furthermore, performing our truths can be "exhilarating" (Smith 2010, 207).

Through spoken word, writers share the stories that matter to them. Many poets who testify and share their pain in supportive spaces experience healing and personal empowerment. In Metropoets, writing, performance, community, and authorship work in ways that actually change lives.

Performing in Metropoets begins with some lines of poetry and the encouragement to be brave. Standing before a crowd, the poet takes a breath and faces emotional vulnerability head on, prepared to share the most personal of stories. Ready to respond with snaps of empathy, the audience is poised to listen to the poet. What happens next may very well be transformational.

APPENDIX A
Interview Questions

Metropoets Interviews

Teaching Artist Interview (Mark and Gabriel)

1. Tell me about yourself. What drew you to spoken word poetry? Were you a good writer in school?
2. What does it take to be a great spoken word poet?
3. How did this spoken word poetry group come about? When? Why? What is the mission?
4. How is the group organized? Who runs it? What happens on a typical day? Over the course of a year?
5. How does the writing process happen in this group?
6. Compare learning in this spoken word poetry group to learning in school. How is it the same or different? What should schools learn from this group?
7. Talk to me about leading this group. What do you like about it? What do you hope to achieve?
8. What features of this group help adolescents improve at spoken word poetry?
9. Recall a time when you observed an adolescent member struggling in the group. How did you help that person?
10. Tell me about the changes you have witnessed in (___) as a result of his/her participation in this group. (Go through adolescent participants one at a time.)
11. Does the group help adolescent members with anything other than writing?
12. Think of a powerful experience you have had yourself, or witnessed, during your time in this group. What happened?
13. Is there anything else you would like to tell me about this spoken word poetry group?

Adolescent Poet Interview #1
(Shawna, Stacey, Jorge, Rafael, Jasmine, and Nicole)

1. Tell me about yourself.
2. I want you to reflect on how you became the writer you are today. Tell me about your writing history. Have you ever been a different kind of writer than a spoken word poet? Explain.
3. How do you feel about yourself as a writer? Is being a spoken word poet part of your identity?
4. What motivates you to write spoken word poetry?
5. Who are your writing role models?
6. Who in your life has supported or nurtured your writing? They don't have to be writers themselves.
7. Does school support the things you like about writing?
8. Think back to a time when you were faced with a writing challenge. What happened and how did you work through it?
9. Next, I have eight short questions that deal with your writing practices and preferences: When do you write? How often? Where? With whom? With what tools? On what topics? In what forms? Any writing dislikes?
10. Do you ever lose track of time when you are writing? Explain.
11. How important do you think writing will be in your future? Explain.
12. What has been the most powerful experience you have had in your spoken word poetry group? Tell me the story.
13. Is there anything else you would like to tell me about your writing past, present, or future?

Adolescent Poet Interview #2
(Stacey, Jorge, and focus group: Rafael/Jasmine/Nicole)

1. Tell me about [this spoken word poetry group]. What is it? What do you do in [the group]? What does it mean to be a member? What are [the group's] goals?
2. Talk about how [the group] is organized. What happens when the group meets? Over the course of a year?
3. Compare learning in this spoken word poetry group to learning in school. How are they similar? Different? What [group] experiences and learning have helped you at school? What school experiences and learning have helped you here? What can schools do to better support writers like you? What can [the group] do to better support your success in school?
4. How did you find out about [this group]?
5. What do you like about [this spoken word poetry group]?
6. I would like for you to comment on some of my observations of [the group] so far: mentoring, connections to the outside world, safe space, and music.

7. Which features of [this spoken word poetry group] are the most important for helping teenagers improve at spoken word poetry?
8. Think back to when you first joined. How has [this group] changed you as a person?
9. How has it changed your writing?
10. What changes have you noticed in each other? Let's discuss one of you at a time.
11. What do your friends and family members say about your participation in [this group]? What changes have they noticed in you?
12. What does it take to be a great spoken word poet?
13. Is there anything else you would like to tell me about [the spoken word poetry group]?

Adolescent Poet Interview #3
(Stacey, Jorge, Rafael, Jasmine, and Nicole)
1. Tell me about the first poem you brought with you today. What is it? When did you write it? Why did you write it? What audience did you imagine? What about the poem are you proud of? Explain any challenges you faced.
2. How does this poem fit with other writing you have done? Is it typical/atypical of your other work?
3. How did you write this poem? Process? Tools? Help from the group?
4. Where does this poem show hints of the writer behind it?
5. Let's view your performance of this piece. As we do so, I want you to stop the video periodically and explain what is going on. Have you watched movie commentaries where directors, actors, or writers comment on their film while it's playing? They give some background explaining what went into the making of the film—the stories behind the work that viewers might not know otherwise. Our process today will work sort of like that, but you can pause the video and talk for a while.
6. Tell me about the second poem you brought with you today. What is it? When did you write it? Why did you write it? What audience did you imagine? What about the poem are you proud of? Explain any challenges you faced.
7. How does this poem fit with other writing you have done? Is it typical/atypical of your other work?
8. How did you write this poem? Process? Tools? Help from the group?
9. Where does this poem show hints of the writer behind it?
10. Let's view your performance of this piece. As we do so, I want you to stop the video periodically and explain what is going on.
11. How are these two works similar or different?
12. Is there anything else you would like to tell me about these two pieces?

Palo Brea Poets Club Interviews

Club Sponsor Interview (Ms. Sanderson and Mr. Casale)

1. How did you become a sponsoring teacher for this club? Year? Path to this role? Any special training?
2. Describe your work as a sponsoring teacher for this club. What do you do?
3. Talk about the club's practices. What happens in this club?
4. How would you describe the club? What are its defining characteristics?
5. What do you like about being a sponsoring teacher for this club?
6. What do you not like about being a sponsoring teacher for this club?
7. What are the benefits of having a school poetry club on campus?
8. What are the challenges of having a school poetry club on campus?
9. Does this club help students grow? Explain.
10. Has working with this club changed your classroom teaching? Explain.
11. Has this club affected school culture? Explain.
12. Recall a powerful experience that you observed in this club. What happened?
13. Is there anything else you would like to tell me about working in this club?

Teaching Artist Interview (Brian)

1. How did you become a teaching artist for this club? Year? Path to this role? Any special training?
2. Describe your work as a teaching artist. What do you do?
3. Talk about the club's practices. What happens in this club?
4. How would you describe the club? What are its defining characteristics?
5. What do you like about being a teaching artist?
6. What do you not like about being a teaching artist?
7. What are the benefits of having a school poetry club on campus?
8. What are the challenges of having a school poetry club on campus?
9. Recall a powerful experience that you observed in this club. What happened?
10. Is there anything else you would like to tell me about working in this club?

APPENDIX B
Poetry Club Planning: Questions to Consider

1. What is the purpose of this club?
2. What would we like to accomplish (in a week/month/semester/year)?
3. How should leadership work in this group? Who runs the group (students/teachers/teaching artist)?
4. How will we communicate with each other outside of this club?
5. Do we need funding? How will we get it?
6. Can we build connections with other groups? Will our district sponsor an event to bring poets from our schools together?
7. What is required to bring a teaching artist into our club (cost/paperwork)?
8. Should the club sponsor(s) write and perform?
9. Are any topics or language off limits in our writing? What? Why? In what contexts?
10. What is the procedure for responding to writing that shows a student is in danger? What if a teacher discovers something when the office is already closed for the day?

WORKS CITED

Abbott, Judy A. 2000. "'Blinking out' and 'Having the Touch': Two Fifth-Grade Boys Talk about Flow Experiences in Writing." *Written Communication* 17 (1): 53–92.
Alim, H. Samy. 2007. "'The Whig Party Don't Exist in My Hood': Knowledge, Reality, and Education in the Hip Hop Nation." In *Talkin Black Talk: Language, Education, and Social Change*, edited by H. Samy Alim and John Baugh, 15–29. New York: Teachers College Press.
Alvermann, Donna E., and Kathleen A. Hinchman. 2011. *Reconceptualizing the Literacies in Adolescents' Lives: Bridging the Everyday/Academic Divide*. 3rd ed. New York: Routledge.
Amabile, Teresa M. 1989. *Growing up Creative: Nurturing a Lifetime of Creativity*. New York: Crown Publishers.
Anderson-Levitt, Kathryn M. 2006. "Ethnography." In *Complementary Methods for Research in Education*, edited by Judith L. Green, Gregory Camilli, and Patricia B. Elmore, 279–96. Mahwah, NJ: Lawrence Earlbaum.
Anzaldua, Gloria. 2012. *Borderlands la Frontera: The New Mestiza*. 4th ed. San Francisco: Aunt Lute Books.
Bakhtin, M. M. 1986. *Speech Genres and Other Late Essays*. Translated by Vern W. McGee. Edited by Caryl Emerson and Michael Holquist. Austin, TX: University of Texas Press.
Barone, Tom. 2000. "Ways of Being at Risk: The Case of Billy Charles Barnett." In *Aesthetics, Politics, and Educational Inquiry: Essays and Examples*, edited by Tom Barone, 181–90. New York: Peter Lang.

———. 2001. *Touching Eternity: The Enduring Outcomes of Teaching*. New York: Teachers College Press.
Beach, Richard, Deborah Appleman, Bob Fecho, and Rob Simon. 2016. *Teaching Literature to Adolescents*. 3rd ed. New York: Routledge.
Bhabha, Homi K. 1994. *The Location of Culture*. New York: Routledge.
Blackmer Reyes, Kathryn, and Julia E. Curry Rodriguez. 2010. "*Testimonio:* Origins, Terms, and Resources." *Equity and Excellence in Education* 45 (3): 525–38.
Blinka, Lukas, and David Smahel. 2009. "Fourteen is Fourteen and a Girl is a Girl: Validating the Identity of Adolescent Bloggers." *CyberPsychology and Behavior* 12 (6): 735–39.
Bradley, Adam. 2009. *Book of Rhymes: The Poetics of Hip Hop*. New York: Perseus.
Brandt, Deborah. 1998. "Sponsors of Literacy." *CCC* 49 (2): 165–85.
———. 2001. *Literacy in American Lives*. New York: Cambridge University Press.
Brenner, Mary E. 2006. "Interviewing in Educational Research." In *Complementary Methods for Research in Education*, edited by Judith L. Green, Gregory Camilli, and Patricia B. Elmore, 357–70. Mahwah, NJ: Lawrence Earlbaum.
Britton, James, Tony Burgess, Nancy Martin, Alex McLeod, and Harold Rosen. 1979. *The Development of Writing Abilities (11–18)*. New York: Macmillan.
Burgess, Amy, and Roz Ivanic. 2010. "Writing and Being Written: Issues of Identity Across Timescales." *Written Communication* 27 (2): 228–55.
Calfee, Robert, and Melanie Sperling. 2010. *Mixed Methods: Approaches to Language and Literacy Research*. New York: Teachers College Press.
Chang, Jeff. 2005. *Can't Stop Won't Stop: A History of the Hip Hop Generation*. New York: Picador.
Charmaz, Kathy. 1983. "The Grounded Theory Method: An Explication and Interpretation." In *Contemporary Field Research: A Collection of Readings*, edited by Robert M. Emerson, 109–26. Boston: Little, Brown, and Company.
Chi, Michelene T. H., Robert Glaser, and Marshall J. Farr, eds. 1988. *The Nature of Expertise*. Hillsdale, NJ: Lawrence Erlbaum Associates.
Cintron, Ralph. 1997. *Angels' Town: Chero Ways, Gang Life, and Rhetorics of the Everyday*. Boston: Beacon Press.
Clandinin, D. Jean, and F. Michael Connelly. 2000. *Narrative Inquiry*. San Francisco: Jossey-Bass.
Collins, Billy. 2003. "Poems on the Page, Poems in the Air." In *The Spoken Word Revolution: Slam, Hip Hop, and the Poetry of a New Generation*, edited by Mark Eleveld, 3–5. Naperville, IL: Sourcebooks.
Collins, James, and Richard K. Blot. 2003. *Literacy and Literacies: Texts, Power, and Identity*. Cambridge, MA: Cambridge University Press.
Common Core Standards Initiative. 2014. "English Language Arts Standards." http://www.corestandards.org/ELA-Literacy.

Corbin, Juliet, and Anselm Strauss. 2007. *Basics of Qualitative Research: Techniques and Procedures for Developing Grounded Theory,* 3rd ed. Thousand Oaks, CA: Sage.

Coulter, Cathy A., and Mary Lee Smith. 2009. "The Construction Zone: Literary Elements in Narrative Research." *Educational Researcher* 38 (8): 577–90.

Council of Writing Program Administrators, National Council of Teachers of English, and National Writing Project. 2011. "Framework for Success in Postsecondary Writing." http://wpacouncil.org/framework.

Csikszentmihalyi, Mihaly. 1990. *Flow: The Psychology of Optimal Experience.* New York: Harper Perennial.

———. 1996. *Creativity: Flow and the Psychology of Discovery and Invention.* New York: Harper Perennial.

Csikszentmihalyi, Mihaly, and Reed Larson. 1984. *Being Adolescent: Conflict and Growth in the Teenage Years.* New York: Basic Books.

Curwood, Jen Scott, Alecia Marie Magnifico, and Jayne C. Lammers. 2013. "Writing in the Wild: Writers' Motivation in Fan-Based Affinity Spaces." *Journal of Adolescent and Adult Literacy* 56 (8): 677–85.

Delgado Bernal, Dolores, Rebeca Burciaga, and Judith Flores Carmona. 2012. "Chicana/Latina *Testimonios:* Mapping the Methodological, Pedagogical, and Political." *Equity and Excellence in Education* 45 (3): 363–72.

Delpit, Lisa. 2006. *Other People's Children: Cultural Conflict in the Classroom.* New York: The New Press.

Denzin, Norman K., and Yvonna S. Lincoln, eds. 2008. *Strategies of Qualitative Inquiry.* 3rd ed. Los Angeles: Sage Publications.

Dewey, John. 1934. *Art as Experience.* New York: Perigee.

———. 1938. *Experience and Education.* New York: Touchstone.

———. 2009. *The School and Society & The Child and the Curriculum.* Lexington, KY: ReadaClassic.com.

Durand, E. Sybil, Tracey Flores, and Wendy Williams. 2015. "Learning Beyond the Classroom: Three Approaches to Youth Community Literacy." Presentation at the Arizona English Teachers Association State Convention. Mesa, AZ.

Dutro, Elizabeth. 2011. "Writing Wounded: Trauma, Testimony, and Critical Witness in Literacy Classrooms." *English Education* 43 (2): 193–211.

Dyson, Anne Haas. 1997. *Writing Superheroes: Contemporary Childhood, Popular Culture, and Classroom Literacy.* New York: Teachers College Press.

———. 2005. "Crafting 'the Humble Prose of Living': Rethinking Oral/Written Relations in the Echoes of Spoken Word. *English Education* 37 (2): 149–64.

Dyson, Anne Haas, and Celia Genishi. 2005. *On the Case: Approaches to Language and Literacy Research.* New York: Teachers College Press.

Eisner, Elliot W. 2002. *The Arts and the Creation of Mind.* New Haven, CT: Yale University Press.

Eleveld, Mark, ed. 2003. *The Spoken Word Revolution: Slam, Hip Hop, and the Poetry of a New Generation.* Naperville, IL: Sourcebooks.

———, ed. 2007. *The Spoken Word Revolution Redux.* Naperville, IL: Sourcebooks.

Ellis, Carolyn. 2003. "The Call of Ethnographic Stories." In *The Ethnographic I,* edited by Carolyn Ellis, 24–57. Walnut Creek, CA: AltaMira.

Emerson, Robert M., Rachel I. Fretz, and Linda L. Shaw. 1995. *Writing Ethnographic Fieldnotes.* Chicago: University of Chicago Press.

Emert, Toby, Katherine Macro, and Pauline Skowron Schmidt. 2016. "Celebrating the Arts in English Classrooms." *English Journal* 105 (5): 11–12.

Emig, Janet A. 1971. *The Composing Process of Twelfth Graders* (NCTE Research Report No. 13): Urbana, IL: National Council of Teachers of English.

Ericsson, K. Anders. 1996. *The Road to Excellence: The Acquisition of Expert Performance in the Arts and Sciences, Sports, and Games.* Mahwah, NJ: Lawrence Erlbaum.

———. 2005. "Recent Advances in Expertise Research: A Commentary on the Contributions to the Special Issue." *Applied Cognitive Psychology* 19 (2): 233–41.

———. 2008. "Deliberate Practice and Acquisition of Expert Performance: A General Overview." *Academic Emergency Medicine* 15 (11): 988–94.

Ferri, Daniel. 2007. "So This Guy Walks into the Green Mill Uptown Poetry Slam (Chicago)." In *The Spoken Word Revolution Redux,* edited by Mark Eleveld, 83–84. Naperville, IL: Sourcebooks.

Fisher, Maisha T. 2003. "Open Mics and Open Minds: Spoken Word Poetry in African Diaspora Participatory Literacy Communities." *Harvard Educational Review* 73 (3): 362–89.

———. 2005. "From the Coffee House to the School House: The Promise and Potential of Spoken Word Poetry in School Contexts." *English Education* 37 (2): 115–131.

———. 2007a. "'Every City Has Soldiers': The Role of Intergenerational Relationships in Participatory Literacy Communities." *Research in the Teaching of English* 42 (2): 139–62.

———. 2007b. *Writing in Rhythm: Spoken Word Poetry in Urban Classrooms.* New York: Teachers College Press.

Fishman, Jenn, Andrea Lunsford, Beth McGregor, and Mark Otuteye. 2005. "Performing Writing, Performing Literacy." *College Composition and Communication* 57 (2): 224–52.

Foucault, Michel. 1990. *History of Sexuality.* New York: Vintage.

Frost, Corey. 2014. "Border Disputes: Spoken Word and Its Humble Critics." *Liminalities: A Journal of Performance Studies* 10 (314): 1–20.

Gallagher, Kelly. 2006. *Teaching Adolescent Writers.* Portland, ME: Stenhouse Publishers.

Gardner, Howard. 1982. *Art, Mind, and Brain: A Cognitive Approach to Creativity.* Breinigsville, PA: Basic Books.

Gay, Geneva. 2010. *Culturally Responsive Teaching: Theory, Research, and Practice.* 2nd ed. New York: Teachers College Press.

Gee, James Paul. 2004. *Situated Language and Learning: A Critique of Traditional Schooling.* New York: Routledge.

———. 2012. *Social Linguistics and Literacies: Ideology in Discourses.* 4th ed. New York: Routledge.

Gere, Anne Ruggles. 1994. "Kitchen Tables and Rented Rooms: The Extra Curriculum of Composition." *College Composition and Communication* 45 (1): 75–92.

Glaser, Barney G., and Anselm L. Strauss. 1967. *The Discovery of Grounded Theory.* Chicago: Aldine.

Goncu, Artin, and Mary Gauvain. 2012. "Sociocultural Approaches to Educational Psychology: Theory, Research, and Application." In *APA Educational Psychology Handbook, Vol. 1: Theories, Constructs, and Critical Issues,* edited by Karen R. Harris, Steve Graham, Timothy C. Urdan, Christine McCormick, Gale M. Sinatra, and John Sweller, 123–52. Washington, DC: American Psychological Association.

Gonzalez, Guy Le Charles. 2007. "The Revolution Will Be." In *The Spoken Word Revolution Redux,* edited by Mark Eleveld, 23–27. Naperville, IL: Sourcebooks.

Greene, Maxine. 1995. *Releasing the Imagination: Essays on Education, the Arts, and Social Change.* San Francisco: Jossey-Bass.

Gutierrez, Kris D. 2008. "Developing a Sociocritical Literacy in the Third Space." *Reading Research Quarterly* 43 (2): 148–64.

Haddix, Marcelle, and Yolanda Sealey-Ruiz. 2012. "Cultivating Digital and Popular Literacies as Empowering and Emancipatory Acts among Urban Youth." *Journal of Adolescent and Adult Literacy* 56 (3): 189–92.

Hagan, Joe. 2012. "The Long, Lawless Ride of Sheriff Joe Arpaio." *Rolling Stone.* http://www.rollingstone.com

Hancock, Dawson R., and Bob Algozzine. 2011. *Doing Case Study Research: A Practical Guide for Beginning Researchers.* 2nd ed. New York: Teacher's College.

Harris, Roxy. 2006. *New Ethnicities and Language Use.* New York: Palgrave Macmillan.

Heath, Shirley Brice. 1983. *Ways with Words: Language, Life, and Work in Communities and Classrooms.* New York: Cambridge University Press.

Herrington, Anne J., and Marcia Curtis. 2000. *Persons in Process: Four Stories of Writing and Personal Development in College.* Urbana, IL: National Council of Teachers of English.

Hill, Marc Lamont. 2009. *Beats, Rhymes, and Classroom Life: Hip Hop Pedagogy and the Politics of Identity.* New York: Teachers College Press.

Holland, Dorothy, William S. Lachicotte, Debra Skinner, and Carole Cain. 1998. *Identity and Agency in Cultural Worlds.* Cambridge: Harvard University Press.

Hudson, Sally A. 1986. "Context and Children's Writing." *Research in the Teaching of English* 20 (3): 294–316.

———. 1988. "Children's Perceptions of Classroom Writing: Ownership within a Continuum of Control." In *The Social Construction of Written Communication,* edited by Bennett A. Rafoth and Donald L. Rubin, 37–69. Norwood, NJ: Ablex.

Hull, Glynda A., and Mira-Lisa Katz. 2006. "Crafting an Agentive Self: Case Studies of Digital Storytelling." *Research in the Teaching of English* 41 (1): 43–81.

Hull, Glynda, and Katherine Schultz. 2001. "Literacy and Learning out of School: A Review of Theory and Research." *Review of Educational Research* 71 (4): 575–611.

———, eds. 2002. *School's Out!: Bridging Out-of-School Literacies with Classroom Practice.* New York: Teachers College Press.

Intrator, Sam M., and Robert Kunzman. 2009. "Who Are Adolescents Today? Youth Voices and What They Tell Us." In *Handbook of Adolescent Literacy Research,* edited by Leila Christenbury, Randy Bomer, and Peter Smagorinsky, 29–45. New York: Guilford Press.

Ivanic, Roz. 1998. *Writing and Identity: The Discoursal Construction of Identity in Academic Writing.* Philadelphia: John Benjamins Publishing.

Jacobs, Greg, and Jon Siskel, dirs. 2010. *Louder Than a Bomb.* Film. Siskel/Jacobs Productions.

Jocson, Korina M. 2006a. "'Bob Dylan and Hip Hop': Intersecting Literacy Practices in Youth Poetry Communities." *Written Communication* 23 (3): 231–59.

———. 2006b. "'The Best of Both Worlds': Youth Poetry as Social Critique and Form of Empowerment." In *Beyond Resistance! Youth Activism and Community Change,* edited by Shawn Ginwright, Pedro Noguera, and Julio Cammarota, 129–47. New York: Routledge.

———. 2008. *Youth Poets: Empowering Literacies in and out of Schools.* New York: Peter Lang Publishing.

———. 2011. "Poetry in a New Race Era." *Daedalus* 140 (1): 154–62.

Johnson, Javon. 2010. "Manning up: Race, Gender, and Sexuality in Los Angeles' Slam and Spoken Word Poetry Communities." *Text and Performance Quarterly* 30 (4): 396–419.

John-Steiner, Vera. 1997. *Notebooks of the Mind: Explorations of Thinking.* Albuquerque, NM: University of New Mexico Press.

Kafai, Yasmin B., and Kylie A. Peppler. 2011. "Youth, Technology, and DIY: Developing Participatory Competencies in Creative Media Production." In *Review of Research in Education: Youth Cultures, Language, and Literacy,*

Vol. 35, edited by Stanton Wortham, 89–119. Washington, DC: Sage Publications.

Kass, James. 2003. "Brave New Voices." In *The Spoken Word Revolution: Slam, Hip Hop, and the Poetry of a New Generation,* edited by Mark Eleveld, 222–24. Naperville, IL: Sourcebooks.

———. 2007. "The 'Youuuuths': At Base, We Humans Want to Connect with Each Other." In *The Spoken Word Revolution Redux,* edited by Mark Eleveld, 198–200. Naperville, IL: Sourcebooks.

Kim, Jung. 2011. "Is It Bigger than Hip-Hop? Examining the Problems and Potential of Hip-Hop in the Curriculum." In *Urban Literacies: Critical Perspectives on Language, Learning, and Community,* edited by Valerie Kinloch, 160–76. New York: Teachers College Press.

Kinloch, Valerie F. 2005a. "Revisiting the Promise of Students' Right to Their Own Language: Pedagogical Strategies." *College Composition and Communication* 57 (1): 83–113.

———. 2005b. "Poetry, Literacy, and Creativity: Fostering Effective Learning Strategies in an Urban Classroom." *English Education* 37 (2): 96–114.

Kirkland, David E. 2008. "'The Rose that Grew from Concrete': Postmodern Blackness and New English Education." *English Journal* 97 (5): 69–75.

Knobel, Michele, and Colin Lankshear, eds. 2007. *A New Literacies Sampler.* New York: Peter Lang.

Knox, Bernard. 1996. "Introduction." In Homer's *The Odyssey,* 3–67. New York: Penguin.

Kooser, Ted. 2007. "Poetry As a Basic Human Need." In *The Spoken Word Revolution Redux,* edited by Mark Eleveld, xvi–xix. Naperville, IL: Sourcebooks.

Ladson-Billings, Gloria. 1995. "Toward a Theory of Culturally Relevant Pedagogy." *American Educational Research Journal* 32 (3): 465–91.

Lankshear, Colin, and Michele Knobel. 2011. *New Literacies: Everyday Practices and Social Learning.* 3rd ed. New York: Open University Press.

Latina Feminist Group, The. 2001. *Telling to Live: Latina Feminist Testimonios.* Durham, NC: Duke University Press.

Lareau, Annette. 2011. *Unequal Childhoods: Class, Race, and Family Life.* Los Angeles: University of California Press.

Lauscher, Helen Novak. 2007. "Compose Your Self: Expression and Identity in the Unsanctioned Writing of Adolescent and Young Adult Poets and Songwriters." PhD diss., University of British Columbia.

Lave, Jean, and Etienne Wenger. 1991. *Situated Learning: Legitimate Peripheral Participation.* New York: Cambridge University Press.

Lee, Carol D. 2008. "Foreword." In Korina M. Jocson's *Youth Poets: Empowering Literacies in and out of Schools,* ix–xii. New York: Peter Lang.

Mahiri, Jabari. 2008. "Street Scripts: African American Youth Writing about

Crime and Violence." In *What They Don't Learn in School,* edited by Jabari Mahiri, 19–42. New York: Peter Lang.

Mahiri, Jabari, and Soraya Sablo. 1996. "Writing for Their Lives: The Non-School Literacy of California's Urban African American Youth." *The Journal of Negro Education* 65 (2): 164–80.

McCarthey, Sarah J., and Elizabeth Birr Moje. 2002. "Identity Matters." *Reading Research Quarterly* 37 (2): 228–38.

Merriam, Sharan B. 2009. *Qualitative Research: A Guide to Design and Implementation.* San Francisco: Jossey-Bass.

Moje, Elizabeth Birr, Kathryn Mcintosh Ciechanowski, Katherine Kramer, Lindsay Ellis, Rosario Carrillo, and Tehani Collazo. 2004. "Working toward Third Space in Content Area Literacy: An Examination of Everyday Funds of Knowledge and Discourse." *Reading Research Quarterly* 39 (1): 38–70.

Moll, Luis C., Cathy Amanti, Deborah Neff, and Norma Gonzalez. 1992. "Funds of Knowledge for Teaching: Using a Qualitative Approach to Connect Homes and Classrooms." *Theory into Practice* 31 (2): 132–41.

Morrell, Ernest. 2005. "Critical English Education." *English Education* 37 (4): 312–21.

———. 2008. *Critical Literacy and Urban Youth: Pedagogies of Access, Dissent, and Liberation.* New York: Routledge.

Morrell, Ernest, and Jeffrey M. R. Duncan-Andrade. 2002. "Promoting Academic Literacy with Urban Youth through Engaging Hip-Hop Culture." *English Journal* 91 (6): 88–92.

Munro, Petra. 1998. *Subject to Fiction: Women Teachers' Life History Narratives and the Cultural Politics of Resistance.* Buckingham: Open University Press.

Nandagopal, Kiruthiga, and K. Anders Ericsson. 2012. "Enhancing Students' Performance in Traditional Education: Implications from the Expert-Performance Approach and Deliberate Practice." In *APA Educational Psychology Handbook, Vol. 1: Theories, Constructs, and Critical Issues,* edited by Karen R. Harris, Steve Graham, Timothy C. Urdan, Christine McCormick, Gale M. Sinatra, and John Sweller, 257–93. Washington, DC: American Psychological Association.

Nelson, G. Lynn. 2004. *Writing and Being: Embracing Your Life through Creative Journaling.* San Francisco: Inner Ocean Publishing.

Nicholson, Cynthia Salley. 2011. "Finding Space, Finding Voice: The Racial, Ethnic, and Spiritual Identity of African American Students in the Urban Southwest." PhD diss., Arizona State University.

Noguera, Pedro A. 2008. "Response to 'Street Scripts.'" In *What They Don't Learn in School,* edited by Jabari Mahiri, 43–45. New York: Peter Lang.

Paris, Django. 2009. "'They're in My Culture, They Speak the Same Way': African

American Language in Multiethnic High Schools." *Harvard Educational Review* 79 (3): 428–47.

———. 2010. "Texting Identities: Lessons for Classrooms from Multiethnic Youth Space." *English Education* 42 (3): 278–92.

———. 2012. "Become History: Learning from Identity Texts and Youth Activism in the Wake of Arizona SB1070." *International Journal of Multicultural Education* 14 (2): 1–13.

Paris, Django, and H. Samy Alim. 2014. "What Are We Seeking to Sustain through Culturally Sustaining Pedagogy? A Loving Critique Forward." *Harvard Educational Review* 84 (1): 85–100.

Polkinghorne, Donald E. 1995. "Narrative Configuration in Qualitative Analysis." In *Life History and Narrative*, edited by J. Amos Hatch and Richard Wisniewski, 5–25. London: Falmer Press.

Pope, Denise Clark. 2001. *"Doing School": How We Are Creating a Generation of Stressed Out, Materialistic, and Miseducated Students*. New Haven, CT: Yale University Press.

Prince Ea. 2014. "Can We Autocorrect Humanity?" https://www.youtube.com/watch?v=dRl8EIhrQjQ.

Prince, Richard. 2003. "Once a 'Virgin, Virgin' at the Green Mill." In *The Spoken Word Revolution: Slam, Hip Hop, and the Poetry of a New Generation*, edited by Mark Eleveld, 139–41. Naperville, IL: Sourcebooks.

Prior, Paul. 2006. "A Sociocultural Theory of Writing." In *The Handbook of Writing Research*, edited by Charles A. MacArthur, Steve Graham, and Jill Fitzgerald, 54–66. New York: Guilford Press.

Reyes, Gerald T. 2006. "Finding the Poetic High: Building a Spoken Word Poetry Community and Culture of Creative, Caring, and Critical Intellectuals." *Multicultural Education* 14 (2): 10–15.

Rivera, Takeo. 2013. "You Have to Be What You're Talking About: Youth Poets, Amateur Counter-Conduct, and Parrhesiastic Value in the Amateur Youth Poetry Slam." *Performance Research* 18 (2): 114–23.

Robinson, Ken. 2011. *Out of Our Minds: Learning to Be Creative*. Westford, MA: Courier Westford.

Robinson, Ken, with Lou Aronica. 2009. *The Element: How Finding Your Passion Changes Everything*. New York: Viking.

Rodriguez, Luis J. 2003. "Crossing Boundaries, Crossing Cultures: Poetry, Performance, and the New American Revolution." In *The Spoken Word Revolution: Slam, Hip Hop, and the Poetry of a New Generation*, edited by Mark Eleveld, 208–12. Naperville, IL: Sourcebooks.

Rogoff, Barbara. 1990. *Apprenticeship in Thinking: Cognitive Development in Social Context*. New York: Oxford University Press.

Ruday, Sean R. 2011. "'It Is Impossible to Sink': Three Adolescent Male Writers'

Experiences at a Residential Summer Writing Program." PhD diss., University of Virginia.

Saldana, Johnny. 2009. *The Coding Manual for Qualitative Researchers.* Los Angeles: Sage.

San Pedro, Timothy J. 2013. "Understanding Youth Cultures, Stories, and Resistances in the Urban Southwest: Innovations and Implications of a Native American Literature Classroom." PhD diss., Arizona State University.

Seidman, Irving. 2006. *Interviewing as Qualitative Research: A Guide for Researchers in Education and the Social Sciences.* 3rd ed. New York: Teachers College Press.

Sitomer, Alan Lawrence, and Michael Cirelli. 2004. *Hip-Hop Poetry and the Classics.* Beverly Hills, CA: Milk Mug Publishing.

Smagorinsky, Peter. 2008. "The Method Section as Conceptual Epicenter in Constructing Social Science Research Reports." *Written Communication* 25 (3): 389–411.

Smith, Ann Marie. 2010. "Poetry Performances and Academic Identity Negotiations in the Literacy Experiences of Seventh Grade Language Arts Students." *Reading Improvement* 47 (4): 202–18.

Smith, Marc. 2003. "About Slam Poetry." In *The Spoken Word Revolution: Slam, Hip Hop, and the Poetry of a New Generation,* edited by Mark Eleveld, 116–20. Naperville, IL: Sourcebooks.

Smith, Michael W., and Jeffrey D. Wilhelm. 2006. *Going with the Flow: How to Engage Boys (and Girls) in their Literacy Learning.* Portsmouth, NH: Heinemann.

Smitherman, Geneva. 1977. *Talkin and Testifyin: The Language of Black America.* Detroit: Wayne State University Press.

Soja, Edward W. 1996. *Thirdspace: Journeys to Los Angeles and Other Real-and-Imagined Places.* Malden, MA: Blackwell.

Sowell, Evelyn J. 2001. *Educational Research: An Integrative Introduction.* San Francisco: McGraw Hill.

Stake, Robert E. 2008. "Qualitative Case Studies." In *Strategies of Qualitative Inquiry.* 3rd ed. Edited by Norman K. Denzin and Yvonna S. Lincoln, 119–50. Los Angeles: Sage Publications.

Street, Brian V. 1984. *Literacy in Theory and Practice.* Cambridge, MA: Cambridge University Press.

———. 1995. *Social Literacies: Critical Approaches to Literacy in Development, Ethnography, and Education.* London: Longman.

Sutton, Soraya Sablo. 2008. "Spoken Word: Performance Poetry in the Black Community." In *What They Don't Learn in School,* edited by Jabari Mahiri, 213–42. New York: Peter Lang.

Sweeny, Sheelah M. 2010. "Writing for the Instant Messaging and Text Messag-

ing Generation: Using New Literacies to Support Writing Instruction." *Journal of Adolescent and Adult Literacy* 54 (2): 121–30.
Taylor, Henry. 2007. "Read by the Author: Some Notes on Poetry in Performance." In *The Spoken Word Revolution Redux*, edited by Mark Eleveld, 44–53. Naperville, IL: Sourcebooks.
Trainor, Jennifer S. 2008. "Critical Cyberliteracy: Reading and Writing the X-Files." In *What They Don't Learn in School*, edited by Jabari Mahiri, 123–38. New York: Peter Lang.
Tucker, Jill. 2014. "James Kass: Visionary of the Year Nominee Takes Poetry to Schools." *SF Gate*. www.sfgate.com.
Tyler, Ralph W. 1969. *Basic Principles of Curriculum and Instruction*. Chicago: University of Chicago Press.
U.S. Census Bureau. 2014. "State and County QuickFacts." www.census.gov/quickfacts/.
Valencia, Richard R. 1997. *The Evolution of Deficit Thinking: Educational Thought and Practice*. Washington, DC: Farmer.
Volosinov, V. N. 1973. *Marxism and the Philosophy of Language*. Translated by Ladislav Matejka and I. R. Titunik. Cambridge, MA: Harvard University Press.
Vygotsky, Lev. 1978. *Mind in Society: The Development of Higher Psychological Processes*, edited by Michael Cole, Vera John-Steiner, Sylvia Scribner, and Ellen Souberman. Cambridge, MA: Harvard University Press.
———. 1986. *Thought and language*. Translated by Alex Kozulin. Cambridge, MA: The MIT Press.
Weinstein, Susan. 2009. *Feel These Words: Writing in the Lives of Urban Youth*. New York: SUNY Press.
———. 2010. "'A Unified Poet Alliance': The Personal and Social Outcomes of Youth Spoken Word Poetry Programming." *International Journal of Education and the Arts* 11 (2): 1–24.
Weinstein, Susan, and Anna West. 2012. "Call and Responsibility: Critical Questions for Youth Spoken Word Poetry." *Harvard Educational Review* 82 (2): 282–302.
Weiss, Jen, and Scott Herndon. 2001. *Brave New Voices: The Youth Speaks Guide to Teaching Spoken Word Poetry*. Portsmouth, NH: Heinemann.
Wenger, Etienne. 1998. *Communities of Practice: Learning, Meaning, and Identity*. New York: Cambridge University Press.
———. 2000. "Communities of Practice and Social Learning Systems." *Organization* 7 (2): 225–46.
Wenger, Etienne, Richard A. McDermott, and William Snyder. 2002. *Cultivating Communities of Practice*. Boston, MA: Harvard Business School Press.
Wenger-Trayner, Etienne, and Beverly Wenger-Trayner. 2011. "Slide: Levels

of Participation." http://wenger-trayner.com/resources/slide-forms-of-participation/.

Williams, Wendy R. 2013. "'Untold Stories to Tell': Making Space for the Voices of Youth Songwriters." *Journal of Adolescent and Adult Literacy* 56 (5): 369–79.

———. 2014. "New Technologies, New Possibilities for the Arts and Multimodality in English Language Arts." *Contemporary Issues in Technology and Teacher Education* 14 (4): 327–55.

———. 2015. "'Every Voice Matters': Spoken Word Poetry in and outside of School." *English Journal* 104 (4): 77–82.

———. In preparation. "Exploring the Art of Spoken Word Poetry with Students: A Sample Unit." In *A Symphony of Possibilities: A Handbook for Arts Integration in Secondary English Language Arts*, edited by Katherine Macro and Michelle Zoss.

Winn, Maisha T. 2011. *Girl Time: Literacy, Justice, and the School-to-Prison Pipeline.* New York: Teachers College Press.

Wissman, Kelly and Lalitha Vasudevan. 2012. "Re-Writing the Stock Stories of Urban Adolescents: Autobiography as a Social and Performative Practice at the Intersections of Identities." In *Reconceptualizing the Literacies in Adolescents' Lives: Bridging the Everyday/Academic Divide.* 3rd ed. Edited by Donna E. Alvermann and Kathleen A. Hinchman, 160–80. New York: Routledge.

Worthington, Kristen Murray. 2008. "Students' Words, Students' Worlds: The Landscape of Adolescent Writer Identity." PhD diss., University of Kansas.

Yin, Robert K. 2006. "Case Study Methods." In *Complementary Methods for Research in Education,* edited by Judith Green, Gregory Camilli, and Patricia B. Elmore, 111–22. Mahwah, NJ: Lawrence Earlbaum.

Yosso, Tara J. 2005. "Whose Culture Has Capital? A Critical Race Theory Discussion of Community Cultural Wealth." *Race Ethnicity and Education* 8 (1): 69–91.

Youth Speaks. 2014. "Brave New Voices." http://youthspeaks.org/bravenewvoices/.

Zimmerman, Barry J., and Andju Sara Labuhn. 2012. "Self-Regulation of Learning: Process Approaches to Personal Development." In *APA Educational Psychology Handbook, Vol. 1: Theories, Constructs, and Critical Issues,* edited by Karen R. Harris, Steve Graham, Timothy C. Urdan, Christine McCormick, Gale M. Sinatra, and John Sweller, 399–425. Washington, DC: American Psychological Association.

NOTES

Introduction: Listening to the Poets

1. Pseudonyms are used for all study participants and group events. The group names, "Metropoets" and "Palo Brea Poets Club," are pseudonyms as well.
2. I typically use the term "Metropoets network" when referring to the larger Metropoets organization (including all of its affiliated school clubs). I use the term "Metropoets group" to describe the group of people who gathered each month for workshops and slams at the library.

Chapter 2: Studying the Poets

1. Data sources generated more than four hundred single-spaced pages for analysis.
2. The participant information form asked adolescents for the following information: preferred pseudonym, grade, gender, race/ethnicity, age, length of time in the group, parent occupation, home language, grade in their last English class, previous experiences with spoken word, and personal background (e.g., hobbies, interests, how others would describe them, how they have changed through their involvement in this spoken word poetry group).
3. Because of the amount of data, I eventually uploaded all materials to the data management program, NVivo, and did my coding there.

Chapter 3: Performing Poetry

1. This slam took place on October 12, 2013, the same day as the writing workshop shared in the introduction. I introduce study participants at the point at which they performed in the slam—except for Rafael, who did not perform, so I added a section

for him after the others. I note poets' entrances with labels for easy reference. The performers in this slam who were not participants in the study have been omitted.

Chapter 4: Participating in a Community of Practice

1. Quotes are from Jasmine's interview on December 26, 2013, and Jorge's interview on December 22, 2013.
2. My study examined the Metropoets group, not Brave New Voices. When the topic of BNV does come up, I focus on how Metropoets writers made sense of this competition. I make no claims about whether poets in this study accurately represent BNV or not.

Chapter 5: Writing and Authorship

1. Shawna is not included in this section because she did not participate in the third interview.
2. Rafael lost many of his poems when he switched phones, so I typed these two poems from our interview recording.

Chapter 6: Weighing Benefits and Challenges

1. There is some variation in his estimates of this trip. At one point in the study he said the trip would be $15,000.
2. The findings presented in this chapter depended on a participant mentioning a specific change (e.g., poetic devices) in response to questions addressing general categories (i.e., writing, academic, and personal changes).

Chapter 7: Exploring a High School Poetry Club

1. Pseudonyms are used for all school, poetry group, and participant names.
2. I consistently refer to the Metropoets network as being run by Mark and Gabriel. Beyond that, I have attempted to keep people in the two studies separate. That is, I do not identify participants from one study in the other space.

Afterword: The Paradox of Emotional Vulnerability

1. Stacey was in the ninth grade during the 2013–2014 Metropoets season.

INDEX

ambassador poets, 55, 66
Arizona, 6, 10–11, 34, 70, 116, 118; featured in poems, 39, 88, 92, 131; House Bill (HB) 2281, 11; research sites, 28, 125; Senate Bill (SB) 1062, 11, 100; Senate Bill (SB) 1070, 11, 102
Arpaio, Joe, 10
authentic writing, 47–48, 107, 109, 153, 156, 159, 167
authorship, 9, 13, 96–107, 148, 156–61, 168

boundaries and brokering, 12, 69, 136
Brave New Voices (BNV), 6–7, 55, 66, 188n2; competing for a spot on the team, 34, 36, 53, 68–69, 114–16, 121, 136; past participation in, 24, 36, 43–44, 60–61, 99, 112, 148

call-and-response, 5, 10, 56
Common Core State Standards, 125, 128, 150, 152
community, 20, 154–56; storytelling and, 13, 19, 112; taking ownership of, 44, 116; in writing classrooms, 154–56, 160–61. *See also* Metropoets
community of practice, 8, 22, 49–78, 110, 120, 130; in the classroom, 155–56
confidence, 4, 8, 19, 26, 41, 111, 118, 137, 151, 167

constellation of practice, 120–21
creativity, 27, 48, 152
culturally relevant pedagogy, 155

duo poems, 68, 92, 95, 132

Ea, Prince, 7, 150
empathy, 8, 19, 40, 43, 47, 52, 83, 112, 118, 129, 168
extracurricular writing, 15–17, 146–47

fiscal agent, 116–17
flow, 13, 96, 103–4
Framework for Success in Postsecondary Writing, 152
freestyle, 18, 91, 94–95
funds of knowledge, 76, 79, 157

grito, 10, 34, 36, 56
ground rules, 73–74, 78, 126, 130, 134–35, 146, 155
guest instructors, 55–56, 61, 69, 98

healing, 8, 51, 99, 112–13, 154, 165, 167–68
hip-hop, 4, 7, 18–19, 57, 97

instructional time, fear of losing, 151–52
intergenerational encounters, 20, 64, 76

Kass, James, 7, 19

189

language review, 1–2, 54, 56, 131
LGBTQ themes and considerations, 11, 20, 75–76, 92, 100
"listen to the poet," 12, 35–36
literacy: in communities, 14–15; sponsors, 22, 63–64, 101–3, 147, 156
local-global connections, 68–69
Louder Than a Bomb, 6–7, 150

mentor texts, 2–3, 18, 50, 54–56, 130–31, 146, 151, 156, 158
Metropoets: citizenship goals, 50, 52–53; community, sense of, 9, 42, 99, 122; competition, 24, 43, 53, 67–68, 99, 115–16; emotional literacy, 41, 52; features of, 49–78, 113, 161; funding, 67, 108, 116–19; growth challenges, 114–15, 119; higher education, 34, 53, 55–56, 61, 67, 108, 111; history, 24; honoring voices, 51–52 ; mission statement, 50, 70; musicians in, 39, 58; network, 3–4, 8–9, 11, 15, 22, 24, 63, 120–21, 130, 136, 147; slams, 24, 28, 40–41, 57–59; space issues, 115–16, 146–47; writing, 50–51. *See also* Metropoets, benefits for youth poets in; Metropoets, forms of participation in; Metropoets, participants; Metropoets, study of; performance; poetry slam; workshops, poetry writing
Metropoets, benefits for youth poets within: academic, 110–11; emotional, 81, 83–86, 100, 112–14; social, 66–67, 111–12; writing, 109–10
Metropoets, forms of participation in: active participants, 59–60; core group, 59; occasional participants, 60; peripheral participants, 61, 155, 167; transactional participants, 61, 167
Metropoets, participants, 29; teaching artist Gabriel, 33–34; teaching artist Mark, 38–40; youth poet Jasmine, 44, 85–86; youth poet Jorge, 36–37, 80–82; youth poet Nicole, 43, 82–85; youth poet Rafael, 45–46, 86–89; youth poet Shawna, 41–42; youth poet Stacey, 40–41, 89–90. *See also* Metropoets, forms of participation in
Metropoets, study of: data analysis, 31–32; data sources, 30–31; gaining access, 25–26; narrative research, 32; research design, 27–28; researcher's stance, 26–27; site, 28–29
music, 4, 7, 10, 20, 44, 58, 91; listening to while writing, 93–94, 105, 107; Palo Brea Poets Club and, 135, 139. *See also* hip-hop

National Writing Project, 159

out-of-school writing, 15–17, 146–47

Palo Brea Poets Club, 8, 10, 16, 121, 123–48, 156; advice offered in, 134, 146; benefits, 136–38, 155; changes over time, 144–46; events, 135–36, 139–42, 144; ground rules, 126, 130, 134–35, 146; Metropoets connections, 126, 134, 136, 138, 144–48; poem feedback, 124, 129–30, 133–34, 145–46; sharing writing, 130–33, 146; writing workshops, 130–31, 146–47. *See also* music; Palo Brea Poets Club, challenges of; Palo Brea Poets Club, participants; Palo Brea Poets Club, study of; performance; poetry slam
Palo Brea Poets Club, challenges of: bureaucracy, 8, 123–24, 140, 147; funding, 139–40; poem content, 141–43; size and nature of club, 138–39; teachers' time, 125, 132, 139–40; tension between group leaders, 143–44; testing, 141
Palo Brea Poets Club, participants, 126–29; sponsoring teacher Mr. Casale, 127–28; sponsoring teacher Ms. Sanderson, 126–27; teaching artist Brian, 128–29
Palo Brea Poets Club, study of: data analysis, 130; data sources, 129–30; gaining access, 123–25; research design, 123; site, 125–26
participation, legitimate peripheral, 22, 61, 167
performance, 4, 7, 27, 30–31, 151–54, 156; in clubs, 122–23, 131, 133–34, 146–47; in Metropoets, 33–48, 58, 77–78, 97–99, 103, 105, 161; in writing instruction, 152–54, 161
poetic devices, 46, 55, 85, 109, 118, 142, 152; metaphor, 82–85, 101, 109, 166; rhyme, 4, 18, 90–91, 109, 133; simile, 55, 109
poetic journey, researcher's, 13, 26, 162–68

poetry slam, 5, 46–48, 150; hosting, 151, 154; judging, 12, 28, 35–36, 38, 44–46, 56–57, 77–78; Metropoets, 28, 30, 33–48, 53, 56–57, 74, 77; Palo Brea Poets Club, 127, 135, 141; warming up the audience, 56–57. *See also* performance
political aspects of literacy, 6, 10–12, 18, 160; in spoken word poems, 4, 8, 38, 45–46, 85, 88–89, 92, 102–3, 150–51
prewriting, 16, 91, 157, 163

role models, 34, 76, 101–3, 113, 147, 156, 158–60

sacrificial poet, 36, 38, 56, 60
safe space, 9, 11, 31, 37, 49–51, 69–78, 118; school and, 40, 127
school poetry clubs, 4, 8–9, 24–25, 31, 43–45, 60, 62–65, 81, 111, 117, 120–48; forming, 67, 139, 143, 155–56; poets' ideas about, 97, 101–2, 109, 160–61
schools, youth poets' advice for improving, 160–61
score creep, 36, 45, 56, 114
self-sponsored writing, 15–17, 146–47
shotgun poet, 40, 114
slam poetry. *See* spoken word poetry
Smith, Marc, 5, 46
sociocultural theory, 21–22
spoken word poetry, 4–8, 70, 152, 168; in after-school vs. out-of-school contexts, 121, 146–47; groups, 19–21, 53, 72
street scripts, 18
supportive practices: encouragement, 77, 101, 146, 154; mentoring, 59, 76–77; poem feedback, 3, 74–76, 122, 133–34; snapping, 33, 37, 42–43, 47, 56–57, 59, 61, 74, 155

teachers as writers, 132–33, 158–60
teaching artists' poems, 33–34, 38–40, 55, 57, 60, 146–47, 158–60; as an element of lesson preparation, 129, 139; responses to, 76, 78, 100, 113, 159–60
teaching writing, 149–61
technology, 7, 57–58, 93, 128
testifying and witnessing, 5–6, 168
testimonios, 6
third space, 16, 56
Town Slam, 24, 42–43, 58, 72, 121, 125; poets' experiences with, 62, 68, 98, 105, 161
trajectories: inbound, 62–65; insider, 65–66; outbound, 66–68, 138, 146

unsanctioned writing, 15–17, 146–47

voluntary writing, 15–17, 146–47
vulnerability, emotional, 6, 81, 83–86, 113–14, 129, 132, 154, 162–68

wounded healing, 154
writing: challenges, 17, 20, 62–63, 66–67, 81, 88–89, 93, 104–6, 164; experiences, powerful, 47–48, 97–99, 149, 168; futures, 50, 62–63, 105–6, 149–50, 152; histories, 97, 156; locations, 95; motivation, 72, 99–101, 156; with others, 68, 92, 95–96, 132; pet peeves, 96, 105–6; schedules and frequencies, 94–95; tools, 18, 21, 32, 49–50, 57–59, 78, 93, 107, 121, 129–30, 156–57; topics, 6–7, 16–18, 46, 48, 76, 92, 101, 106–7, 109, 131, 134, 151, 157, 168
workshops, poetry writing, 1–3, 25, 83, 99, 118, 151, 155; Metropoets, 3, 24, 28, 30–31, 41, 50, 53–56, 61, 66, 78, 116; school clubs, 43, 63, 69, 122, 130–35, 144, 146–47

Young Chicago Authors, 6
youth literacies, 10, 17–19
youth literacy groups, supporting, 117–18
Youth Speaks, 6–7

zone of proximal development, 21–22, 50, 63

WENDY R. WILLIAMS is assistant professor of English education at Arizona State University. She studies out-of-school literacies, multimodal writing, youth authorship, and teacher education. Her research has appeared in *English Journal, Journal of Adolescent and Adult Literacy, Contemporary Issues in Technology and Teacher Education,* and *Pedagogies: An International Journal.* Dr. Williams is the founding director of Young Authors' Studio, a program for writers in grades 5–12 that is administered by college students. In addition, she has organized Sparky Slam poetry events at ASU to celebrate youth voices. Before earning her PhD, she taught middle school and high school English for nine years.

www.ingramcontent.com/pod-product-compliance
Lightning Source LLC
Chambersburg PA
CBHW030138240426
43672CB00005B/173